PURE GOLD

MY AUTOBIOGRAPHY

The Ultimate Rags to Riches Tale

PURE GOLD

MY AUTOBIOGRAPHY

The Ultimate Rags to Riches Tale

DAVID GOLD

WITH BOB HARRIS

Published in 2006 by Highdown,
an imprint of Raceform Ltd
Compton, Newbury, Berkshire, RG20 6NL
Raceform Ltd is a wholly-owned subsidiary of Trinity Mirror plc

A CIP catalogue record for this book is available from the British Library.

ISBN 1-905156-21-9

Cover designed by Tracey Scarlett

Interiors designed by Fiona Pike

Printed in Great Britain by William Clowes Ltd, Beccles, Suffolk

DEDICATION

I dedicate this book to my wonderful mum, Rosie.

Acknowledgements

There are many people I would like to thank for their advice, support and, perhaps above all else, patience in helping me write the story of my life. Firstly, thank you to Bob Harris my writing partner for – more than anything – being such a good listener! Also, to Andy Newbold for putting the pictures to the words and to publisher Jonathan Taylor and his team at Highdown for making it all happen.

My thanks also go to my friend Vince Ellis for burning the midnight oil with me, to Victoria Fuller and everyone at Pitch PR, to Gary Shaw for his technical support and to Gio, my PA, for her unfailing support day in day out, rain or shine.

I would also like to thank all of my friends and family for their love and laughter throughout the years. I hope you enjoy re-reading many of the fabulous times we've shared, as much as I've enjoyed recounting them. And to my lovely Lesley, and to the next chapters of our life together.

David Gold
April 2006

CONTENTS

PROLOGUE

THE STENCH OF POVERTY

Every day I take a short walk that reminds me who I am, and where I came from. This is not some stroll around the East End, or around the gardens or golf course at my lovely house in Surrey. Nor does it involve a trip to one of our shops, or to John Adam Street, where I ran my first bookstore so many years ago. It has nothing to do with the airport, where my fleet of jets take off, or stockrooms, or printing plants, or football pitches. It's a much simpler walk than that, out of my bedroom and down a short flight of stairs. There, on the landing, is a mirror, and every single morning, without fail, I pause in front of it for a few moments to straighten my tie, and look myself in the eye. On the wall to my left are photographs from my childhood. On the wall behind me are more. Grainy black-and-white pictures of us as children with our stunning mother; one of me with Mum and our tin bath hanging from the wall next to the outside toilet at our home at 442 Green Street; and pictures a few years later, again with Mum, this time looking worn out, exhausted. But she is still smiling, despite everything we endured.

I think humility is very important, and it is good to have Lesley, my fiancée, watching over me, making sure I don't become Billy Bigtime, as my friend Tom Ross often calls me. One day Lesley and I were shopping at Harrods in London. When we'd finished, my driver Mark pulled up outside and with the help of the doorman loaded up the boot with our purchases. Mark opened the car door for Lesley and the Harrods doorman opened mine. I gave him a tip.

As we drove off, Lesley turned to me and said, 'I'm surprised you didn't thank Albert the doorman.' Only Lesley would be kind enough to remember the doorman's name.

'But I did,' I replied. 'I gave him a tip.'

'You gave him a tip, but you forgot to say thank you. It's not the same thing. I have never known you do that before with waiters, doormen or anyone else. A tip on its own is not a thank you.'

I reassured her I hadn't reached a point where I don't have to say thank you. I would hate for that to happen to me, as it has happened to others. That's why I look at those pictures of us at Green Street: they remind me of where I came from, and I believe it is what keeps my feet on the ground.

I have never forgotten the stench of poverty. It is like no other. It is insidious, creeping, all-consuming. It hovers so heavy that no ray of light, no glimmer of hope can pierce it. We were a family of four, with no breadwinner. Repairs were left undone. A leak in the roof would drip until mildew developed behind the wallpaper and the smell permeated the house. Normally the man of the house would put such problems right. If you could afford it, you brought in a professional to fix it. But we were too poor, and there was no man around most of the time to do the job.

The war years made life even more difficult, not just in our house but in the air-raid shelter, a dank, damp, corrugated-iron construction in the back yard. There you could encounter the true stench of poverty, not to be mistaken for the unclean smell of filth. The bombsites had a smell of their own. That too would seep into the house, reeking of damp, leaking roofs, blocked gutters, broken drains and cracked manhole covers. Nothing was ever fixed. When the bombs fell, the shrapnel would fly, breaking tiles and cutting through anything in its way, making no distinction between brick, wood and flesh. The skies would fall silent only for the drip, drip, drip of the leaking roof to start up again. All we could do was put a bucket underneath it until the rain stopped.

Throughout it all, my mother was meticulous. I saw her on her knees scrubbing the lino on the cement floor with carbolic soap, even when she was desperately ill. The house was deteriorating around us, but she kept it as clean as she could.

The stench of poverty embraced all that was going on around you. We were poor, hungry and cold. The awful smell of an empty grate was a constant reminder. Briefly, when the fire was roaring and the strength-sapping cold was held at bay, we could lose ourselves in the dancing flames and the warmth. Even the stench of poverty would be temporarily overwhelmed, replaced by the wonderful aroma of burning wood. But in the mornings, most mornings – most days and nights, in fact – the stench of poverty returned with the stink of the damp ashes as the rainwater came down the chimney.

There are so many elements to poverty. There is hunger, which on its own is not soul-destroying. Combined with a biting chill and frequent illnesses, it can quickly become so. No fire, damp beds and stomach-cramping hunger is real poverty. We had little chance of heating because we were too poor to afford coal and all the wood has been used up from around our house. This was poverty in the East End of London 60 years ago, and it only became relevant to me when I saw others living different lives in better places, warm and well clothed. I can remember times when I did not have a belt to keep my trousers up. There were holes in my shoes and the soles flapped. Every time it rained my much-darned socks got wet. I could feel despair grabbing me, when I looked around at everything and nothing seemed right. I was not the kind to give up, but when I wasn't feeling well, when all of my family had dysentery, when I couldn't stay warm, when hunger gnawed at me – that was when I knew something in my life was wrong. As a young child I could not have defined poverty because I had nothing with which to compare my situation. But when it has been there, in your face and your ears and your nose – especially your nose, this stench of poverty – for years, and you start to understand that it really does not have to be this way, that's when you wonder what else could possibly go wrong.

Inevitably, something did. And every morning, just a short walk from my bedroom and down the stairs, I stop, I look in the mirror, I straighten my tie, and I remember who I am, and where I came from.

CHAPTER ONE

ABJECT POVERTY

My clearest, earliest memories of being a five-year-old living in the bomb-ravaged terraced houses of the East End of London during the war years are the cold and the hunger, but there was no way of knowing that my family and I were enduring abject poverty because it was all we knew. It is only now, many years on, that I know exactly what it was. There are people who are hungry, those who cannot afford the simplest of luxuries, and many who are cold, but to suffer all at the same time is abject misery.

I recall as a small child waiting for my mother, Rose, to come home after going out to work. She was basically a single mother because my father, Godfrey, was a philanderer who spent a good deal of his time away from home either as a travelling salesman or in prison, because he was also a petty criminal. As a consequence we did not see him for long periods of time. My abiding memory is waiting for my mother to come home from her part-time job on a Friday evening, after she had been paid, because it meant she would return with food, which was a real treat. Half a loaf of bread with either jam or dripping, or, as a special treat, bread and margarine with a little coarse-grained sugar sprinkled over the top.

We returned home one day to discover that our house in Hampton Road had been bombed; the walls and roof had collapsed and it was now completely uninhabitable. That presented us with two pieces of good fortune: firstly, of course, we were all out of the house at the time; the other was that we were given another house around the corner in Green Street where I spent the rest of my young life. I was probably about six years old when I arrived in Green Street, thinking this was a great adventure, moving to a new home. It all sounds very exciting, swapping our old house for another, but when we arrived there was a huge tarpaulin over the roof where a bomb had gone through. We were going from one bombed house to another, though Green Street was less bombed and the tarpaulin stopped the leaks.

Hampton Road was a back-street dwelling, and the odds were we would be moved to another back street, but Green Street lifted us up one notch from the bottom of the ladder of life because we found ourselves on a main road, though not the major thoroughfare it is today because there were so few motorised vehicles; indeed, you were more likely to be run over by a horse and cart. Our front garden had been cemented over and was a natural spot to set up an old trestle table, which was always breaking, to display goods to sell. I was the one designated to repair the table when it collapsed – a regular occurrence as the screws always somehow seemed to work their way loose. On Fridays and Saturdays we would sell whatever we could lay our hands on, whether it was buttons, comics or, in season, Christmas decorations. Originally my mother made Christmas garlands for an uncle who would sell them on to shops. They were, of course, wholesale prices, and it was only later we put them up for sale ourselves on our forecourt. All this would never have happened but for that one piece of luck – a German bomb.

I have often wondered whether this was a subconscious turning point in my life, for it provided me with early experience of selling. While we were selling we never celebrated our luck in gaining a house in such a good position, but it was definitely a time when skills began to emerge for both my brother Ralph and me, when we asked ourselves 'Can we make it cheaper?' or 'Can we make more out of it?' We did this from the age of nine upwards, at weekends and when we were not at school, trying to catch the shoppers and the Hammers supporters after their Saturday-afternoon football game at nearby Upton Park. I wonder now whether Ralph and I would have ever developed into entrepreneurs if we hadn't had this facility to trade from our front yard.

We are not talking about adding luxury to our lives or extra pennies to put away for special treats; we are talking about earning enough money for the family to survive, and even then it was very much touch and go. In addition to the stall I did a paper round in the neighbourhood for a pittance. Ralph also had a paper round. We would give Mum all the money we earned and she would give us pocket money. They were truly desperate times. Other children from families with a little more – namely, a father bringing in a regular wage – would keep all they earned. But we did not grumble nor complain. We knew the score. We worked to survive.

There was little doubt we quickly learnt the value of the money we earned. Every single penny was important. It was counted and allocated, and if we could do something to save spending one of those precious coins we did, even to the point of making our own toilet paper out of old newspapers and paper bags. It was nothing, no big deal at all; just part of our lives. I couldn't even tell you where the newspapers came from, because we didn't buy papers. We would use any kind of wrapping, even the paper the bread came in.

It was extraordinary in the sense that it was an adventure, although certainly not for my mother. These are bad memories for me, but were they bad times? Apart from being hungry and cold, as a child I didn't know it was poverty because my entire world was only a couple of square miles. You understand poverty if you have something with which to compare. We had nothing. It is only looking back now that I realise how desperate my mother was with so little help from anyone. Poverty often brought with it poor health, and with money needed for food and no National Health Service, illnesses developed unchecked. My poor mum had to have all her teeth removed. That kind of surgery would have been bad enough for someone who could afford two weeks in hospital and specialist care, but a poverty-stricken woman like my mother had no access to that level of treatment. She had the bottom set out in the morning and was back at home in the afternoon. I honestly thought she was dying. I looked on in horror at all this blood in the bucket by the side of her bed and on the bedclothes as she lay there in agony only hours after the operation. Then, just two weeks later, she went through it all again and had the top row extracted. I discovered later that she suffered from pyorrhoea, a disease of the gums. But there was no time for her to complain or moan for she knew she had to get up and get back to work so that she and her children could survive. There was no such thing as sick pay or paid holidays in the part-time menial jobs she combined to feed her family. I recently went back to the house in Green Street for a television documentary and went into the bedroom where I pictured her lying in bed with her mouth oozing blood. They were terrible days, near the end of the war when there wasn't much of anything in the way of work, help or money.

I, my younger brother Ralph and my lovely little sister Marie, carried on what was to us a normal life. We did things together whenever we could, and rather than go to the zoo or the picture house, which cost too much money, we did things together that cost nothing. The only interruption came when we fell ill. I remember when all three of us suffered dysentery at the same time and we were put in an isolation ward in Samson Street Hospital in the East End of London. Dysentery, I learnt, was the illness of the poor, and it was all a great burden to my mum because when she wasn't working there was nothing coming in. At least the hospital fed us and gave us warm beds. I was in there for six weeks, as was Ralph, and I was in isolation for a month. My sister also contracted scarlet fever while she was in hospital; she had come in a week later than us boys but stayed an extra week. They were all isolation wards, but she had somehow managed to wander around to contract a second illness. My brother and I were in the same room, but my sister was goodness knows where.

I seemed to be under a handicap from the outset as I was a premature baby of less than four pounds at birth, and with incubators not yet available in Stepney for the likes of us it was a toss-up from the start whether I would survive or not. Certainly it was the beginning of a long battle against everything life could throw at me and my family. I also lost two teeth, because we didn't have any money to have them treated so they simply pulled them out. There was an abscess, but instead of prescribing an expensive course of penicillin, which we could not afford, the dentist pulled the offending molars out. The pain was gone, but you lost your teeth for ever. It was tragic. My mum should have been in her prime, but at the age of 30 she was an old woman with no teeth.

I can clearly see her lying in her bloodstained bed. She could have died, and at the time I thought she might. But not only did she survive, she is still going strong, in fact stronger than ever: she is now into her nineties. My mother also survived lung cancer. She smoked 50 Weights cigarettes a day – a small cigarette about the same size as Woodbines and Park Drive, and just as noxious. There were no filter tips, and there wasn't anybody telling you how it could affect your health. In fact, in those days the tobacco companies blatantly boasted of how it could help your health and self-esteem! It is remarkable she survived the illness almost 40 years ago, at the age of 53. I am told today there is still only a 2 per cent survival rate. It was a miracle none of us expected. At one stage I went to the hospital with Ralph to say a final goodbye to her. The surgeon came out of the operating theatre after a long, gruelling operation, shaking his head as he told us he had done all he could and had gone as far as he dared, and adding darkly that he wasn't hopeful. When I went in to see her I burst into tears, put my hand on her and said goodbye as though she were already dead.

I did the same thing on another occasion when my sister Marie's husband, Kenny Mould, a dedicated ambulance driver and a dear friend, drove his beloved motorcycle into the back of a parked lorry coming home after a late shift. It didn't kill him straight away and, incredibly, there was hardly a mark on his body. He was kept in intensive care at Atkinson Morley Hospital, and weeks later, when all hope was lost, he was moved to Mayday Hospital in Croydon, where we watched him pass away peacefully. I put my hand on Kenny's body as a goodbye gesture then too, and thought back to when I believed my mum would not survive until morning. Some time later I put my hand on my dear friend David Tearle's dead body as I sat alone with him for an hour after he died. I gave the eulogy at his funeral and told the story he had told me a couple of months before he knew he was dying of cancer. He told me how lucky he was. He had two beautiful children and a grown-up son from a previous marriage, and had decided to marry Karin, his long-time partner and mother of his two young children, only a few days before he died.

My mum must be the strongest woman in the world, and she has certainly made up for the lost years. She looks and acts many years younger than she is, and is a vibrant person. She loves being interviewed by the local papers. A while ago Barry Fry, our former manager at Birmingham City, and his wife Kirsten sent a chauffeur-driven car over to pick her up and took her out for lunch. I knew nothing about it until she came back and told me, and that she was planning to take a holiday in Tenerife for ten days with the Frys.

When I look back over those early years, I really do appreciate why we owe her so much. It was a fact of life that the poorer families suffered far more illness than their richer neighbours. Poor diet, draughty houses and little access to medicine meant a high death rate for those in poverty. The dysentery was bad enough, and hardly uncommon, but the real threat was from tuberculosis. I suffered from the disease as a child, and my mother had to care for me. There was no one else. It meant I was a sickly infant unable to ward off illnesses, and I suffered with this particular malaise as a five-year-old child right through until I was eight. I suppose overall we were fortunate. It would probably have meant little to anyone had one of the three Gold children passed away, as so many did with tuberculosis in those days. The details are a little hazy, but if I recall correctly, I had two operations and I went back and forth for treatment for many years; certainly my stay away from home was a lot longer than it was when I had dysentery, and I was in and out for operations, then convalescence. I used to have ultra violet light treatment and wore huge goggles with green lenses to protect my eyes. Mum still remembers the clinic in Church Road in Manor Park, close to where my gran lived, where I would go for my 'sunshine'. I was also in Black Notley Sanatorium for many months. The room I was in looked like a garage with two beds. I and the other sick children were wheeled out into the gardens whenever the weather permitted. During and after the war they would put patients with tuberculosis on the embankment because they believed the cure was fresh air, which we now know could do more harm than good. The buildings were single storey and all the beds would be pulled out in the mornings on an open walkway. Was I there for weeks or months? I don't know; time has little meaning in such circumstances. All I remember was the terrible loneliness.

All these things, the sickness, the hunger, the cold, added up to what could have been a tragic young life. But we survived. On top of all those troubles my school was bombed and I missed important lessons when I was evacuated, as kids were from the inner cities under threat of the German bombs. But because my mum would come and get us we were only ever away for short periods at a time and spent most of our early life in our houses in the East End. How much easier it would have been for Mum to have left us in her home town of Doncaster, where we were evacuated. It would have meant she had only one mouth to feed instead of four, and it would have given her precious time to herself. Clearly she never once countenanced the idea.

I have great empathy with my mother for the way she fought and managed to scrape a life of survival, with three children to bring up and a husband in prison. Now, if you have no money you go to social security and they will give you enough to survive, put a roof over your head and enough food to fill your belly. My mother's first job in her home town of Doncaster was as a bus conductress. She had only a basic education and no special skills, so even from her early years life was about survival. She had no experience of gaining state support until she discovered the RO, which was like today's social security. RO stood for Relief Office and gave us the chance to improve our situation – but even that came with caveats. They did not give her money but tokens, which she could then exchange for food, clothes and shoes. I remember going into the shoe shop where the only footwear we could purchase with our tokens were big, chunky shoes like army boots with metal cleats on the toes and heels. One style, and one colour, black. They were known as 'Blakey's', and everyone knew where they came from. It was like a badge. You always knew when someone was wearing RO boots because you could hear them clip-clopping along, spelling out the message 'Here comes a scrounger', because in those days, if you received any kind of government hand-out it was because you were considered a scrounger not because you were unfortunate. Everything seemed to conspire against me, even the wooden block floors at school. When the pupils were called out in alphabetical order to pay their five pennies for a week of school dinners, I always went out last with my RO ticket. As I walked to the front I imagined a big finger pointing at my head saying, 'Here comes the scrounger, clip-clopping in his RO boots.' The noise told everyone I was different. It was awful for a youngster in front of his peers. Yet nobody cared or was sensitive enough to believe this little boy would be deeply hurt by it all.

School meals were to me appalling anyway, and as hungry as I often was I would rather go without. They usually consisted of lots of gristle and very little meat. I simply couldn't eat it, so I surreptitiously put the fatty bits into my handkerchief and took them home with me to throw away, still hungry! I just couldn't stomach the idea of swallowing them, which puts the lie to the old wives' tale that a poor man will eat anything. Even at home when Mum served meat I was a picky eater and would carefully take off the fat and the gristle and simply eat the best part. It sounds strange for someone as poor as I was, but if I ate it all I felt ill. I am a picky eater even now, but then, even though I was hungry, I would rather eat a crust of bread than a meal with its main constituent being fatty meat. In a way I was fortunate not to be eating those foods, which we now know are bad for you. I did not eat food that was high in saturated fats – not that I knew what the phrase meant at the time. Instead, I ate a lot of apples, plums and pears, and they were a meal for me on their own. At school there was a period when we weren't given free meals and with my five pennies I would buy fruit. When I didn't receive the money I would steal the fruit from the market stalls because I dreaded school dinners. Fruit from the market was more readily available, often picked up as bruised items thrown on the floor by the market traders. I even remember my first ever banana after the war – probably because it made me sick!

At weekends I would sometimes work down the market, and when the stallholder, in order to display the best of the vegetable, ripped off the leaves from a cabbage or a cauliflower and threw them on the floor, I would scoop them up, put them in a bag and tell him I was taking them home for the rabbit. Mum's job was as a part-time cleaner in a local café, wiping down tabletops, cleaning the floor, washing up and collecting dirty plates. But there was a bonus: she would bring home a brown paper bag full of bones, which she put in the stockpot. They would be boiled with my vegetables and it would provide us with a delicious piping-hot broth. She told her employers the bones were for the dog because she was too proud to admit they were to feed her family, but it was nourishing and good for us. Of course, we had no pets at all. How could you afford to feed pets when you could hardly afford food for the family? Needless to say, memories are fragmented; whether the bones and the greens came at the same time I am not sure. Inevitably I have tried to push these memories to the back of my mind. But there is every chance the two coincided, and they were all put in a pot, which would boil for days to feed us. At home I would probably have had hot meals almost every day, even if it was only toast for breakfast – and that would have been toast on its own, with no such thing as a boiled egg or crispy bacon to go alongside it. There was no butter either, only margarine, and not much of that, and it was a rare joy if sometimes there was the addition of a blob of marmalade.

When I was sick with tuberculosis we were given huge free jars of cod liver oil and malt, which was dark brown with the constituency of the old Tate & Lyle treacle in the green tin cans. I thought it was delicious. The malt had a special taste and I would spoon it into my mouth. It didn't do me much good weight-wise though, as might be expected, because I was the skinniest little wretch you have ever seen; I did not start putting on weight and filling out until I was in my thirties. So there are redeeming features in these things. I am, in my sixties, as fit as a fiddle, healthy and well, and I thank the powers that be for that after such a rough start to my life. Maybe it was not having the bad things like fast food, fried eggs, fatty bacon and black pudding; we were probably healthier than most modern kids on their bad diets. I shudder when I see the obesity in the young these days. Poverty, war and rationing had its benefits – but having said that, I wouldn't wish them on anyone.

Occasionally on Sunday we would go to my grandmother's in East Ham for a treat. It was in her neat and tidy home that I discovered there were things to eat other than bread and jam. My father was Jewish, and his family had a problem with the fact that he married outside his religion. For a while my mother was ostracised – not that I realised it at my age. But when we three children came along we would be invited to my grandmother's where we would have glorious Jewish chicken soup, a fantastic treat. My grandmother would produce huge bowls of this nectar after carefully removing the skin and bones, leaving slithers of delicious tender chicken. The smell in the house for Sunday lunch was wonderful. Huge bowls, which we just gobbled up. The best meal we got at home, the one we would look forward to, was Christmas Day lunch when somehow Mum would scrape together enough for us to have chicken and roast potatoes with brussels sprouts. Just the smell of a roasting chicken now brings back memories of the past.

By the time I was ten the war was over, and for my birthday I was given a football – the poorest quality you could imagine, but a real leather football nonetheless. Goodness knows how Mum found the money to pay for such an obvious luxury. All my friends knew I had been given a leather football and were waiting outside on Green Street, a busy main road, ready to play the FA Cup final all over again. I ran proudly out of my house and kicked the ball towards the boys. The next thing I heard was a loud bang – a trolley bus had run over the ball and burst it. It was brand spanking new, only kicked the once. I was reminded of this terrible moment in my young life when driving past Hurstpierpoint College one day. A rugby ball bounced out of the hedge in front of my Bentley. I slammed on the brakes to avoid running over the ball, and a young boy of about ten years emerged through the hedge, scooped it up and called out, 'Thank you, sir.' I tell the story because my ball, all those years before, was in the middle of Green Street for what seemed to be an eternity with the trolley bus bearing down on it, but it didn't stop. It just ran over it. I would have been mortified if I had run over that boy's rugby ball.

Meanness of spirit sums it up. When I see someone running for a bus these days, for instance, the driver will stop and wait; when I was a kid they would drive off. But it has not gone away with the passing of the years, as I saw recently when I was in traffic and I watched a woman with two children, one in a pram and the other holding her hand, waiting to cross the road. It could have been my mum with my brother Ralph and me. The traffic went past the lady and her children at no more than five miles an hour. They would not have lost a place in the queue or a second of time if they had let this lady and her children cross, but a dozen drivers didn't. That is the modern meanness of spirit, perhaps not much different from the old. When I reached her, stopped and waved her across the road, she smiled. A huge reward for such a small effort on my part.

Another thing I learnt that day in Green Street was how fickle friendship can be. All my friends melted away when the ball exploded. There must have been fourteen of them waiting for the new ball and shouting to me, 'Come on, Goldy, come on. Let's go and play football!' Within a couple of minutes I was left standing there holding my burst ball, on my own, with tears running down my cheeks.

Sport was important, even though we had no national or international idols to look up to because we had no radio or television. One of the benefits of living in Green Street was that we had a yard at the back of the house with a wooden fence. The fence was multi-purpose, sometimes providing firewood but also sporting equipment: I can remember making a cricket bat out of one of its planks. All the kids in the street would play cricket in the summer.

But the real adventure for six-, seven- and eight-year-old kids was exploring a bombed house. As soon as it was cleared of possessions and dead bodies we would be in, stripping the wood and anything else we could lay our hands on. We never thought of it as stealing, we were scavenging. We could not afford coal, so we collected wood for the fire. Being sent out to look for wood was simply part of growing up.

Number 442 Green Street was a basic terraced house in East London (the house number didn't carry the same footballing connotation then as it does now). There was a black stove in the living room which burned wood or coal; it was used for cooking and, to make use of the valuable heat, there was always a filled kettle on the go. There was also a copper boiler in the kitchen where Mum did the washing, hanging out the clothes to dry on a pulley-operated rack that could be raised and lowered. The entire heating of the house was generated downstairs by the stove and the boiler, but as I said, my memories are of the place being cold and damp, the fire always going out. It was the very devil to get the thing started again, probably because the chimney needed sweeping so badly that there was little air circulating up or down. We had no facilities to cope with such an exercise and certainly no money to pay anyone to do it. It was such an effort to relight the thing. Sometimes my mum would announce that we were going to have a sack of coal delivered and the house would be a little warmer than usual for a while. Looking back, during November and December we would be paid by my uncle Dave for the Christmas garlands we had made.

I realised later that the money helped to pay for coal during the coldest months. Not that we made a lot, because we had to buy the goods to make the garlands and then, when we sold them on, it was to a middle man who still had to make his profit. We made more on those we sold on the stall, but what sort of money did you make in an area like ours? If we were lucky we would sell five or six at a shilling apiece with the cost of the material eating up most of the profits, but I guess it was enough for a sack of coal.

My strongest memories, however, are of the days when we had no coal at all. Those are the days etched into my memory. When the fire was out you really felt the cold, and the hunger. You'd go to bed in your clothes because you couldn't bear to take them off as the bed would not only be cold but also damp. I can remember doing it time and time again, and if my mum came up to tuck me in she would scold me and make me undress for bed.

But if I could get away with it I would go to bed in my socks, my trousers, certainly my pants, and a shirt. And more often than not it was freezing cold standing outside by the stall. So cold, in fact, that we invested precious money in a second-hand paraffin heater – something else that constantly needed repairing.

Mum received much of the stock for the stall through my father, Godfrey. He would reappear from time to time with odds and ends for us to sell. He once brought a parcel of buttons and we sat and stitched them on to cards to make up sets. He would pick up any number of things like this on the cheap. He might bring back a parcel of metal plates or jugs, perhaps a clearance line, which we would clean up and put on sale. Other items he brought were in need of repair, which I would do. And there were other products he brought home, like a comb with a mirror. You would pull the comb out of its case and there would be a mirror. That sort of item we could sell at the market. They would go quite well if we pitched them at the right, rock-bottom price.

Godfrey never had a regular pitch when he was at home but would move from market to market. He was no bigger than five feet five inches tall, in fact not much taller than Mum, but this little man would stand up to anyone. He was a small-time criminal, and Ralph and I were fortunate not to follow in his footsteps. The Queens, our local pub, was infamous for all the local villains, young and old, and we were lucky we did not get mixed up with them. Our neighbours, like Mum, were honest, down-to-earth people, and they influenced us in our early years.

I'm not saying I was whiter than white though. If I could steal an apple off a market stall down the road, I would. Some may say there is little difference between taking an apple from someone's orchard and stealing from a stall. There is. Running like the wind after picking an apple from a tree is one thing, but taking an apple from a stall in the Queens Road Market, which was about a hundred yards from our house, is another. While I could tell Mum about an apple I had taken from someone's garden, I certainly couldn't tell her about stealing from a stall. I am ashamed to say I became quite proficient at it, and I am sure when I became a pacey left-winger a lot of it was due to the training of pinching an apple and sprinting to escape the stall holder. It was a huge market and I would go to a different part each time. An apple was tea on the run. I would go to the market at lunchtime when they were busy, particularly on a Saturday when it would be hard to spot me, being such a little lad, and I would bring home a couple of apples to share with my brother and sister, but at the same time keeping them away from Mum who would have marched me back to the market by my ear to give them back. Mum will probably still give me a clip around the ear when she reads here how I stole apples. She was mortified at her husband being a petty criminal, especially as she loved him so much.

They met when my dad was selling door-to-door in the north. He had travelled up to Doncaster from the East End to change his pitch and met mum at the local Plaza Ballroom. He swept her off her feet, this handsome young man from the big bright lights of London, no doubt jangling money in his trouser pocket. It was, from her point of view, true love, and it remained solid and unshakeable through thick and thin, despite everything he did to her. She adored him and would have done anything for him, such as bringing up three children in appalling conditions. She would scream and shout at him when he returned home after one of his long absences though, and I could never understand why the volume would suddenly decrease and softer noises would emanate from behind the closed bedroom door. As I grew older I understood that these were the sounds of my parents making up and making love.

While mum adored Godfrey when he was there, it was still mainly arguments and rows, usually over lack of money or his womanising. He was a gambler, a philanderer and a petty thief, and when he was at home he was a disruptive influence in the household. I would try to blank him out of my thoughts. When he was home it was better in the sense that money was coming in – not a lot, but something for essentials like coal and food – but all the arguing and squabbling would spoil it. We, as children, always expected him to stay when he came back, but he would soon vanish again, whether to prison or on one of his excursions we never quite knew. Mum would protect us from the details, especially the womanising. He had a very high success rate with women, we learnt as we grew older. There was, of course, much choice as many women were alone either because their husbands were away fighting or because they had become widows. For those willing to look in such circumstances, the pickings were rich. It was of the time.

Despite my father only occasionally being at home and my mother never having a penny to spare, there would always be presents for the three of us on Christmas Day, but they were, by necessity, minimal. Occasionally we had a pillowcase at the end of the bed for Father Christmas's visit, and Mum did her best to fill it with an apple, an orange and other odds and ends and bits and pieces, but they were so small it is hard to remember what they were. I can, however, still recall the wooden aeroplane Mum gave me once. It was the most wonderful toy I had ever received. Ralph, Marie and I always treasured those presents. We knew my mother would have gone without to buy them. Perhaps that's why I find it so hard to watch children on Christmas Day now. They open a gift, and before they have appreciated the care and love that went into choosing it, they have tossed it aside and begun tearing open another.

Christmas was always exciting for the kids around us, but it was no big deal to the three of us in the Gold household. To us, despite the roast chicken dinner, Christmas was not a big day because there wasn't anything particularly special about it. Christmas morning we would have scrambled eggs for breakfast, but even then they were usually powdered eggs out of a packet. The streamers we made were to sell, not to put up, apart from a few rejects; and there was no tree with coloured baubles dangling from the branches. We couldn't have a tree for the simple reason that we couldn't afford one. After the early years the front room became a shop. I was good with my hands and built all the fixtures and fittings. Later, when I opened my own shop, I built all the shelving and racking, just as I had done for my mum. But once the shop was opened we were left with a tiny living room and an even smaller kitchen. I have no recollection of sitting around there opening presents, but we did listen to the King's Christmas speech.

One Christmas, when I was around twelve, I saw a gleaming black Sunbeam Talbot – a dream car – parked in the street outside our house, and I thought to myself, 'One day I will own one just the same. I will buy myself one for Christmas.' It was, I suppose, my first real taste of ambition. But, to be honest, there was no burning desire at the time to get out of Poverty Street. Maybe it was because there was only one way to go – up! I always had energy and I always had drive, but it wasn't until I started out in business at the age of 21 that I began to make my move forward. Once I had my own business, I knew I could be a success. Before then it was all about survival.

People may not quite understand this when they see me now, but the truth is that well into my teenage years all I worried about was how Mum, Ralph, Marie and I would survive for the next 24 hours. Marie was someone who had to be looked after. She was the family responsibility. Ralph and I would have to baby-sit her while Mum was at work, and there was a communal commitment to the entire family with everything anyone earned going into the pot. There was no 'I'm going to climb out of here at all costs' feeling; there was no jealousy or envy of other people, even now, when we talk over the past as a family. We wanted things, of course we did. I wanted a bike, but there was no envy of the boy a couple of doors away who was given one for Christmas.

To my shame, when I was very young and we were evacuated up north, I kept a three-wheeler bicycle hidden for two days behind the outside toilet. I can remember it to this day, a glorious, new, shiny black thing. I was never caught, but they found it after a couple of days and returned it to its owner, a boy called Johnny. I was too young to experience guilt. It was just a wonderful feeling to have had it and ridden it for two days. So yes, there was plenty of want and desire, but no real envy. I believe that is the right way. Envy can encourage criminal intent, whereas wanting something can spur you on to greater efforts.

CHAPTER TWO

THE AIR-RAID SHELTER

Everyone of my age will remember the old air-raid shelters we scrambled into when the sirens began to wail. There were all sorts, from the underground stations in London to expensively designed shelters dug under the ground, right down to our air-raid shelter, which consisted of a sheet of corrugated iron stretched over a hole in the backyard. Anderson shelters varied hugely from street to street, even house to house. Fathers or grandfathers would fashion these little shelters into second homes so that their families were as comfortable as possible.

I can still picture our air-raid shelter. In fact, I can still see the bunks in which we slept in my mind's eye. The floor bunk was six inches above the damp ground and the second around two feet six inches above that, leaving just enough room to climb in and little clearance even when you were lying flat. Once in, it was rather like a coffin. The shelters were corrugated iron, semi-circular, dug out about three feet below the ground; the earth taken out was piled up on top leaving just a front entrance. Most had doors. Ours, however, had no door, just a couple of planks you pulled up behind you when you crawled in and then propped up against the doorframe. It was draughty, cold and damp, and needless to say we would be inside for as short a time as possible, scrambling out as soon as the noise died down, whereas other families would stay in their shelters for the remainder of the night making themselves comfortable so that they were not disturbed again if another wave of bombers came over.

Our shelter was simplicity itself with its four bunks and its damp dirt floor inside a corrugated-iron tube. When the sirens wailed we would scurry off to it. Mum would carry the bedding down from the house when the sirens sounded because it would get too damp if it were left down there.

If it rained, the water ran in, and if you needed something as basic as the toilet, you didn't! We were so frightened we had to hold on and run to the outside toilet at the first opportunity.

I remember vividly going to a friend's shelter and looking at it in amazement. It was like going into a home, only a much better home than the one I lived in. It had electricity, a wooden floor covered in carpet, a paraffin stove and running water – things we did not have in ours, which was basically a hole in the ground with a metal roof. They were designed only to protect us from shrapnel, or if parts of the house were to collapse on to the shelter. We would not have had a prayer if we had taken a direct hit from a bomb or a doodlebug. But at least some shelters were habitable, warm and comfortable, the families having taken the trouble to make them a home from home.

If it rained, there was an inch of water on the floor of ours, and it was cold with a musty smell at all times. Unlike other shelters, which were like a kids' camp, ours was not somewhere to play because there were spiders and various insects living there. In fact, it was a horrible, scary place to go, and we had to be bundled down there reluctantly whenever the air-raid sirens sounded. We lived only a few miles from the docks, facing West Ham United's football ground, and the German bombers would fly overhead and aim at the docks. If they missed by a small margin, we had bombs landing in the street. Sometimes those sirens would sound every night for a week because the Luftwaffe were bombing the docks, and in those days anything exploding within a couple of miles of the target was considered a hit for Jerry. Sometimes the raids went on and on, hour after hour of bombers coming overhead. They would come down the Thames Estuary and some would turn left, but most turned right over West Ham, East Ham and Canning Town. The noise was relentless. I can only wonder how the soldiers survived on the front line in the First World War.

It is frightening now to think about it, but as kids, despite the terror of these nights, we had this extraordinary feeling of invincibility, that we would survive everything. If they had given me a gun at the time I would have been ready to go and kill the Germans and win the war on my own. Even when neighbours and their children were killed in the raids it made little difference to that sense of inner strength. The horrors of war were quickly erased from our minds. Maybe it was this remarkable feeling of being indestructible. Death was simply not going to happen to us; it was something that occurred to other people, not to me, and definitely not to my family. I suppose it is a safety mechanism all children possess, especially in war time. There were no thoughts of being killed, even when others nearby were killed by the bombs or collapsing buildings. Death was not an option. As far back as I can remember I have been blessed with this inner strength, a feeling that nothing will beat me.

CHAPTER THREE

ABUSED

As if we did not have enough problems in our young lives, Ralph and I had to suffer more pain and suffering, this time at the hands of our uncle John Cenci, my mother's stepbrother, who beat and abused us. He came to stay while my father was in prison. He was always hitting us when we were in the way or had committed some perceived offence. But that was just the beginning.

There are bits in your life you are not proud of, like stealing half a crown out of John's pocket to buy Mum a birthday present when I was a kid, 'borrowing' that tricycle for two days, and pinching those apples from the market. I suppose most kids do something similar, but if you are going to tell a story you have to tell it all. The hitting and slapping I could endure, but the sexual abuse has haunted me for the rest of my life.

It happened during a time when Ralph, Johnny and I were all sleeping in one bed. There had been bomb damage to the roof and one of the bedrooms had had to be evacuated. It ended up with Mum and Marie in one bed, and the three males in the other. It was there that I suffered the appalling indignity of being molested by Johnny. With my father away, he should have been a trusted guardian; instead he took advantage of his position to satisfy his own urges and make my childhood even more miserable. There was no penetration, but I would wake up to discover this drunken man fiddling with me. Any event that contributes to the deprivation of a young boy's life should not be missed, which is why I mention it. It also explains why I hated the man for so long.

But even a child cannot keep that amount of resentment bottled up for ever, and after one particularly savage beating I rebelled. John would normally lay into Ralph and me after a skinful in the pub on a Sunday. He would come back and go to bed, not remembering anything he had done in his drunken state. Ralph was a devil and would poke fun at John after he had passed out. The big naughty word for us in those days was 'penis', and Ralph would call him 'penis head' to show his contempt for the man. On this memorable day he overheard us taunting him, and to our surprise he came running out of his room. In a desperate attempt to run away from him I fell over Ralph, which allowed John to catch hold of me and beat me remorselessly. He left me sprawled on the ground while he went back into the house and into his bedroom.

Ralph was distraught. He felt responsible because of his name calling and accidentally tripping me up. I did not look a pretty sight. I was only around eleven at the time and Ralph coming on nine, though streetwise we were years older than many other kids in our neighbourhood. Ralph had no idea how to help me as I lay nursing my wounds. He suddenly appeared with, of all things, a newspaper. 'What the bloody hell is this for?' I yelled, and he started to cry, begging me not to tell him off, saying I was always shouting at him and it was not his fault. He had brought the newspaper as something of an offering, but I told him it would be far more helpful if he could find a damp cloth so I could wipe away the blood and clean myself up before Mum returned.

Johnny was a thug, but what could we do? He was paying Mum eight shillings and sixpence a week to live in the house, and that went a long way in terms of feeding the family. So I couldn't tell my mother.

Eventually Ralph, as if reading my mind, as he has done so often in our business life, asked, 'What are we going to do, Dave?'

I looked at him and said firmly, 'We're going to kill him!'

Was it bravado? Did I really mean it? Maybe all the abuse he had put me through, physical and sexual, explains why I thought of killing him.

Ralph wiped his nose on his sleeve and sniffled. 'I ain't never killed nobody. I can't do it, Dave.'

I answered calmly, 'We don't have to do it now.'

I had heard from Mum that Johnny was going blind. It was a fact. So, I decided, we would wait, and when he was blind and helpless we would kill this awful, brutal man.

Fortunately, before any plan could ferment in my young mind, Johnny left and went back to his wife. My cracked ribs gradually improved and I got over the beating. He only beat me badly the once, the other incidents were whacks, but they hurt. Johnny might have had deteriorating eyesight, but he was a big, strapping, intimidating man, a roof tiler by trade, used to working physically every day. I was only a kid, but I still thought of killing him. Was it that wrong? Didn't Roy Rogers, the American movie cowboy and my boyhood hero, and Dick Barton, Special Agent, kill bad guys too? Wasn't that the rule of the Wild West? It certainly was in the cinema on a Saturday morning, once I'd sneaked in through an open door. I despised this man for his brutality towards my brother and me.

More than 40 years later I went to Green Street on my way to see a football match. I popped in to see Mum, and she was crying. She had just heard that Johnny had cancer and was dying. I have to admit I thought to myself, 'So what? Who cares!' This man never lifted a finger to help. I remembered him only in anger, and my memories of him were all bad. A drunk, violent and aggressive man. But I bit my lip and said, 'Mum, that's very sad.' I discovered that she had been paying for him to be in a nursing home because he had been virtually blind for some years. She revealed she had been paying £200 a week but had run out of money and didn't know what to do. 'What about his son?' I asked. 'What about his ex-wife?' No. He was all on his own – and I wasn't surprised. So Ralph and I gave her the money to look after him, thinking he would probably be dead within a year or two. We were giving Mum £10,000 a year to cover the nursing-home costs of our childhood abuser, and he lived for another eleven years. Mum paid the bills and went to see him regularly, but we stayed away. I did not feel terrible about the half a crown I stole from Johnny to buy my mum a blue butterfly brooch from Woolworths for her birthday because he would never have known as he was so drunk, and I certainly paid it back a million times over all those years later.

Johnny's sexual abuse happened on three occasions and counted heavily towards my attitude towards him. I also hated his drunkenness and the way he treated my mum. He would borrow money from her for drink, there would be arguments over him not repaying her, and he treated her like a skivvy, not like a sister. But Mum's loyalty and love for her stepbrother, and indeed my father, remained unmoved. She had, and still has, a loyalty which is unsurpassed.

CHAPTER FOUR

ON BEING JEWISH

As a young boy living in the East End of London, I was something of an enigma. My surname was Jewish, my dad was Jewish and my paternal grandparents were avid, practising Jews, but my mother and her family were not. I didn't go to a synagogue, and I couldn't speak Hebrew. I had no religion then, and neither do I now, but I am Jewish by birth and background. When you are as poor as we were, religion is the last thing on your mind. It was simply not part of our lives.

But, of course, what influenced us meant nothing to other children, and it made me different in their eyes. They always associated Jews with being well off, but I was the only boy in the class receiving RO (Relief Office) free meals. I've spoken already of the awfulness of clip-clopping along the wooden block floors at school, RO ticket in hand, when the pupils were called up to pay their school dinner money. This was the first time I encountered anti-Semitism. The fact that we weren't wealthy Jews mattered not; instead, we were seen not only as Jews but also as scroungers, not to be tolerated by society, as I learnt from other kids baiting me. They could only have learnt of such hatred from their parents. They simply couldn't understand the correlation between the words 'Jew' and 'poor'. I was a total enigma, so they beat me up.

I remember my school friend little Sammy Warzofski when we were both about ten. He never said an unkind word. He was from a better-off family than most of us and would share his sweets, his apple and sandwiches with anyone. But Sammy was always being picked on because he not only looked Jewish, he went to synagogue every week. He was also the only boy in the entire school who was dropped off at the gates in a car driven by his father. No other kid I knew had a car, and unfortunately for

Sammy it put him on the wrong foot immediately with the others. He was regularly beaten up, and as a little studious guy he found it difficult to defend himself against the bullies. I would step in when he was being picked on and more often than not end up being beaten up as well.

Sammy was extremely bright, and when we took our eleven-plus exam he finished halfway through the allotted time and spent the rest of the time reading a comic. He passed with flying colours. I failed miserably, which was probably not a surprise as the preceding six years of my formative education had been interrupted by deprivation, poverty, pain, tuberculosis, dysentery and a bombed school – with a little child abuse thrown in. There is not the same kind of closeness among children as there is among adults; there is more of an easy come, easy go attitude, especially among kids who are about to move on to separate schools. But when it was time for Sammy to go off to grammar school, he came over to me, hugged me and said, 'Good luck, Goldie.' It was the last time I ever saw him, and I would love to know if he fulfilled his potential. I'm sure he went on and became a surgeon or a captain of industry. I want to know that the good guys do well and the bad guys get what they deserve, just as they do in books and films. Unlike Sammy, I headed for the nearest thing to a borstal. I remember just before I left Creden Road School to go to the big boys' school, the head teacher Mrs Green looked at my results and announced, 'Gold, you will never amount to anything!'

There were so many kids at Burke Secondary Modern who came from the families of villains and tough guys. It was a tough place, a breeding ground for future criminals, and needless to say, the kids soon formed themselves into gangs and there were many trials of strength. This was the era of the young Richardsons and Krays; in fact, these were the formative years of London's most notorious and violent gangs. There were razor gangs prowling the back streets looking for mischief. Seeing guys with badly scarred faces was not unusual, especially in South and East London, which were the most infamous parts of the country with no-go zones like Cable Street and the Old Kent Road. I could touch and smell the evil, but the nearest I came to it was my brutal uncle Johnny. He drank in the Queens pub on the corner of Queens Road and Green Street and frequently found himself involved in trouble. Godfrey, of course, was a petty criminal, and to some a lovable rogue, but, thankfully, not involved in the violence and intimidation that went on. We also had friends who became involved because we were surrounded by deprivation, and poverty breeds criminality. History shows that crime increases during times of depression and recession. Looking back, it would have been so easy for Ralph and me to be drawn into a life of crime, but we were both determined to fight our way out of poverty, to get ahead relying on honesty, hard work and chutzpah – a wonderful Jewish word meaning extreme gall.

I was nine, going on ten when the war began to draw to a close, and instead of wave after wave of bombers there were the dreaded unmanned doodlebugs making a frightening noise as they sped through the air; when that noise suddenly stopped, you knew they were plummeting to earth. I wasn't on my own in my fear of these monstrous robots: everyone living in London was going through a similar nightmare. But at that age you don't think of others, you think of yourself. It was a sad time in my life – sad when I think of the little boy and wonder, how much more could he have taken? How much worse could it have got? When you are a child, you look at the poverty, the handouts, no shoes, your Jewishness … they all seemed part of it. I admit that at an early age I was ashamed of being Jewish because of the perception and insults. It was bad enough being poor, having no shoes and no money, and being cold and hungry, but then to have someone spit on you because you are a Jew is devastating. But as I continually say now, I am what I am. I have an affinity with the Jewish people and I am comfortable with what being Jewish means, but as a youngster I never could be. Being Jewish simply led to bullying on top of everything else I had to face. Then it was tough, now it is part of my life.

I can remember years later as a young man going to my first black tie function. It was a boxing dinner, and an associate at the table told a joke that was derogatory to Jews. I falsely laughed to be one of the crowd and felt awful doing it. The feeling lasted a long time. Later still, during the Yom Kippur War in 1973, when they were raising money after the Arab nations had attacked Israel, there was a great surge of sympathy for the nation and I sent more than I would for any other cause because I felt an affinity. It was there in the blood. I didn't have the guts to stand up and say I was a Jew when I was young, but as I grew older I felt a pride. That Jewishness is important to establish.

And it wasn't only on the home front that I had to face my Jewishness. I remember bunking into the Green Gate cinema and seeing pictures on Pathé News of the holocaust. The stark black and white images made it even more terrifying. It was the most traumatic experience of my young life, and even now, 60 years on, the memory still haunts me. I have subsequently seen the same footage again on the History Channel on television. The scenes I saw as a child were repeated and were equally terrifying as I took in the horrors of Belsen, Auschwitz and the other concentration camps. It was when the Allied forces were going through Germany and Poland and the pictures were coming back for the first time. Although we know now that there were many other nationalities involved, it seemed as though it was Jews, Jews and more Jews who were being liberated. But thousands lay dead or dying. The pictures were harrowing.

I went to my grandmother, Miriam, afterwards and asked, 'Why are people killing the Jews? Are we so bad?' I had been told at school we were responsible for killing Jesus. Now Jews were being killed, and I wanted to know why. Maybe, I thought, that was why the kids wanted to beat me up, and when I was older they would want to kill me for being a Jew. I had always felt indestructible as a small child; suddenly I realised I might not be. I had seen these bodies piled up at the camps and it made me feel extremely vulnerable. As I watched the images on the film screen I was mesmerised; my eyes were on stalks. You half turn away, fingers over the face, and squint your eyes – but you still watch. The film report was clearly meant for adults, not for small children sneaking in through the cinema's emergency exit. I was seriously troubled, and I needed my grandmother to tell me why the Germans were killing the Jews. 'Am I next?' I added. 'Are they going to kill you, Grandma?'

Those questions must have broken my grandma's heart. She had escaped persecution in Poland when her father, my great grandfather, Goodman Goodman, escaped with his family to England. Yet he committed suicide just a few years later, driven to despair by the amount of anti-Semitism he faced in what he had hoped would be a safe refuge. My grandmother was ten years old when her father was found hanging, and there she was, nearly half a century later, listening to another distraught ten-year-old wondering if anti-Semitism would blight his life too. She cried, because she couldn't find the words to explain. She became even more upset when I asked her whether they were going to kill us. I didn't have a clue where Germany was, how close or how far. I didn't even know how far Birmingham was. Grandma tried to tell me a story about the war and the Jews but couldn't finish it because she was crying so much. It left a deep impression.

It was difficult all round, of course, because of Godfrey marrying out of the faith. There were problems over the marriage, and all of his family were bitterly against it. My father was the first one of their children to get married and Grandma had hoped they would all marry into the faith, but it was at a time when everything was changing because of the war, and the anger eventually went away.

Sadly, my grandmother died at the age of 61 of sugar diabetes. Whether there was medication available I don't know, but I do remember she was terrified of injections and wouldn't have anything to do with them, thus contributing towards her own death. I only really knew her for about eight years, and even then I only saw her on the occasional Sunday. She was an old lady at a young age, as was my mother. When my mother was ill at the age of 30 she looked about 60. This was not just the false vision of a young child but something very real.

That jerky black and white newsreel was a sad and meaningful moment of my life. There was confusion and persecution, and I felt it. Jews were being exterminated, and I was being picked on. I was one of them. To be Jewish in the East End of London during and shortly after the war was difficult anyway, of course: we were despised as it was perceived we were taking jobs from other, local people – a totally irrational notion considering our poverty. Thankfully, anti-Semitism started to collapse after the war when radio and the new medium of television told of the contribution made by the Jewish people to the war effort. The civilised world was stunned when the concentration camps were discovered and finally liberated and the scale of the holocaust emerged.

CHAPTER FIVE

TOMMY GOULD, VC

One Sunday afternoon during the war I visited my grandmother, and when I arrived she had just finished reading a letter, and what she had read had clearly excited her.

'What is it, Grandma?' I asked.

'Your cousin Bill has been awarded the Victoria Cross,' she answered. 'He's a hero, and you should be proud a member of our family is to receive such an honour.'

'A hero, Grandmother?' I asked, my interest aroused. 'What did he do?'

'He saved a submarine with fifty men on board,' she replied, sending shivers racing up and down my spine.

When I told my friends at school that my cousin was a hero, the classroom was buzzing with excitement. Mrs Green, our teacher, wanted to know what all the commotion was about. I proudly told her: 'Bill Gold, my cousin, is a hero and he is going to receive the Victoria Cross from the King.' Everybody wanted to know more, and for once I was the centre of attention. A couple of days later I was brought back down to earth when Mrs Green, in front of the entire class, asked me if I was sure my story was true. She had looked up the VC awards in *The Times* and there was no mention of a Bill Gold. I was devastated. Did she think I was lying? I had seen the letter myself.

It was only recently that I discovered, quite by chance, there was a Tommy William Gould who won the Victoria Cross in February 1942. The medal is on display at the Hendon Jewish Military Museum. I visited the museum to find out more about Thomas William Gould. He was born in Dover on 28 December 1914.

Tommy died in 2001 at the age of 86, and was the only Jewish recipient of the Victoria Cross in the Second World War. When he won it he was a 27-year-old Petty Officer in the Royal Navy serving on the submarine HMS *Thrasher*. At about midday on 16 February 1942, HMS *Thrasher* was on patrol off Suva Bay on the north coast of Crete when she torpedoed and sank an enemy supply ship of some 3,000 tons that was escorted by five anti-submarine vessels. The escorts, with support from enemy aircraft, counter-attacked and 33 depth charges were dropped, many of them exploding close to their target. Miraculously, *Thrasher* survived the attacks, and that evening after dark she surfaced to recharge her batteries.

In the early hours of the morning, while still on the surface, *Thrasher* altered course across the swell and began to roll heavily. Clanging noises were heard from above, as though some heavy object were loose and rolling about. To everyone's horror it was discovered that there was a bomb, probably weighing about 100lb, lying on the submarine's outer casing in front of the four-inch gun mounting. Lieutenant Peter Roberts and Petty Officer Tommy Gould volunteered to go on deck and remove the bomb. Tommy was in charge of the stowage of gear inside the casing (a light, metal, free-flooding structure erected on top of the submarine's pressure hull). There was clearance of some two or three feet between the casing and the hull which contained a tangle of pipes, wires and other gear. At any moment the bomb might roll off the casing on to the saddle tank below and detonate. While Tommy held the bomb still, Roberts put an old potato sack around it and tied it with a length of rope. The bomb was too heavy to be thrown clear of the saddle tanks, so they manhandled it a hundred feet forward to the bows where they dropped it overboard, while *Thrasher* went full astern to stay clear.

Looking more closely at the casing of the submarine, they found a jagged hole, and inside it another bomb, resting on the hull. This was a different matter altogether as it was clearly not possible to manhandle the bomb up through the hole. The only way was through a hinged metal grating about twenty feet away. The two men lowered themselves through the narrow opening and wriggled on their stomachs to where the bomb lay. If it exploded, the submarine and all her crew would be lost. Furthermore, *Thrasher* was off an enemy coast and the enemy knew there was an Allied submarine in the area. If a surface vessel or aircraft were sighted, *Thrasher*'s captain, Hugh Mackenzie, who later became Vice Admiral Sir Rufus Mackenzie, would have to dive and the two men would be sacrificed and left to drown.

Tommy lay flat on his back in the pitch dark with the bomb in his arms while Roberts lay in front of him, dragging him by the shoulders as he crawled along. By the faint light of a shaded torch, the two of them worked the bomb along the narrow casing, easing it up through the grating. The bomb made a disconcerting twanging noise whenever it was moved and it took fully 40 minutes before the two men had it clear and could wrap it in a sack, carry it forward and drop it over the bows.

'I never expected to get the VC,' Tommy said. 'When we came down from the casing that night, we were soaking wet and all the captain said was, "You'd better get yourselves dried."' Mackenzie did not make much of the 'bombs incident' in his patrol report, merely commending Roberts and Gould for their 'excellent conduct'. The incident was virtually forgotten until several months later when, as Mackenzie recalled, he was 'surprised by the news that Roberts and Gould had each been awarded the Victoria Cross. A great personal honour to themselves and to their fellow submariners.'

The VCs were awarded on the recommendation of the Commander-in-Chief of the Mediterranean, Admiral Sir Andrew Cunningham, but were opposed by the Honours and Awards Committee in London, who argued that the acts of bravery had not been performed in the presence of the enemy, as VC Warrants stipulated, and the George Cross would be more appropriate. Admiral Cunningham, however, retorted that two large enemy bombs in a submarine off an enemy coastline constituted quite enough enemy presence. As a VC hero, Tommy was later interviewed by the Marquis of Donegal, who asked him what he had been thinking while busy with those bombs. 'I was hoping the bloody things wouldn't go off,' Tommy replied.

From my research, I discovered that Tommy Gould had joined the Navy on 29 September 1933 and had served on the cruisers *Emerald* and *Columbo*. He joined the submarines in 1937 and served on HMS *Regent*, HMS *Pandora* and HMS *Regulus*. Later in the war, on 4 June 1943, he was mentioned in dispatches after the submarine *Truculent* sank the German U-boat U-308 off the Faeroes. On 13 January that year Tommy had been made an Honorary Freeman of Dover, and in March, after his investiture at Buckingham Palace, he went home to St Albans, where he then lived, to a civic reception by the mayor and Corporation. After being invalided from the Navy in October 1945, Tommy became a business consultant and was for some years chief personnel manager with Great Universal Stores. He kept up his interest in the Navy and the Jewish community, taking part in Jewish ex-servicemen reunions. In July 1946 he was at the front of a march through London to protest against the government's policy towards Palestine. He was also commissioned as a Lieutenant RNR and commanded the Sea Cadet Corps at Bromley in Kent, where he was then living. In May 1965, Tommy's name was in the papers again, this time as 'a VC on the dole'. He had lost his job as personnel manager, because of 'a clash of personalities', and remarked that he was finding his VC a liability. 'Incredible though it may seem,' he said, 'people in top management seem to shy away from me. I think it might be because they are afraid a man with such a record could show too much embarrassing initiative. If it is the VC which is frightening people away from me, I wish they would forget it. Those days are over.' Tommy's VC was eventually sold at Sotheby's in October 1987 for £44,000 and is now held by the Association of Jewish Ex-Servicemen.

For several years Tommy was president of the International Submarine Association of Great Britain and was an active member of his local Royal Naval Association and of the Victoria Cross and George Cross Association. He was also an active Freemason. He was a quiet, conscientious man of great personal presence. Meticulous in his habits, he was always smartly dressed, and in later life grew a luxuriant naval beard and moustache. His father, Reuben Gold – the brother of my grandfather Morris, Miriam's husband – changed his name from Gold at the turn of the century to avoid anti-semitic persecution, which was rife at the time. He was killed in the battle of the Somme in 1916. I also discovered that Tommy's family nickname was Bill!

How I wish I could have met Bill Gold VC, and how I wish I could have introduced him to Mrs Green and my classmates!

CHAPTER SIX

FIGHT OR FLIGHT

A lan 'Pikey' Pike, even at the tender age of thirteen, was heading for a life of crime. He was huge, as hairy as an ape, a very grown-up boy hailing from a family of villains. He looked certain to follow in their footsteps and was one to avoid at school. We were the same age and in the same class. My brother Ralph was in the year below us and, hopefully I thought, out of the firing line.

Unfortunately he wasn't so lucky. One day Pike intercepted Ralph at lunchtime and said, 'You're Goldie's brother, aren't you? Another f***ing Jew!' He promptly grabbed hold of Ralph, climbed on his back and made him piggyback him across the schoolyard until Ralph collapsed under the weight. Then Pikey and his mates held him down and subjected him to the local torture: a knuckle twisted into the chest, inflicting great pain. I saw what was going on and ran across, screaming and shouting, pushing and shoving through the gathering crowd until I got to Pikey, who looked me up and down and simply said, 'After school, Goldie, after school.'

The school was mixed, but the boys and girls were only allowed together during lessons; we were segregated at break and lunchtime. There was even barbed wire on top of the walls between the two playgrounds. But everyone, it seemed, boys and girls, knew about the pending fight. They were fairly regular events, with one big fight at least once a month, and all well attended. The venue was a bombsite just outside the school grounds, and word raced around that Pikey was going to kill Goldie.

It was all very gladiatorial, and half the school were there by the time I arrived. I knew I had to go through with it as I had accepted the challenge and there was no way out because so many people knew about it. I knew the score only too well, because I had been in the circle myself watching

41

others fighting. My only hope was that Pikey wouldn't turn up. He might have found himself in trouble with one of the teachers and been kept in after school. But no, there he was, this huge, ugly, ape-like character waiting to tear me apart. I was small, but fortunately I was fit while Pikey was big, fat and out of shape.

I immediately made out I was boxing and shaping up to counter-attack, but all I was really doing was keeping out of the way of his wild swings. The first punch he landed almost floored me, and my circling and dodging were as much to allow me time to regain my senses as to wear him down. This went on for some minutes, and I could see his huge, hairy chest heaving and hear his breath escaping from that ugly mouth in ever shortening gasps. At that moment I thought I might yet survive. Apart from the first punch he had scarcely touched me, other than a couple of wild swings that had brushed my shoulders. I was feeling good while he was gasping for air, and it dawned on me that if I could continue to avoid his wild swings I could actually win.

I saw my opportunity when he summoned up the energy for one last effort. He came in swinging, throwing punches for all he was worth. I ducked underneath them, held my right fist rigid and let his momentum carry him into me. He went down on his knees, spitting blood from his mouth, breathing heavily like a downed bull. He was not knocked out, but it was the end of the fight.

Afterwards he had a grudging respect for me. He thought of me as a good, brave boxer with a knockout punch. I believe I got lucky. If any of his swings had caught me I would have gone, but he kept missing, sapping his own energy. It also changed the Gold brothers' status in the school, and it took the pressure off both of us. The pride of the young sibling in his older brother was also noted. Ralph wrote in his autobiography, 'From that day on the Gold name took on a new light.'

Three weeks later my newfound status was challenged, this time by Derek Moon, son of a local gangster and another from a family of villains. It was a bit like being Billy the Kid: I had beaten the bad guy and now all the local gunslingers wanted to take a shot at me. I hated being in this position – I had beaten Pike out of necessity – but now there was nowhere to hide.

The venue was the same, but this time my opponent was wearing a big ring on one hand, and clearly this was to be used like a knuckleduster. He was ready for me, sleeves rolled up, flexing his muscles, when there was murmuring from the crowd telling him he had to remove the ring. He eventually agreed, but then claimed he couldn't get it off. For a moment I hoped it would mean the fight being called off, but this was not a bout organised by the British Boxing Board of Control conforming to the Queensberry Rules. With a shrug, he launched himself at me, landing a punch on the side of my face, splitting my cheek with his ringed finger. The cut was so bad that I still have the scar to this day. I went down, but whereas today you would be kicked, at that time you were allowed to regain your feet, even in these unauthorised bouts. I was hauled to mine. The fight was stopped and there was another effort to get the ring off. It failed again, and the fight continued.

I decided all I could do was keep out of the way because I knew one more punch would finish it. But, like Pikey, gradually Moony tired and I was able to take advantage, raining punches to his face and body until, suddenly, he stopped fighting and looked ready to burst into tears – something which would have been unforgivable had he done so. I didn't go for the final blows even though the crowd of kids were urging me on. His hands, one of them still with that huge ring on – were hanging lifelessly by his sides. He looked pathetic. I just walked away.

It was my last fistfight ever – well, almost! The final fight, more of a one-punch cameo, came much later in life when I was driving to work and cut into a line of traffic to make a turn. This was in 1966 before road rage officially existed, and I was quite surprised when at the next set of traffic lights a guy got out of the car I had overtaken. I wound down my window to apologise, but this knight of the road clearly wasn't about to accept such an easy conclusion. He was taller but older than me: I was 30 and still fit, and he was probably twice my age. Today I would have locked the door and wound the window up, especially as he was frothing at the mouth, but he opened my door, pulled me out and lifted me up off my feet. In those days I wore fancy waistcoats, and I heard mine rip. Until then I was wondering what the hell he was doing and how I should respond. The chances were he was going to hit me, so after I heard my waistcoat tear I took a swing at him. Surprisingly, he went down like a sack of potatoes. Another man ran over claiming to be an off-duty police officer, and I thought I was going to be arrested. Instead, he said he had seen everything and told me to get in my car and be on my way. I never found out what happened to the angry driver, but I vowed it would be the last time I was involved in any physical confrontation.

The most important result of the fight with Pikey was its effect on the relationship between Ralph and me. We walked home together, and from that moment on we became much closer. Prior to the incident the age difference had been noticeable. I was the older brother and a good deal taller than Ralph, but on the way home I had my arm around his shoulder and he had his around my waist. We realised we were going to have to stick together if we were going to get through all of this – our father being in prison, anti-Semitism, poverty, illness, a poorly mum. The fight was the catalyst that brought these two Jewish brothers, these two ordinary cockney lads from the East End of London, together.

While I was able to take care of myself, Ralph was younger and he was beaten too often for his liking. He realised he would need to be able to defend himself, so he took up amateur boxing. He subsequently gained respect through his skill and determination, especially when he was on television in the Amateur Boxing Association Championships. He became something of a celebrity in the local area due to his success in the ring and was respected as a boxer just as I was as a footballer.

I can remember coming home one night from the YMCA when Ralph was a junior ABA champion, together with our friends Jimmy Brown, Charlie Cross, Iris and Millie, who I was in love with. Suddenly we were picked on by a group of bullies. The last thing we wanted was to get involved in a fight with six lads. The biggest guy picked on Jimmy, who was the biggest lad in our group. The guy who foolishly decided to take on Ralph quickly found himself out of his class and on his backside. Seeing Jimmy struggling, Ralph then took on his opponent. He was a good six inches taller than Ralph, but it only took a minute or so for the big guy to realise he was out of his depth and up against a serious boxer. The whole episode only lasted a few minutes but I was immensely proud of my younger brother. How we had moved on since Pikey! He saved me from getting involved in my third fistfight. This time I never had to throw a punch. I was simply a bystander.

Ralph was well respected in the neighbourhood. His picture appeared regularly in the local paper and everyone knew what he had achieved. At the same time I was getting publicity in the local press through my football. But the real coming together as a team was when we started working together, which is when we became best friends. We knew we had different qualities, and as we got older we took them into our joint business ventures and made them work for us. Neither of us would be where he is today if we hadn't teamed up, especially after breaking up with my father and facing the possibility of going out of business.

CHAPTER SEVEN

A VISIT TO DARTMOOR

My father wasn't really a bad person and he didn't do really bad things. He was just a spiv, the sort of man they now make television programmes about. I suppose one of the reasons I didn't like him was the way he treated my mother. I remember him, for instance, putting some jam on a slice of bread and pushing it into her face. But I guess that was the worst incident; I certainly never saw him strike her. Over the years I grew to dislike him more and more. As a kid you don't want to disapprove of your dad, and I fought it, but gradually I discovered I disliked everything he stood for.

He was sent down several times, the biggest sentence coming when he was used as the getaway driver of a lorry for a gang that was stealing a barge of copper from the River Thames at Greenwich. He was found guilty and sentenced to four years in Dartmoor for his crime. I was casually listening to the radio when I found out what my father had done and why he had been sent away. It was a sort of early Crimewatch programme, and I heard that my father Godfrey was the driver for a gang who pulled a barge off the Thames, up a creek, and stripped it of its cargo of copper bars. (Bizarrely, many years later my friend David Tearle opened a comedy club called Up the Creek on the banks of the very creek where Godfrey and the gang were arrested with their haul of copper.) Apparently there had been an informer within the gang, and to my humiliation I learnt how my father had been caught asleep at the wheel of the getaway vehicle.

We would go to see him when he was serving his various prison terms in and around London. When I went with my mum to these prisons she would put tobacco in my pocket and I would sit on Dad's knee so he could surreptitiously sneak it out of my pocket and into his own. This would have been at places like Wandsworth and the Scrubs. Dartmoor was something completely different. I guess he was sent there either as the result of repetitive crimes or maybe because the copper barge was a much bigger crime than the scams he was normally involved with.

When I was just into my teens and my sister Marie was seven or eight, we went to visit him at Dartmoor on our own. Imagine, just the two of us, nothing more than kids, going to the scariest prison in England. For the life of me I don't know why I went. I can only think my mother was poorly, or simply couldn't afford the time off work. Godfrey was permitted a monthly visit at Dartmoor, and because he was so far away and we were so poor we were given free tickets for the train, but on a specific date and a specific train. If my mother was ill it would stand to reason the ticket would not be wasted and I would go in her place.

It was no big deal, because even before my teens I would be left in charge of both my brother and sister when my mother was out working. In fact, when I was eleven I was going on 27; I even had pubic hair at that age, and at thirteen, at school camp at Yarmouth, I stood out physically from the others when we were showering because of my advanced puberty. I suppose camp was a little like prison. It was free for me, but I was still not quite part of it. I would see my pals receiving a daily food parcel and a letter from their mothers, but there would be nothing for me because my mother could not afford to send anything. The food at camp was adequate and filling, though, with plenty of porridge for breakfast. It all sounds pretty Spartan, but at least it was a change of scenery, and I enjoyed the sports. I even won the cross-country and was awarded a Churchill Five Shilling piece, which I cherish to this very day. I felt I had a talent for cross-country, but it was a difficult sport in which to progress in my circumstances and it lacked the popularity of sports like football and cricket. Besides, there wasn't a lot of country to run through in the part of the East End where I lived.

I have to admit there were moments in my life when I yearned for my father. I disliked him, but I yearned for him. I had this deep pain, probably purely a chemistry thing. I desperately wanted to believe him when he told me things were going to be different. He was always going to change things, and there were moments of hope that he would make those changes, but he never did. He would tell us that next time he came home he would make things up to us. I remember him coming home from prison once and I was so sure in my mind everything would change and he would make us all proud of him as he had promised. But I was always disappointed, and at school, to cover my shame, I told my friends he was away fighting in the army. Later, because they were asking me when he was due home on leave, I even told them he was dead, embellishing my tale by adding that he had been killed in action. I was so ashamed of him being in prison, I lied. I received some sympathy from my school chums – but then he was released and he reappeared. How do you reinstate a dead father? I had to lie again and say he had been missing, presumed dead, but had miraculously survived. In fact, my story made him an even bigger hero.

I just couldn't admit my father was in prison when other fathers were coming back from the fighting with tales of heroism and adventure. When he wasn't there, particularly when he was in Dartmoor for so long, I had to make up more stories of where he was and what he was up to. I told the tales so often I almost believed them myself. I just wanted a dad who was a hero, someone I could believe in, be proud of and look up to. Godfrey was no hero. He was in jail because he was a crook. To a degree I got away with my stories because the other children would eventually become bored and want to talk of other things.

I always hoped he would change, but my and Marie's visit to Dartmoor was one of those occasions when I had a wave of heartache come over me. Despite all that had happened I still wanted to have a relationship with my father, but there was this dull pain in my heart while I gradually built up my dislike of him for what he had done to my mother and, later, to my brother and me. At that stage of my life I simply lived from day to day. Those years from fourteen to twenty, when I felt the world was against me and every day was a battle, seemed to take for ever to pass. The year from twelve to thirteen, when I desperately wanted to be a teenager, just took forever. Yet the months between 49 and 50, when I needed every second because there was so much I wanted to achieve, felt like they were over in the blink of an eye. The other thing that seems to make time go quickly is happiness. If life is going well it flies by, but if you are in prison or, worse, a hostage, can you imagine how long it must take? Every day would be an eternity. People's perception of time differs, and knowing what is ahead helps.

Dartmoor stands out in my memory of the many things that happened in my formative years. I was carrying a small case with the items visitors were allowed to pass on to the inmates they were going to visit. This time there was no tobacco hidden in my pockets, or in Marie's, because this was Dartmoor and it was too scary to try anything like that. It was an awesome task for a young lad when we arrived. I was holding Marie's hand not knowing where we were going. We had to go through the security checks, and though it was an adventure it was a grim one, laden with the cold chill of being in this infamous prison and looking after my sister on my own.

Dartmoor left a lasting impression. It was a huge prison, especially in the eyes of a young boy from the slums of East London. There were massive walls keeping my dad in there, and bars at every window. It is the vastness of it all that stays in the mind. From a child's aspect everything was scary, for wasn't this where they hanged the really bad people? There were gallows for sure, and murderers lived there.

I tried hard to keep up with the other visitors as we walked along the corridors to the distant room where visitors met the prisoners face to face. My shoes were making a loud noise on the shiny stone cobbles, louder even than at school. Whenever I started to fall behind as a result of looking around, I hurried to catch up the others in case we were snatched by one of the prisoners. It was all in my imagination, of course, but it was frightening, and the memory of it has an almost haunting effect.

As the curtain was lifted we saw our dad, and he was clearly pleased to see us because his expression softened. He was not wearing a ball and chain as I'd imagined, but a grey suit. As children we were allowed into a room with him without bars or even a grille between us. There was just a small table, with him sitting on one side and us on the other.

I handed over the little suitcase to one of the guards and he took away things like letters and other packages to be checked before they were passed on to Godfrey.

I can recall sitting there for ten minutes with Dad, holding hands and saying nothing. I was glad when it was all over. Those 45 minutes seemed to be an eternity.

The tangible elements of the visit were bad enough; the psychological side was more powerful. I was ashamed my father was in there at all, and because of his actions I had been driven to lying to avoid stigma and to protect myself and the family. Weren't we in enough trouble being poor without having our father in prison? I had never taken any note of the routine when I went with my mother to other prisons, but at least I was no stranger to it, and I suppose it helped on that traumatic visit.

When we travelled with my mum she would take sandwiches and

maybe jump off the train at a station to buy other bits, like drinks or sweets, from a platform trolley. On our journey home from the prison Marie went on and on about how hungry she was. The train stopped occasionally, and seeing those little barrows on the platforms selling apples and sandwiches only made it worse for her. I was thinking of jumping out, but I asked myself what would happen to Marie if the train departed before I could get back on board. Hence, I took on the responsibility of taking her to the Pullman dining car for a meal. We both ordered food knowing I couldn't pay for it: I had looked in my pocket and there were just a few shillings remaining after the outward journey. But I knew exactly what I was going to do because I had seen it all happen in a movie.

When the steward approached us with the bill, I quoted the line from the film: 'Sir, I find myself financially embarrassed.' He was not impressed with this precocious statement. It did not go down at all well with this servant of British Rail. He was very officious, and muttered something about kids getting away with murder these days. He then fetched the conductor who was even more obnoxious, demanding my name and address in a very loud voice so that all the other people in the dining car could hear. I took my medicine and did not answer back.

All these years later I still don't know why I committed such a foolish prank. But it had been such a traumatic day, travelling to one of the country's worst prisons to visit my father. Maybe I just took a chance to cheer up my little sister and myself. And all the embarrassment was worthwhile. It was a meal I shall never forget. We finished it off with treacle pudding. There was even a little pot of custard to go with it. But who needed custard when there was hot treacle dripping down the sponge and pooling at the bottom of the dish? Three weeks later, my mum received a bill from British Rail, which she paid.

CHAPTER EIGHT

RUN RABBIT RUN

Football was my escape from the poverty trap, the first time in my life I found something I was really good at. I had failed my eleven-plus, and failed it miserably. I didn't even get close to passing. I bet my papers provided the worst results in the entire county – it was that poor. Remember, I missed much of my schooling because of illness, and there was no way I could catch up on lost time. My mum was too busy making garlands or out working and too tired to help me. Both my brother and I were too busy helping to keep the family afloat to catch up on lost schoolwork.

My brother would sell fresh mint – easy and quick to grow in great quantities – round the market while I would be helping my mother to make the garlands, or getting on a bus to a wholesaler to buy comics to sell as we began to add products to our stall. This was a further sign of our entrepreneurial spirit. We were always asking ourselves the question, 'Can we buy something cheap enough and sell it on the stall for a profit?' It wasn't so much the regular comics like the *Beano* and *Dandy* I went for because those could be purchased in any newsagent; what I sought was the newly offered American comics with superheroes like Superman, Batman, Captain Marvel and Spiderman. These were the very early imports, colourful and very collectable.

At the same time, football was a growing passion, but as a skinny little eleven-year-old kid I couldn't get into the school team and I was always a reserve, passing around the oranges at half-time. There were no substitutes in those days so I used to travel as a first reserve in case someone failed to turn up or became ill. I took my boots, but I never seemed to play as there were always eleven boys, and I was left to cut up the oranges. This went on for two years until, at the age of thirteen, one of the boys was injured. Then, suddenly, I found myself plunged into the team, and far from being nervous I revelled in the opportunity. The ball felt good at my feet, and I quickly realised that, small as I was, I was faster than most. If there was a chase for a ball twenty yards away, I would win it. I had genuine pace. I still wasn't sure how well I could play football, but I knew I was quick.

The other factor in my favour was that I was left-footed – the only one in the team. It was noted, and instead of standing shivering on the touchline, I became a regular in the first team. They tried me at left-back, left-half, inside-left, and finally on the wing. Bingo. I was suddenly the next Tom Finney. I sped down the line so quickly they nicknamed me The Rabbit, after the West Ham first-team winger Eric Parsons. I was selected to play for West Ham Boys just seven months after playing my first game for the school. It was wonderful. It was such escapism going to West Ham United on a Tuesday and Thursday evening for training. Wow! After training I loved going in the big bath the players used in those days. In fact I still carry a chipped tooth as a souvenir from when I dived in. It looked deeper than it really was.

The master who first picked me for West Ham Boys took me under his wing. He must have felt sympathetic towards a local lad from a poor background, but the kindness he showed me on a visit to play Norwich Boys – knowing I was from a Jewish background, he arranged for me to have something other than ham for my lunch – though it was well meant, left me once again with the big finger pointing at me saying I was different from the other lads. It was like the Blakey's I wore at school, the free boots that marked me out as I clip-clopped my way to pick up my ticket for a free lunch. He was so caring and worrying, which was unusual, yet it was causing me more problems. Maybe he was Jewish or his wife was; maybe he was just trying to look after me. But it was ill conceived because it made me stand out from the others, and that, at the time, was what I was trying to avoid.

Still, I loved my days playing football from the moment I first kicked a bundle of rags. In fact, I loved sport. I enjoyed swimming almost as much as I loved football, and we used to go with my father. He was the type who said 'You can do it', and would then throw you into the water to prove it. Sink or swim. It was a good East End philosophy in those days, and not just in the local baths. In the summer Ralph and I would go to Wanstead

Flats to swim in the duck ponds, paying our twopence on the bus. It was a great treat, and we swam with one towel for the two of us. Coming home on the first occasion we only had twopence between us. We caught the number 40 bus, which should have taken us all the way home, but the conductor realised we were going further than our penny tickets permitted so he kicked us off and made two young boys walk the length of Green Street to get home.

Sport turned our lives around, Ralph with his boxing and me with my football.

Until then the only thing we had been successful at was surviving. Ralph won the ABA Schoolboy Championships and went on to box for England and Great Britain, and almost won a place in the famous GB v. USA match at Wembley when Britain won 10–0, Billy Walker becoming an overnight sensation after knocking out a massive American heavyweight. It was the equivalent of Wycombe Wanderers beating Real Madrid 5–0. I remember it well as I watched on a little black and white television, hoping to see my brother box. He was first reserve and didn't make it, but to this day he expresses his relief that he wasn't picked just in case he had lost and the match had finished 9–1! Ralph was an international on many occasions but refused to turn professional because by then we had made our start in business. He considered the prospect several times but eventually turned his back on a boxing career.

He boxed for West Ham Boxing Club. He was up before six a.m. most mornings to run along the sewer bank and trained at least two nights a week in the gym. He reached the Schoolboy Finals, but his big night was the London Championships at the Royal Albert Hall in 1961 with the fights being shown on live television. He was even interviewed by the legendary Harry Carpenter. The cameras were idle when he beat Ernie Wiles against the odds, but before the start of the finals the then young, up-and-coming Harry Carpenter interviewed every competitor. The problem was my nervous brother couldn't remember his Christian name and called him Paul. Carpenter responded by calling my brother Larry. It was hilarious, because Ralph had Harry mixed up with the film star Paul Carpenter, and Harry got his own back by using the name of famous band leader Larry Gold. Ralph suddenly remembered it was Harry, but dropped the 'H', so Harry dropped the 'R' and called him Alf. But Ralph had the last laugh when he beat the favourite Keith Waterhouse in the final to become London ABA champion. Everyone in our area seemed to have seen the bout on television or read about it in the newspapers, especially *Boxing News*, the fight game's bible.

We were travelling in parallel, him in boxing and me in football. It was wonderful for us, bringing pride and achievement into our lives and our home for the first time. Everything before then was failure, from my eleven-plus through to the fact that we were poor and had no possessions to speak of. Football took me out of that life and put me on a level playing field, if you will forgive the pun. People say we did terrifically to get along, and the mind of a young boy surrounded by the worst house, the worst furniture, the worst garden, the worst food and second-hand clothes is terribly aware of all these things. Sure there were others who were poor, but I was the poorest of all those around, and it showed. Some of those memories are really bitter, but football was a great leveller.

I played for West Ham Boys for three successive years between the ages of thirteen and fifteen. I was selected for every game and never missed a match. I was also picked for Essex and London Boys and began to dream about what the future might hold for me. I could picture myself running out at Old Trafford or Highbury with the Hammers. One of the great regrets I have, and the reason why I now hoard every single item from my life, is that when I was a kid I didn't continue to keep every programme, poster and cutting from the local papers. I started out doing it, but as the pile grew I began to believe I was going to become a star so I stopped collecting because I thought there would be so much more to come. Now I keep everything that's written or televised about my family and me. I suddenly thought it was a good way to diarise my life. This is an important time, and I know I will regret it if I don't keep notes and references. This book, of course, does all of that for me – it brings it all together.

My early teens was a great time in my life because suddenly I became somebody, even if it was only a small somebody. I remember riding my bike to school as a fourteen-year-old when a complete stranger, a man of about 40 wearing a cloth cap typical of the time, suddenly called out, 'Hey, Goldie! Well done, son!' He must have been a fan at the game the previous Saturday, when we beat East Ham Boys at Upton Park and I scored two of the goals. I felt a million dollars when he recognised me; I was ten feet tall. For the first time in my life, instead of an insult I was being complimented. Suddenly I wasn't a scrounger or a poor boy without any ambition in life. I existed, and it was a wonderful feeling. It was quite a special moment in my life, and I was filled with pride, as was my mum, who used to get the cuttings from the paper and go over to Ethel, her friend, to show her.

People say you don't hear the crowd when you are playing, but when I turned out for London Youth at Selhurst Park against Glasgow Youth, despite there being 12,000 people in the ground, I can recall distinctly hearing people call out, 'Come on Rabbit!'

That's what people did then. They would turn out for reserve and youth matches in almost the same numbers as for the first team. It gave me a great sense of achievement to be out in front of all these people and, better still, to be recognised. It was wonderful, and travelling to play football also allowed me to see something of the world beyond the East End. We went where the professional teams went. Travelling to Sheffield by coach, for instance. The journey took all day as there were no motorways in those days. We'd stay overnight in a hotel and play at Bramall Lane the following morning. It was a great thrill. As you got on to the coach you sat in a comfortable seat, you were treated well and equally in the hotel, and could enjoy the luxury of a hot bath after the game. All we had at home was the old tin bath once a week, or even once a fortnight, and I was third behind Marie and Ralph, with all that that entails! I loved those baths after football. There was even a massage before a game if we wanted one, and if you had a sore foot, on came the physiotherapist to sort you out.

I progressed to the West Ham A team, which was a huge stride for a sixteen-year-old, playing alongside full-time professionals, players I had watched from the terraces. The A side was not a team for the kids but for the seniors who were trying to find a bit of form, or who were working their way back after an injury, players like my great hero Bert Hawkins at centre-forward, who I played alongside a number of times. I remember to this day him calling out to me when I got the ball, 'Goldie, on me 'ead! On me 'ead, son!' I was desperate to follow the others in the team and become a full-time professional, and I thought my time had come when the great Ted Fenton, the famous manager of West Ham United, one of the all-time greats, called me into what I remember as a huge office. 'Gold,' he said, 'I have had some great reports from the A team. I have some forms for you to take home to your parents for them to sign so you can become an apprentice professional.'

At that precise moment everything that had gone before was forgotten. I had achieved my dream. At least I thought I had. That, in fact, was as far as I got on my yellow brick road to football stardom, for my father, in his wisdom, refused to sign the forms. Here was this alpha male who had hardly ever been at home trying to show that when he was there he was the boss and his word was law. There was no other reason I could think of then for him refusing to sign. Maybe it was because there was at that time in the game a maximum wage of only £20 a week and no prospect of playing on to your old age, but I don't think so. After all, what was the alternative? At the time I was an apprentice bricklayer who ran errands for other builders and earned even less.

I do believe, however, that a degree of jealousy was involved. I remember being in the garden kicking a ball against the shed, using both feet and generally practising my skills. In those days there was no trickery on public display, but I could juggle the ball with foot, head, thigh and chest. I was improving my ball control for the sheer enjoyment of it. But one sunny Sunday afternoon out of season my father came out into the back garden and told me to stop showing off. It was a shock to me. Who was I supposed to be showing off to? There was no one else there. He considered it was the big-head syndrome. So him saying no to his son becoming a professional footballer certainly could have been envy on his part, especially when I learnt that as a youngster he aspired to be a boxer and never made the grade. Then again, how you can be jealous of your son is beyond me. If one of my daughters does anything of note, I burst with pride.

Perhaps at a later stage of my life I would have argued the case, but you simply did not do it then and I had to go back to Ted Fenton to tell him that my dad wanted me to complete my brickie apprenticeship. Fenton asked if I would bring my father in to meet him so he could discuss it. I went home and told Godfrey what he had said and he turned round and replied, 'There ain't nothing he can say to me to make me change my mind.' He wouldn't even go and see him, and that was the end of the matter as far as he was concerned. The irony is, had it been during one of the many long periods when Goddy was absent from the family house, my mother would have been only too delighted to sign the forms for me, knowing how much it meant. Perhaps I should have bypassed my father and gone straight to Mum, but it just wasn't the sort of thing you did in those days.

I was naturally devastated, but I was still like the kid in the air-raid shelter – invincible. I was still optimistic, I felt I was good enough eventually to become a professional footballer, and I was convinced my chance would come again. So I carried on playing football. The youth team manager I had got on so well with at West Ham left Upton Park for Leyton in the Isthmian League, and I went straight into the first team there.

I remember playing against Hendon shortly before they were due to play at Wembley in the Amateur Cup final against Bishop Auckland. The manager of Hendon came into the dressing room before we played in front of a full house and said, 'Chaps, I just want to say that next week Hendon are representing the Isthmian League at Wembley, so today should be a game of football with nothing aggressive.' In other words he was saying, 'Don't kick us!' As soon as he went out of the door our giant of a centre-half spat out, 'Not f***ing likely!' And out we went to kick seven bells out of the opponents, our centre-half whacking their centre-forward to hell and back. But they gave as good as they got and were probably a better prepared team for it. Even so, they lost 2–0 at Wembley as the famous north-east team began a run of three successive Amateur Cup victories.

Then, as a seventeen-year-old, I went with the coach to Fulham, still determined to make the grade. I met the great and much-lamented Johnny Haynes at Craven Cottage – the thrill of a lifetime. After winning the 1953 Senior Cup at Craven Cottage and receiving my winner's medal, I went upstairs to the 'Cottage', the famous building at Fulham Football Club, for a drink before making my train journey home. Playing on the snooker table were Johnny Haynes, Jimmy Hill and two other players. The phone rang and the barman called out to Johnny's partner, 'You are wanted downstairs.' To my surprise and delight, Johnny turned to me and said, 'Goldie' – I was thrilled he knew my name – 'it's your shot next. You're my new partner and we're ten points behind.' We went on to win the game, and afterwards he bought me a drink. I have many times since told people that I once played with Jimmy Hill and the great Johnny Haynes when I was at Fulham and often neglected to tell them that the sport was snooker, not football.

Soon after that the coach left Fulham, and again I moved with him. In fact, between the ages of sixteen and 21 I did the rounds, playing non-league football for Leyton, Leytonstone and Barking, and for Fulham, Charlton and West Ham in an effort to break into the game as a professional. Charlton was a very brief affair as the coach who looked after me did not stay long himself. The club offered me an apprenticeship, but my heart was still with the Hammers. It was all I dreamt about, and I still felt I could make it. Playing professional football is every young boy's dream, both then and now.

But my football life finished when I was in my early twenties because by that time I was dedicating myself to my new business. Of course in some ways I regret the decision. If I could have had everything, I would have played for West Ham and England, been better than Tom Finney, and still been a success in business. But the reality is that you cannot have everything in this life. You can pursue it, you can chase the pot of gold at the end of the rainbow, but only at your peril, because if you pursue too much you might achieve nothing. My life has gone the way it has, though of course I would change the odd thing here and there if I could. I would have liked to make love to more women, for instance – or more love to fewer women – but I would still want to end up with my lovely Lesley. I often say to her that I wish we had met when I was sixteen.

So at the age of 21 I decided I wouldn't sign on again for Leyton and would concentrate solely on the shop I had just acquired. Saturday was going to be my busiest day and I needed to throw everything into it. That was when my life changed and football, sadly, receded into the background. I did play again however, for Biggin Hill some twelve years later, and it was wonderful to put on a pair of boots again, with plastic instead of leather studs, that fitted beautifully and were really comfortable to wear. Even kicking a ball that didn't weigh a ton when it was wet was a new pleasure I had not experienced before. As a nippy young winger it would have been wonderful to play in lightweight boots under those conditions and not be ferociously tackled from behind. I still have the scars from those tackles which blighted the game when I was trying to make my way. They were considered missed tackles then! What a joke. They were brutal methods of stopping a winger, and were widely practised.

But always at the back of my mind is the belief that with the right opportunity I could have become a professional footballer. The reason I say that is because I was a wide left player where there was, and remarkably still is, a dearth of left-footed players. I was blessed with pace, good control and a great left foot. All I would have needed was more fitness, daily training and good coaching.

CHAPTER NINE

SLAVE LABOUR

Back when I was fifteen and still playing for West Ham Boys, I couldn't wait to leave school and start earning my living properly, to contribute to the household funds and make life easier for all of us, especially my mum. When Ralph and I started working – he as a clerk in an Inland Revenue office, me as an apprentice bricklayer – suddenly we were both contributing a couple of pounds a week to the household instead of a few shillings from our paper rounds. In fact we had moved up a rung or two because by that time we had converted the front room of the house into a little shop from where Mum sold sweets, books, comics and cards for many years. We were just looking out for each other, something we will continue to do for the remainder of our lives. With Ralph and me earning and Mum in her shop there wasn't the acute poverty we had suffered during the war years and directly afterwards, but we were still very poor, even in comparison to some of our neighbours. Still, we had, at last, started to climb the ladder, though we were not aware of any amazing transformation.

It did not all happen at once, because when I left school at fifteen I was out of work for a year, which was a terrible burden to carry for a young man desperate to pay his way. Even when I eventually found a job it was only as an apprentice bricklayer, which was nothing short of cheap labour. I was asked, or rather ordered, to do all the rotten jobs none of the men wanted to do, and even when I finished my apprenticeship at 21 I wasn't the greatest bricklayer because I was used and abused rather than properly trained. I was seen as a handy gofer to run all the errands, make the tea, fetch the newspaper and anything else too menial for the men. I eventually received my diploma to say I was a fully qualified bricklayer, but I knew I was nothing more than a glorified labourer.

To this day I remember the company – how could I forget them? They were called Jerrams of East Ham – horrible people to work for who treated me like slave labour and gave me little in return, not even an education in the job. If someone had built a wall six inches too high it was me who was sent to chisel it down to the right level. Rather than creating I was always clearing up in the wake of others or running errands. I loathed the experience and couldn't see any way of escaping it because I was locked into the apprenticeship. It was almost reminiscent of my childhood: here I was, on the verge of manhood, and I was still cold, laying bricks in all kinds of weather for next to nothing, and what's more I wasn't very good at it because of a lack of instruction. But I tried – how I tried! I never once sat on my backside feeling sorry for myself. I was always doing something, even though I was earning a pittance compared with those around me. As an apprentice bricklayer, I was on £4 a week working next to a man earning three or four times that amount, and in a day I was probably laying as many bricks as him as well as making the tea and fetching his *Daily Mirror*.

Still, from the moment I became an apprentice bricklayer, as menial as it was, I was earning twice as much as I'd earned from all the other jobs I did while waiting to be accepted, like sweeping up and carrying boxes of fruit in the market (ironically, for the same people I'd stolen from when I was a boy). Now I had more fruit than I could eat, with all the bruised apples and other items not quite good enough to go on sale. After the market I would clear up as the stallholders packed their things away and would be paid extra to carry all their goods back to their yards.

When I started working full time on the building site, I would see the governor arrive in his chauffeur-driven car. He would walk around without knowing I existed. He never once acknowledged me in five years. I loathed the man, but I thank him for teaching me a strong lesson on how *not* to treat people. There was of course no reason why he should have said hello – other than out of politeness for a young man who worked for him for so long for so little. When I go to visit a workplace with 200 of my employees I will know half of them by sight and the other half by their Christian names. It is a different culture now. We were just a form of cheap labour when I was young with few or no rights at all. We could be sacked at the drop of a hat and no one would have bothered or cared.

In the year before I was given an apprenticeship I would go to Jerrams and other building sites and wait every day to see if there was an opening. I was going to be a bricklayer, and nothing else entered my mind because that was what was expected of me. I had it firmly in my mind how important it was to learn a trade, something drilled into me by my mum and the teachers at school. I had been to the School of Building and done half a day a week at different trades, and I was best – or at least I thought I was – at bricklaying. I had a dream of building the new St Paul's Cathedral once I became fully qualified as the best brickie in East London.

My friends were great while I was unemployed. I wanted to be a full-time, fully paid employee so I could pay my way and contribute to the housekeeping fund, but they understood my position, and if we were going to the pictures or a football match they would all chip in and pay for me. These were my friends from school, people like Jimmy Brown, Charlie Cross, Victor Phillips and others, all of whom found jobs soon after they had finished school. For a time I was the only one out of work out of our group, but they looked after me, and I am friends with Charlie to this very day. Sadly, my best friend Victor, who married Ann Harwood, left for Australia in the late 1950s and I have never heard from him again.

Charlie wrote to me more than ten years ago to tell me he was going to my mother's 80th birthday party. I walked into the West Ham United supporters' club where my mother was having her celebration – a typical East End knees-up; it was like travelling back in time – and as I arrived I looked across the room and there was Charlie standing at the bar. It was fantastic to see him, and I discovered he still lived locally, was still a West Ham supporter and was now a semi-retired brickie. The bond of friendship was still there and we have been close friends ever since. We often speak on the telephone, he stays over at my house, and I take him to see games at Birmingham. One weekend I was going to a game at Manchester City and planned to take off from Biggin Hill and land at Stansted to pick up David Sullivan, co-owner of Birmingham City Football Club, and his partner Eve before flying on to Manchester. I was talking to Charlie on the Wednesday before the game and invited him to travel with us, suggesting that he meet me at Stansted. He arrived an hour before I landed, and waited in the luxury VIP lounge. We had coffee, waited for David and Eve to arrive, then climbed aboard our Gold Air HS125 jet, registration GOLD D. Charlie was thrilled by the experience. Two ex-brickies sitting on board a private jet flying north to watch a game of football! We enjoyed every minute as we were picked up at the airport and driven to the brand-new stadium, which had been built to stage the 2002 Commonwealth Games, where we were entertained in the boardroom before watching the match from the directors' box. How good a feeling it was for me to be able to entertain Charlie all those years after he had helped me when I was out of work.

We all learnt to dance, because in those days until you knew how to dance you had no chance of meeting the girls. There was nowhere else to meet them socially once you had grown out of the youth club years because it was mainly men and older women who went to the pubs. Clubs and discos simply did not exist. Sadly, I was a hopeless dancer with no rhythm and no confidence – and, consequently, no girls! At least I was now earning enough to give Mum some housekeeping, have a little left for the bits and pieces most young men waste their money on, and to buy a motorbike.

Yes, the first passion of my life, at the age of eighteen, was not, as with most young men, a young girl, but a motorbike. The Ariel 350cc was my first great extravagance in life, it cost me £60, and it took me three years to pay for it. It was worth every penny and every one of those years. It opened up the whole world for me – well, at least the part of the world I had not previously experienced through football. I could drive to places I had never been before for just a cupful of petrol. The greatest joy of all was when I went to Butlin's at Skegness for my first ever holiday. Three of us made the journey on our bikes as I went with a couple of male friends – all of us virgins. Sadly, I was the only one to come back the same as I went out.

I loved the freedom of the concept: by the sea, away from the slowly recovering East End, no boss telling you to make the tea or fetch the newspaper, no mother worrying over you. We took full advantage, sleeping in until midday, dancing until the early hours, then trying our luck with the girls. Lots of youngsters went to the holiday camps with the express purpose of experimenting with the opposite sex. The joke doing the rounds was about the security man hammering on the chalet door of a young man and demanding, 'Have you got a girl in there?' When the answer came back in the negative, the guard was reputed to have responded, 'Hold on a minute and I'll go and get you one!'

Of course it was never as easy as that, and for me it was all a learning experience. I managed to fumble around for a few nights with a couple of girls, but I got no further because I didn't know what I was doing. I recall vividly the three of us taking three girls back to the chalet and my friend Terry, on the upper bunk, leaning over and asking me if I had a spare contraceptive. I had a pack of three Durex in my wallet which I had carried around for about two years. God knows how safe it was. It was clear I was going to have no use of it that evening so I passed it up. The bed above me shook for a couple of minutes, then all went quiet except for the giggling of the other two girls. The next night it was my other friend who rattled his bed against the walls. But though I persevered, nothing happened for me.

It was all part of growing up, some girls and boys a little more advanced or braver than others. Today many kids seem to lose their virginity by the time they are teenagers and are married with a child by the time they reach an age when I was still fumbling about without any success. I have watched many things change as I have grown older, and nothing is more remarkable than the difference between teenage boys now and in the 1950s. Nowadays a typical lad of sixteen or seventeen can be over six feet tall and wise to the world. He has probably already been to America for his holidays and is well versed in women, sex and designer beers. But we were still considered kids at that age, suppressed and held in our place, seen and not heard, as they used to say. Now you have a seventeen-year-old earning a couple of hundred pounds a week and living with a girl in a flat. That was unheard of in the fifties. Still, I guess I must be one of the few boys in their late teens who went to Butlin's and came back a virgin.

But they were great memories, particularly riding down to Skeggy on our motorbikes for my first proper holiday, away from home for more than a day for the first time in my short life. Yet in truth there is little to tell of those five years of my life to the age of 21. It was just about playing football and going to work to earn enough money to pay for my beloved motorbike and play my part in helping to keep the home together.

CHAPTER TEN

HANK JANSON TO THE RESCUE

I suppose if there was one person who changed my life it was an American private eye who went by the name of Hank Janson. He was smooth, smart, full of great one-liners, and made out with the ladies as if they were going out of fashion. He was a latter-day James Bond. He always solved his cases, he put me on the road to riches, and he was, of course, totally fictional.

When I finished my apprenticeship as a brickie my brother Ralph, who was by then a book and magazine salesman, told me that one of the shops he served had gone out of business and the landlord had told him that if we found the outstanding rent, for no more than a couple of hundred pounds we could have the shop and the stock left in it. It was, I reasoned, too good a chance to miss, so I reluctantly sold my motorbike for around £150 to pay for the lease (I still have a photograph of my Matchless 500 twin, in a prominent place in my house), Ralph contributed £150, we borrowed £100 from my mum, and suddenly I was in my own shop on John Adam Street, just around the corner from Charing Cross station in the middle of London.

The shop had barely enough stock to open its doors, and consequently sales were poor. I discovered why the previous owner had gone bust after taking just £37 in the first week. I wondered what I had let myself in for. The key to the future was obtaining credit so that we could keep the business going and provide some additional stock, so the £37 went straight back into replenishing magazines and books. I had to forget about the telephone bill, the rent, the rates, even eating.

I put all my skills as a maintenance man into building racks and shelving. There was no front door to the shop. Entrance was gained through a side door, so I had to put the book racks outside every morning so people could see what I was selling. When I first moved into the shop it had some shelving, but I wanted it to look better so I would work on it when it was quiet or after closing time. To utilise the little space I had I would open the window on to the street and serve through it like a kiosk, hanging all my racks on the outside wall. It was more like a newsstand than a shop, as the customer not only had to enter through the side door but also to turn into a corridor to get into the shop. I also invested in a canopy to pull down over the street so that I didn't have to bring my stock in when it rained.

But a couple of months into the business I knew we weren't going to make it. I was making no profit, and the only encouragement I had was people telling me it would pick up in the summer when the tourists arrived. But I was going to run out of cash before then. I simply wasn't going to survive.

That was when I took my courage in my hands and decided to go to bank manager David Witchall to ask for a 'monkey' to help me keep the business going. I was petrified, and he was mystified. He hadn't a clue what a monkey was, and I had no business plan to show him. But he obviously liked what I had to say as, in my broad cockney accent, I explained what a monkey was. He not only lent me the £500 I needed but an additional £200 on top.

But it was still not enough, and I was plummeting downhill financially. Then came my second stroke of luck. Ralph was due to pick me up to go to Mum's for our weekly chicken soup dinner, but he rang in a panic to tell me he would be late because his van had broken down. I told him not to worry; I would wait in the shop for him to arrive. As it turned out I was waiting for him from six until 9.30, and during that three-and-a-half-hour spell I took more money than I had taken for the entire week. That was the luck that probably changed my life. The light came on – literally. It was dark by seven o'clock at that time of the year and my little shop was so close to the main road that it caught the eye. Everyone who walked down Villiers Street towards Charing Cross station saw the lights and many came to see what was still open. The shop, although small and almost hidden down a side street, stood out like a beacon, especially from the busy main road and the bustling railway station. We were just two shops down, and I could see people looking down the road at my brightly lit shop. Don't forget, in those days shops didn't stay open late; even restaurants closed early in the city. But my shop beckoned everyone who passed to come and have a look at what was going on.

The following day I stayed open late again and waited until my last train at ten o'clock. The same thing happened again. The difference in takings was immense. Instead of opening at ten in the morning until six in the evening I started opening at noon and staying open until ten p.m., except for Friday and Saturday when it would be midday to midnight: on the first Friday I'd decided to open until the last customer left, which was midnight. The money rolled in.

I couldn't get home so I slept in the shop. I promptly went out and invested in a sleeping bag. I had a paraffin heater in the shop, and in the back was a toilet and hand basin. I knew I couldn't live like that for long, but it was the only way I could prove there was regular late-night trade. Once I had proved it conclusively to myself I found better accommodation. I tried the odd small hotel but they were too expensive, so I settled for digs round the corner.

The customers were a strange, eclectic mix. During the day there was the usual assortment of tourists, couples and singles of both sexes, just as if I were running a shoe shop, but at night the clientele became predominantly male. They were salesmen, working-class men, in fact all sorts who found themselves on their own in a city as big as London, or catching a late train home and killing time before the last departure. My entrepreneurial flair began to emerge. I went to Kosmos, the local wholesaler, and bought his entire stock of Hank Janson books at half price because the publisher had been sent to prison. Until then I had been working all hours fitting up the shop and breaking off to serve my customers, but now I was spotting what was selling and developing my business. I was buying Hank Janson books in bulk to cut my costs while at the same time increasing the cover price from two shillings and sixpence to three shillings and sixpence. What is more, I was selling lots of the more expensive titles.

I knew what the customer wanted because I read everything myself. I quickly learnt that you cannot tell a book by its cover. While some Hank Jansons were erotic, others had no erotica in them at all and were simply detective novels. I separated them and increased the price of those that were erotic, and my customers quickly became aware that if a Janson book had a white serrated label with a black price on it the contents were spicy. I eventually extended this practice beyond Janson. The customers paid more, but they knew what they were getting.

I bought a couple of thousand Janson books from the wholesaler, who had been trying to return them to the publisher. I then discovered the address of the publisher's warehouse and introduced myself to the manager, who was looking after the stocks of thousands of books. I started to buy them direct from him, bypassing the wholesaler. I was selling something most people were afraid to sell because they were sexy, though they could scarcely be described as pornographic. I couldn't believe two men had been sent to prison for publishing them. It was outrageous. Hank Janson quickly became my biggest seller. The late-night shoppers often sought out erotica, particularly those Janson books. Call it what you like – one man would call it erotica while another would call it porn – but it was clearly what these men wanted to read (there were, of course, no pictures other than the cover). My only regret is I didn't charge five shillings instead of three and sixpence.

The dirty raincoat brigade didn't exist – except on television and maybe the odd undercover policeman. The customers were normal working people dressed in their work clothes, whether it was a suit or a donkey jacket. I only saw people in macs when it was raining, and they were going into restaurants and hotels as well as my bookshop. But the expression will probably last for ever, perpetuated by the media and comedians like the late Peter Cook and Dudley Moore. It is the same sort of expression as 'dirty magazines' and 'mucky books' – where did those terms come from? I think it is a misnomer reflecting a complete lack of understanding of the reality and the facts. I can say that the smartest, most elegantly dressed man about town was just as capable of buying erotica as Dudley Moore in his guise as a dirty old man. Nothing was more pornographic than the Pete and Dud audiotapes, which happened by accident. The sort of stuff they used was gratuitous filth, particularly in the second tape, which hardly lived up to the spontaneity of the first.

Admittedly there wasn't much erotica in the country at the time, and not much in my shop, but it did not take a genius to realise that the product selling most was erotica. This was what late-night selling was all about in 1958. By this time, alongside the Janson books I had also started to sell pin-up magazines – *Carnival, Pep, Spick and Span* and the like – which were considered sexy and sold well. Incredibly, there wasn't a nipple to be seen, except in *Health and Efficiency*, which airbrushed out all the other so-called 'naughty bits' as the men and women played volleyball and tennis. Compared with today's top-shelf magazines they were mild in the extreme, but the fight against authority continued for the next 30 years. What a terrible waste of public money, and what a waste of time for the police and the courts.

Because there were no clear definitions at the time, *Cosmopolitan* magazine through to hardcore pornography could be called erotica by one person and pornography by another. They are only words, and it was Lord Longford, after a year of constant campaigning, who changed the name from erotica to pornography. At one time in the industry, as in much of the media, there was a generally understood definition. For example, *Jane*, the scantily-clad beauty in the *Daily Mirror* cartoon strip, was considered erotica, not pornography. But it all became very cloudy and difficult to interpret as you went from *Jane* to *Health and Efficiency* and other magazines, which showed breasts and the occasional nipple but, hilariously, no pubic hair. There was nothing generally available beyond that until American-influenced magazines like *Playboy* and *Penthouse* became available, and then erotica suddenly branched out into expressions such as soft porn and hardcore. Then along came Lord Longford, who embraced the entire spectrum from live sex shows to the harmless and popular *Tit Bits* and categorised them all as pornography. During his year-long investigation into the sex industry he visited a live sex show in Hamburg, and when asked what he thought of it he answered wittily, 'I have seen enough for science and more than enough for pleasure.' But what Lord Longford did in a short period of time was transform the media and public's perception.

I believed my interpretation was common sense, that magazines like *Light and Shade*, *Reveille* and *Health and Efficiency*, followed by the early pin-up books like *Spick and Span*, were nothing more than titillating erotica. Not so long ago I went with Lesley to Greenwich market in London – which we own along with David Tearle's family – and we bought a pack of the sort of pin-up books I used to sell for a shilling and sixpence. They cost me considerably more this time round, but it was a pleasant exercise in nostalgia. Not only that, it also showed how harmless these magazines really are. There is a lot more sex in today's Sunday papers.

The problem when you were fighting against the Lord Longfords of this world was that no one out there would offer their support. No one in Parliament, for instance, stood up and argued for more freedom for erotica once Lord Longford had got up in the House of Lords and attacked it. Their lordships were frightened of being labelled for any support they might show for the so-called sex industry. But how many of their lordships purchased what Lord Longford deemed pornography? I can tell you: most of them.

I was hauled up in court on a number of occasions, but in business you have to have courage as well as luck and opportunity. When people ask what are the elements for success, one of the things I promote is courage. I had to have it otherwise the business and my future would have collapsed. Some laws are not good, and as a young man I couldn't understand why I wasn't allowed to trade at such times. Who was I hurting? The potty law was in the way of me making a living. Why should anyone tell me I couldn't work after six p.m. if I wanted to, and if my customers wanted me to? If I had conformed I don't think I would be in the position I am today.

I have every respect for the law, but throughout my entire life I can demonstrate occasions when the law has been an ass. There was a time when we would shake our heads and mutter about the iniquities, but times have changed and people won't stand for stupid laws any more. I tried opening my shop during prime hours on Sunday but it turned out to be the worst day of trading, and anyway, I needed to take a break. Eventually I only traded on Sundays in the summer months when the tourists were about. I even became an employer as, ultimately, I brought someone in to work on Sundays. He was a busker who would simply fill in for me while I did the bookwork, and I would pay him a commission on the books he sold. He worked whatever hours he wanted.

It wasn't the police I had trouble with so much as the council, what would now be called Trading Standards. I was regularly hauled up in front of the local magistrate and fined £30. Every time I paid up, walked away and completely ignored them. Had it been a serious law with any depth of meaning they would have increased the fine each time, but they didn't. There would be spells when one person would make it his job to come and get me. They were like modern-day traffic wardens. They could have put me out of business by fining me every day, but as I said, the magistrates never increased the fine and seemed to understand when I explained that this was my business, how I earned my living.

Here was a crime with no victim, and that was to plague me for a good deal of my working life. Whenever I was arrested for selling so-called pornography, there was no victim. Who was the victim? Certainly not the person buying the book or magazine.

If I asked a forum of 100 people who had driven along a motorway at four in the morning, hands up all those in the room who drove at no more than 70 miles an hour? I doubt if many hands would go up. So all those people in the room thought the law was an ass as well. The 70 miles an hour limit was introduced 40 years ago when there was no MOT, no ABS breaking systems and minimal street lighting. The cars and motorways have improved dramatically, so what are we doing still limiting speed at 70 miles an hour? And during rush hour on a wet or snowy evening with swirling fog or black ice and lots of cars on the road, why is it still 70 miles an hour? Variable speed limits and common sense are needed, it seems to me.

I broke the law in my little shop because I thought it was a stupid law, and I suppose I was fined around twenty times, but it never discouraged me. I was young and defiant. I was never going to stop doing what I thought was right. Though that, of course, was once I had overcome the trauma of my first appearance before the beak. I was absolutely terrified. I could hardly answer the magistrate when asked whether I was guilty or not guilty. When I pleaded not guilty he demanded to know how I could be not guilty when the shop was open at 9.30 on a Wednesday evening. It must have sounded as silly to him as it did to me. But if I hadn't appeared so often before one particular magistrate I would never have discovered a way of getting round the crazy laws that were hampering my business. 'Not you again, Gold,' I remember the grey-haired magistrate barking out as I stepped into the dock. He had thieves, muggers, drunks and other serious criminals to deal with and he was clearly fed up with me taking up his valuable time. So he craftily gave me this piece of advice, which would enable me to beat the system: 'You wouldn't have to be here if you sold newspapers and periodicals,' he said, realising I was a hard-working young man trying to earn an honest living.

This was more than a throwaway line – it was the answer to my problem. By stocking periodicals I could justify staying open as long as I liked, and no council official would check whether customers were walking out with a magazine or a book. I added periodicals to my stock and the council harassment stopped. It was all I needed: one opportunity, and I grasped it. The magistrate had no need to tell me, but he did, and for the final two years in that shop I was not fined again.

But those court cases were awful early on because they came at a time when I was just beginning to make money and things were going right for us. Ralph always used to say with some truth, 'Beware of the leveller! Nothing is for ever.' They, whoever they may be, will not let you have a free ride; you have to work every step of the way. There is always adversity coming into your life, but if you have the resolve it eventually strengthens you. Be down for a day, but bounce back and start again; give in, and you will fail. I learnt to accept the challenge.

I dedicated myself to that shop for more than three years with a serious work ethic and little involvement in anything else. Needless to say I had a very restricted social life. I smoked a little and drank even less – just the occasional glass of red wine because, fortunately for my wallet, I couldn't stand the taste of beer. In my entire life I have hardly set foot in a pub, until they started selling decent food. After sleeping in the shop for the first few weeks, I went home during the week but stayed in my digs on a Friday and Saturday when I knew I would be busy late into the night. It was three years of virtually non-stop work, six days a week with a break on Sunday when at least half a day was spent doing the accounts. Sunday, like late-night trading, was illegal, and the powers-that-be were even keener to hunt me down on a Sunday than they were on weekday nights.

We were on our way in the business world, but, as Ralph predicted, nothing is for ever. Again, I got very, very lucky. I could have still been in the same shop today if the landlord had not come along and told me he was giving me six months' notice. I was distraught and pleaded to keep the shop, even offering him more rent, but he pointed out the redevelopment clause in my lease. (He never did redevelop the site as he claimed; he clearly got a better deal with one of the betting companies and tripled his rent.) I was devastated. I was doing so well. We were building up cash, turnover was increasing, everything was so promising, but there was no getting around it. There was nothing I could do to stop it happening. But it proved to be the best piece of fortune I could have had.

I have long lived by the mottos 'It is what it is' and 'If it's to be, it is up to me', so I picked myself up and set about looking for a replacement store. I went to the local estate agent and told him what I wanted. I swore I would never take a lease again (although I now have hundreds around the country) and I went out and bought, with the money we had made from my little bookshop, four stores with a substantial deposit on each. The first one I looked at was perfect for what I wanted, then up came another, then another, and another. Two of the stores we still have today, one in Wardour Street and the other in Brewer Street. Both are now Ann Summers shops. The other two stores were four or five doors apart in Tottenham Court Road. We bought the freehold for £20,000 each and sold them ten years later for £3 million.

CHAPTER ELEVEN

THE BLIND BEGGAR

The East End of the Swinging Sixties was a land of myth and legend. Bobby Moore, Martin Peters and Geoff Hurst led West Ham United to glory in the FA Cup and the European Cup Winners' Cup, and England in the World Cup; Henry Cooper challenged the newly renamed Muhammad Ali, formerly Cassius Clay, for his world heavyweight title from his gymnasium down the Old Kent Road; pop music threw up stars like Joe Brown, Mick Jagger, Dave Clark and my dear late friend Adam Faith. And the Richardson brothers and the Kray twins dominated the cockney underworld.

While we celebrated our sporting achievements and led the world in popular music, the underworld was a different matter altogether. These gangs were all about awe and fear. The Krays had a reputation that was chilling; there was nothing like it before, and there's been nothing like it since. People are powerful today because of political, media or financial clout. You think of Richard Branson as being powerful, Tony Blair, the Duke of Westminster, Rupert Murdoch – powerful because they are successful. But the power when I was a young man lay with the London gangs. They were the terrorists of their time. There was nothing glamorous or attractive about those gangsters, no matter how much they loved their mothers, as the Krays undoubtedly did. The best people like Ralph and me could do was to keep our heads down and avoid their attention. But it almost didn't work. We came desperately close to being sucked in until a violent murder in a London pub saved us at the last minute.

For a while Ralph and I were in business with our father Godfrey, and it was my father's flirtation with the criminal fraternity that exposed us to the nightmare of organised crime and the notorious George Cornell, first lieutenant of the Richardson brothers, the sworn enemies of the notorious twins Ronnie and Reggie Kray. The Richardsons, it seems, were every bit as dangerous as the Kray's 'Firm'. Mad Frankie Fraser, in particular, was an extremely violent and remorseless criminal who was never afraid of taking on the infamous twins, while Cornell was not far behind him.

It was early March 1966 when the drama began to unfold. I took a call in my office in our new premises in Dock Street. A gruff cockney voice demanded rather than asked to speak to Goddy Gold. I handed the telephone to my father. We could only hear one end of the conversation as Dad first of all asked who it was. It was George Cornell. It was a name I was not familiar with at the time, but Goddy knew exactly who it was and was clearly shaken. Then, after listening for a few moments, he said stiffly, 'I ain't got to do nuffink.' The one-sided conversation went on for a few minutes before my father broke the connection, saying, 'I'll be there.'

Godfrey Gold was a thief, a petty crook and a womaniser, but he was no coward. He had demonstrated this fact to us when Ralph and I worked with him down the local market. He was only a flyweight in boxing terms but he hated bullies and would stand up to guys two stone heavier and six inches taller if they tried to muscle in on our early-morning pitch. My father was not a violent man. He was known as a lovable rogue and was certainly not a murderer. I make no secret of the fact I did not have a lot of time for him for the way he treated my mother, and I despised him more when he left her. But, to his credit, he was always a man who stood up to bullies. It was something I discovered was in me as well. It was not just the way I'd stood up to Pikey, but also the establishment bullies who subsequently tried to take my living away from me.

But this was a different sort of enemy. The establishment don't hit or knife you or threaten your family. This was different to anything we had taken on before. This was the murderous criminal world of Ronnie and Reggie Kray, Mad Frankie Fraser, Jack McVittie, Charlie and Eddie Richardson, and George Cornell, gangsters and villains all who between them ruled the East End and beyond. They committed every conceivable crime, including murder, and the fear they generated ensured that the police rarely had a witness to call on while they were in their pomp.

Goddy told us he had arranged to meet Cornell outside Bloom's, the Jewish restaurant in Whitechapel High Street, the following day, 10 March. It was obvious what the meeting was about – protection money. The usual stuff about not wanting your factory or your warehouse burned down. The protection racket was run jointly but separately by the Krays and the Richardsons who extended a long arm into the East End and beyond, not just with businesses like ours but clubs, pubs, restaurants, in fact anywhere that made money. We did not want to be associated with them and certainly did not want to give them money, which was hard enough to come by as it was. Ralph tried to persuade Goddy to ring Cornell back and try to put him off for a week. But he wasn't interested and planned to go ahead and meet the hard man. We were well aware any contact could only lead to further and more dangerous involvement. As I drove home with Ralph that night we were worried sick and desperately trying to think of a way to wriggle out of what threatened to be a life-changing problem. But what could we do? Ring the police? That was clearly not an option because it would threaten every member of our family, especially us. The words 'concrete boots' and 'Thames' sprang quickly to mind. I dropped Ralph off outside his home in Orpington around eight o'clock.

Needless to say, that night I couldn't sleep. My wife at the time, Beryl, was in bed unaware of the drama unfolding, and the radio was softly playing in the background as I tried to think of a solution. Suddenly my attention was drawn to the radio as the music programme was interrupted with an announcement: East End villain George Cornell had been shot in the head in the Blind Beggar pub just up the road from our warehouse. He had been taken to Maida Vale Hospital where he was found dead on arrival. My immediate and certain thought was that my old man had killed him. Hadn't he always made a point of standing up to bullies? Clearly he had done so again. Cornell had obviously threatened him over the telephone, and clearly the meeting at Bloom's was to sort out how much we should pay.

I immediately telephoned Ralph to tell him what I had heard, and how I was convinced Goddy had killed Cornell. My brother was just as stunned; in fact, he could hardly take in the dramatic turn of events. To make matters worse, we could not contact Goddy, and for a couple of hours we panicked. There were, of course, no mobiles or any other way of contacting people in those days; all we could do was keep trying his home telephone number or wait for him to call us.

It was not until one a.m. that we eventually got in touch with him. It quickly became evident, to my great relief, that Goddy had not been involved in the death of the villain he was due to meet the very next day. Had Goddy been the killer the repercussions would have been horrendous.

As it was, incredibly, the gangland war between the Krays and the Richardsons had given us, if not Cornell, a last-minute reprieve.

It was only much later that the full story came out. Cornell had been shot by Ronnie Kray himself at 8.33 p.m. on the night of 9 March 1966 in the public bar of the then notorious Blind Beggar pub. It was rumoured that Ronnie killed him because Cornell had called him a 'big fat poof'. It is more than possible because Cornell, six feet tall with a neck like a tree trunk, was not afraid of anybody and had grown up with the twins in the back streets of the East End. He was big, strong and aggressive, a heavy drinker prone to violence at the drop of a hat. He teamed up with Charlie and Eddie Richardson and their enforcer Frankie Fraser in the fight against his former neighbours for control of gangland London and the West End. The uneasy truce between the warring factions had ended after the shooting of the Richardsons' cousin Dickie Hart, and it was only a few days after the killing that Cornell and Albie Woods stopped off at the Blind Beggar following a visit to Jimmy Andrews, who had lost a leg in a previous shooting.

The Kray twins were in the Lion pub in Tapp Street when they were told Cornell was in the area. Ronnie immediately told Reg he was going to 'do' Cornell, and he, John 'Scotch Jack' Dickson and Ian Barrie picked up their weapons en route from one public house to the other. Ronnie and Barrie walked into the bar where, without a word, Kray took out his 9mm Mauser pistol and shot his rival three times in the head. Barrie let off a volley but hit nothing more than the ceiling and the jukebox, which promptly jammed on the Walker Brothers record 'The Sun Ain't Gonna Shine Anymore'. It certainly wasn't going to for the late Mr Cornell! Ronnie changed his clothes and moved on to the Chequers, and although the police picked him and his two henchmen up, there wasn't a single witness who would place them at the scene of the crime, and they were released.

The Krays were eventually arrested and appeared at the Old Bailey in 1969 where brother Charlie received a seven-year sentence while Reggie and Ronnie were put away for life with a minimum sentence of 30 years. Ronnie died in prison in 1996 and Reggie in 2000, a free man, after serving 31 years. He had been released earlier that year on compassionate grounds because he had cancer.

We had escaped becoming part of this evil empire by the skin of our teeth, but even before this incident we'd met up with the Krays face to face at Ralph's home. The event was a house-warming party thrown by Ralph and his wife Joan in their new property in Chingford – very smart, as it was the only detached house in a road full of terraced properties. There was a little dancing and drinking in the front room, a typical party of its type and of its time, with maybe a sprinkling of Ralph's boxing friends to add a little colour and glamour. The party was well under way and all invited guests had arrived when the doorbell rang. There on the doorstep stood four men, two minders and Reggie and Ronnie themselves, every bit as recognisable as football favourites Bobby Moore and Geoff Hurst.

They were welcomed at the door by one of Ralph's friends, Freddy King, who introduced them to Ralph. The Krays were ordinary in their behaviour but their reputation was huge and their aura stunning. They looked very gangsterish, one of the minders wearing a trilby throughout the visit. No one laughed or asked him to take it off, and we didn't ask about the bulges under their jackets. The two minders brought in with them half a dozen bottles of spirits, and the four stood in a corner watching people dancing nervously and casting glances at the brooding villains. It was clearly not the sort of party the Krays had expected, and after a short time, no more than twenty minutes, they very politely thanked Ralph, shook his hand and, to everyone's great relief, left. To this day we do not know who invited them, but Ralph had a pretty good idea it was Joan's hairdresser and her husband Archie, who seemed to know them both. Ralph handled it all very well, and the one bonus was that they left all their booze behind. I guess there was plenty more where that came from!

The sixties was a dark era as far as criminals and gangs were concerned, before the police and the people of the East End brought it to a halt after years of black marketeering, extortion, gangs and organised crime. I guess I am lucky it was my only brush with the other side of the fence because it was absolutely terrifying when we suddenly got involved. It was only a miracle that saw us come through unscathed. There were some very unsavoury and violent people around us, and for a while it looked as though we might be dragged into this murky underworld. And just imagine if I had been right about Goddy doing the killing. We would have gone from one nightmare into another much worse one. I guess the story of my life is about good luck and bad luck, and this episode was undoubtedly good fortune, for who knows what might have developed from that meeting between Cornell and Goddy.

It is remarkable how the names of those East End villains live on and how the myth surrounding them remains unchanged. Even Tony Blair was guilty during the run-up to the last general election when, talking at his daily news conference, he argued that the criminals of the past operated according to a 'code of conduct'. 'Back in the fifties there were certain rules or a code,' he said. 'It wasn't of the same nature as some of the really appalling, ugly, violent crime that you get today, linked often with drugs.' Sorry, Mr Blair, this is not nostalgia, but a bloody history that ruined many thousands of innocent lives and at the same time corrupted a large portion of our London police force. Perhaps the Prime Minister should have spared a thought for those innocent businessmen, shopkeepers and restaurateurs before he talked about this 'code'

CHAPTER TWELVE

UP CLOSE AND PERSONAL

I was still a virgin at the age of 20, a quiet young man following the traditions of Hollywood film stars like James Dean, Alan Ladd and Robert Mitchum and other heroes of the day. The strong, quiet hero of the time was in vogue. There was little or no humour between the male and female leads in the movies, and the quiet chap always won the girl. But, of course, in real life that was not the case. In real life the man who gets the girl is the man who gets her to smile or laugh, the one with the great chat-up line. I still have a friend named Millie who is the same age as me and who I was desperately in love with when I was an innocent sixteen years old. But she fell for a chat-up line of a friend called Ken, who made her laugh, told jokes and looked more like Elvis Presley than Alan Ladd. He also turned out to be something of a rascal, as I found out when Millie came to Birmingham City Football Club with two other old friends from the East End, Charlie Cross, his wife Pat and Barbara Weeks. I discovered that Ken and Millie's marriage had lasted for no more than a few years.

I married my first girlfriend, Beryl. It was a disaster for both of us, almost from the very start, but in those days if you made a mistake you kept quiet and stayed together. I went to my mother-in-law and told her it wasn't working, but her response was that the moment Beryl had a baby she would be a different person. I believed her, and a year later we were blessed with my daughter Jacqueline. Unexpectedly, seven years later, Vanessa was born. They were and always have been a great delight to me. Jacqueline was named after President Kennedy's beautiful First Lady, while Vanessa was named after the beautiful actress Vanessa Redgrave. And my mother-in-law was exactly right about the fact that my wife would change after having a baby: she was even less interested in me as a lover from that point on.

We just weren't lovers, a fact I became aware of, sadly, from the first day of our honeymoon in Majorca in January 1960. Beryl wouldn't fly, so we spent a day crossing the Channel being sick, then got on a train to Barcelona, and then on another boat for a day and a night of being sick again. When we finally arrived at our destination the taxi had to drop us off a couple of hundred yards from the hotel because the storms, which had tossed our boat about in the Channel and the Mediterranean, had thrown the beach and the shingle right across the road, making it impassable to cars. We had to walk with our cases to the hotel, and I recall giving the bemused taxi driver an English sixpenny piece as a tip. I returned to the hotel a few years ago. It was still there, and is now served by a four-lane motorway.

I knew from that first holiday that our marriage was doomed, but I was determined to try and save it and make the best of the situation, as many people did in those days. But there were dark days. I remember driving home to my parents on my motorbike from our flat in Beckenham, six weeks after getting married to Beryl. My father was back with my mother at the time, and when I revealed my problems to him he told me I had made my bed and had to lie in it. This was another time when I needed my father to say he was supporting me and offer me a bed upstairs, just as he could have signed the forms Ted Fenton offered me to turn professional at West Ham. He was never there when I really needed him. That was the one time he was at home when I wished he hadn't been; now here he was being a big shot and offering great words of wisdom from father to son. Could I rely on him? No. I ended up getting back on the motorbike and headed once again for my loveless marriage. But had I left home then, I would never have had Jacqueline and Vanessa. Now the greatest joys in my life are my two daughters and my lovely Lesley, the lady I have waited for all my life.

Beryl and I just weren't made for each other, and my work ethic was not conducive to a marriage, so I don't blame her. The fact that we were married but weren't lovers drove me deep into the arms of my business, and her deep into the arms of a lover, as I was to discover to my huge dismay. One day at work I had a blistering argument with my father over the direction in which the business was going. I was absolutely livid after telling him basically he was mad if he carried on the way he was, buying too much product, and that we would soon have a warehouse full of merchandise and no money. I told him we should discuss our business differences as, after all, we were all equal shareholders. He turned round and said, 'No you f***ing ain't.' There's more to say on this in a later chapter; the point here is that but for that row I would never have returned home early from work and arrived unannounced in the middle of the day. I walked through the front door into the study and stood looking out of the window down on to the swimming pool, and there in the pool were my wife and my best friend, John, having sex. Intrigue and betrayal, all in one shattering day.

What should I do? Should I confront them as the outraged husband? No. I got back into the car and returned to the office without saying a word. They never discovered that I had seen them. I returned to work because I knew being at home would achieve nothing and could only hurt my daughters in their formative years. I was neither angry nor distraught, just rather numb. I was 32 years old, and I'd continued with a sham of a marriage for so long out of necessity. When I saw them in the pool I knew it was the end. I kept it to myself, but I moved out of the matrimonial bedroom. John and Beryl would orchestrate dinners and parties so they could be together socially without knowing I knew what was going on. But it wasn't as painful as it sounds because our love and desire for each other was poor from the beginning.

Then came the strangest of incidents. I was at a party thrown by my wife's best friend Sue, the wife of Beryl's lover John, when Sue made a great play for me, flirting and teasing. She was 21 years old and I had difficulty coming to terms with what was happening, especially when she came over and asked if I wanted to swap! Apparently it had already been arranged between John, Beryl and Sue; it only remained for me to agree! I liked her, and knew I had nothing to lose because my wife was having an affair. Sue had realised something was going on and she was no more impressed with John than I was with Beryl. We had flirted with each other prior to the 'arrangement', but it had never occurred to me she would find me sexually attractive because of the age difference. Beryl eventually married John and lived happily with him until her untimely death, which has freed me to tell the story of this unusual part of my life. Sue and I were together for a while, but I don't know what happened to her after that.

The affair between Beryl and John carried on for, I suppose, a couple of years, and it was all born out of trying to keep the façade of a marriage together in the eyes of Beryl's family, and, more importantly to me, to bring up the children in as stable an environment as possible. Beryl was my first relationship of any note, so I didn't know how a loving relationship could be fulfilling and rewarding. We stayed together for the children and to avoid the local social stigma that would certainly have been attached to us had we broken up, especially to the voyeurs behind those twitching curtains.

Even without the affair I believe my marriage would have collapsed anyway. In fact I don't think either of us was ever in love with the other. We fumbled around as a courting couple, and people kept asking when we were getting married and when we were going to name the day. Before I knew it I was walking down the aisle wondering what the hell I was doing. While we were travelling to Majorca on our honeymoon I was still thinking the same thing. And it was cold and wet when we arrived, despite the travel agents telling me it would be hot and sunny. We had ten days stuck in each other's back pockets knowing we faced another rough trip home. The door had closed, and I was locked into a marriage neither of us wanted.

When I eventually left home, John immediately moved in. I broke up with Sue because it was never going to work as the relationship was built purely on convenience. It wasn't on the rebound in my case because I knew my wife had initiated the exchange to suit herself. At the time I just looked over at this attractive 21-year-old and it was a question of whether I went to bed on my own or with her. Eventually Beryl and I divorced, but there was some animosity because she demanded so much. I gave her the house, the land, and paid all the bills, but to be fair to her everything turned out OK, though I suppose I was a bit disappointed because I was being blamed. We were equally culpable, but she was saying I wasn't living at home, I had broken up the marriage and I was the bad guy. Even then I did not reveal that I had seen John and Beryl having sex.

In the summer of 2003 I sat with my dying ex-wife, the mother of my two lovely daughters, in a nursing home in Caterham. It was a harrowing experience. I held her hand and selfishly thought to myself, 'Please don't let me die like this, not in agony and distress. I would rather die like a pet dog, put to sleep, peacefully.' It seemed a long time since I used to return to the house every Thursday to see the girls. Whenever I arrived, John would disappear. Vanessa would sometimes come downstairs and sit on my knee and chat to me, but Jacqueline was distant. As a teenager, she was having a difficult time and wondering why her dad had left. She blamed me for not being there. She had some issues with John, who was very strict with the girls. Jacky was demanding more freedom but they were confining her to the house.

One day things came to a head when Jacky climbed out of the top-floor window, slid down the roof, dropped to the ground and walked from Biggin Hill to my house in Croydon – a distance of ten miles, at five o'clock in the morning. I had arranged to go skiing that day and was all packed and ready to go when she turned up on my doorstep with a policeman who had picked her up on the road. I put her in the car and drove her back to her mother's. John nailed up her bedroom window after that experience, and no doubt my daughter felt I was at fault for taking her home instead of keeping her with me. Beryl, in fact, was paranoid that Jacky would be kidnapped or killed and protected her to the point of stifling her. She wouldn't even allow me to take her on holiday because she was frightened I wouldn't bring her back. Should I have taken her in and cancelled my holiday? I don't know. Had I not been going away I would probably have driven her back to her mother's anyway. There was little else I could do with a fifteen-year-old girl who was still at school and whose clothes and personal belongings were at home. I don't think she held it against me, but I hated myself.

CHAPTER THIRTEEN

FRENCH KISS

Several months after the trauma of seeing my best friend John and my wife Beryl having sex in my swimming pool I met Ann-Marie, a petite Jewish French girl who was working as a representative for a magazine company. She visited our warehouse in Dock Street near Tower Bridge once a month to deliver her magazines, pick up her cheque and take an order for the next issues. I found her both attractive and interesting – a somewhat explosive combination given my circumstances at the time.

After concluding our business we would go across the road for a glass of wine and a sandwich, and this went on for a few months. We chatted about business and other things we had in common. One of the things we both had a passion for was Jewish food, so I invited her to the famous Bloom's restaurant in Aldgate for dinner. We had a fantastic evening, laughing, joking and flirting. After dinner I walked her to her car, embraced her, kissed her, and said we must do this again. Driving home that evening, I couldn't get her out of my mind.

Two or three days later my private phone rang and to my surprise it was Ann-Marie. When she said, 'I just need to confirm the orders,' I immediately knew this wasn't the reason for the call – the orders had already been confirmed! 'Thank you for a wonderful evening,' she continued. 'The food was great, and so was the company.'

'My pleasure, Ann-Marie,' I replied. 'I had a wonderful evening too. Would you like to have dinner there again some time?'

She surprised me by answering, 'Well, I was thinking maybe I could cook lunch for you at my apartment.'

'That would be fantastic – but only if you cook chicken soup,' I joked.

She gave me her address in Commercial Road, Mile End, and asked me to meet her there at noon one day the following week. She added that she would be taking the afternoon off, implying that we would spend the rest of the day together.

I couldn't wait for the days to pass, and when the day came I made my excuses to my secretary. I told her I was visiting a supplier, I wouldn't be back, and I would see her tomorrow. The day was perfect, and the chicken soup she served for lunch was the best I had tasted since my grandmother's. As we chatted I discovered she was married and had a home in Paris; her husband worked for an oil company and was away from home on a regular basis. I tried to discover whether the marriage was good or bad, but she shrugged and led me to believe that it was neither happy nor unhappy. I could only draw my own assumptions, especially as lunch progressed to something more physical. That same afternoon, we made love. I was like a teenager, because this was the only woman I had made love to other than my wife, and it was a fantastic experience. As we relaxed afterwards I had to ask myself if I was falling in love. That was my last thought before we drifted off into a blissful sleep.

The whistling kettle woke me, and as I stirred Ann-Marie called out, 'One sugar or two, *chérie*?' (That was the first time she had addressed me like that, but from that moment on she always called me *chérie*. She would often say, 'How is my *chérie* today?' It was very endearing.) She climbed back into bed, we drank our tea together, and made love again. She was a joy, a delight. I wanted to stay with her in her little flat for ever. Afterwards she got out of the bed, slipped on a dressing gown and offered to run a bath for me. I was just too relaxed and sated to move and, lighting a cigarette, told her to go ahead and bathe first.

She ran the bath and I heard the bathroom door close. I climbed out of the bed and walked to the window where I sat on a window seat looking out on to the Commercial Road. It was early afternoon and still relatively quiet. I idly watched two tramps talking to each other, but with my mind still heavily engaged on more recent, pleasant matters. But, gradually, I focused on the two knights of the road and noticed that the larger man was drinking from a bottle while the smaller man had clearly lost a hand in a recent accident and was heavily bandaged. The larger man eventually passed the bottle to the one-handed man who proceeded to drink copiously from it, much to the annoyance of his friend who grew irritated and tried to grab the bottle away from the smaller man. It crashed to the ground. The big man was clearly furious and proceeded to punch the other man ferociously, while he attempted to defend himself by raising his arms in front of his face and head. One of the punches struck his damaged stump, and although I couldn't hear I could literally see him scream out in pain. The large man continued to rain punches about his head and face until he fell to the ground, where he then attempted to kick him but missed. Somehow the smaller man managed to regain his footing, which probably saved his life. The large man stepped back half a pace and lunged with his right fist towards his erstwhile friend, but at the same moment the smaller man swung his right fist with all his might, connecting with his assailant's chin. Unbelievably, the large man dropped to the ground like a stone. The man with the stump seized upon his opportunity, kicking the man's head time and time again until blood was spurting from his face and neck. It was sickening.

I was transfixed, rooted to the spot, telling myself I must do something. At that moment a nurse riding her bicycle arrived on the scene. She dropped it on the road and rushed over to the man lying on the ground. Was he dead? Bizarrely, the man with the stump stood looking down at his victim while the nurse attended him, not attempting to run off.

I could hear Ann-Marie singing in the bathroom. I picked up the phone and dialled 999.

'Which service do you require?' I was asked.

'Police,' I replied.

'Please hold, I'm putting you through.'

'Police here, how can I help?'

'There's been a fight just across the road.'

'Yes, sir. Can I have your name and address?'

I slammed down the phone in panic. Seconds later I picked it up again and dialled 999. When I was again asked which service I required, I replied, 'I think a man has been killed on the corner of Commercial Street and Mile End Road. Please send an ambulance and inform the police.' Then I put down the phone. I was shaking. My cigarette had burned out in the ashtray. I lit a fresh one.

The entire episode must have taken less than ten minutes.

'I'm finished in the bathroom, *chérie*,' Ann-Marie called out. 'Who were you phoning?'

'Oh, just calling the office,' I lied. 'I do need to get back.' Despite my best efforts, my voice was quivering.

Her head popped around the door with a towel wrapped around it. She looked stunning as she asked, 'Are you all right, *chérie*?'

Composing myself quickly, I replied, 'Yes, I'm fine, Ann-Marie.'

I bathed quickly, and left. I had to get away, I had to think. I had just witnessed either an act of grievous bodily harm, a killing in self-defence or a murder, and I was running away. A large part of my concern was, of course, involving Ann-Marie, and I was asking myself, 'How can I tell my wife? What was I doing in an apartment on a Wednesday afternoon in the East End of London?' My mind was racing and I couldn't sleep that night worrying about the consequences of my actions. Should I go to the police and ask for anonymity? Should I phone and tell them what I saw without disclosing my name? I just didn't know what to do.

The following morning I went to the office.

'David, you look awful,' said Ralph.

'No, I'm fine,' I lied. 'I just had a bad night.'

'Well, if there's anything I can do, just ask.'

As usual, Ralph was always there for me if I needed him, but this time I felt the need to get this straight in my mind before sharing it with my brother. In a strange way I felt like a criminal and I didn't want to implicate him, but I had already meticulously written down the events of that extraordinary day.

Later I climbed into my car and drove to the scene of the crime where all was peaceful, almost surreal. If it hadn't been for the bloodstains on the pavement it could all have been a bad dream. I walked round the corner and purchased a number of papers including the London evening papers, the *Evening News* and the *Standard*. I frantically turned the pages, but there was nothing. Not a mention. It was as if it had never happened. What more could I do? I had another bad night.

Come Friday morning, sitting in my office, it dawned on me. While the national and London newspapers might not have covered the event, surely it would be featured in the local paper. I hurried out of the office, sped off to Mile End Road and purchased the local paper. There it was, on the front page; my worst fears were realised. 'MAN ARRESTED FOR BRUTAL KILLING' screamed the headline. The story went on to say that the arrested man, Alan Smith, was to appear at the local magistrates court for the killing of Kenneth Cunningham.

Some time later I found myself sitting in the public area of the local court. The big question now was whether the prisoner was going to be charged with murder, manslaughter or killing in self-defence. I was sure in my own mind and from what I had seen that it wasn't murder. But was it self-defence or was it manslaughter? I would not have liked to judge that. There he was, sitting in the dock no longer looking like a tramp. He was now clean-shaven with clean bandages on his stump, staring into space.

The clerk of the court stood up, looked at him and said, 'You have been charged with ...'

'Please, please, not murder,' I was whispering to myself. If it was murder I knew I would have no alternative but to own up and face the consequences. I could not let this man be charged with murder, get sentenced to death – still the penalty for murder at that time – and do nothing. My hands were sweating. I felt sick.

'... the murder of Kenneth Cunningham. How do you plead?'

The reply was hardly audible. 'Guilty.'

No, no, surely not! There were gasps around the courtroom. A man who I assume was his lawyer rushed over to Smith and spoke to him. The lawyer then approached the judge and a whispered conversation took place. The judge turned to the clerk of the court and asked him to repeat the charge. This time the defendant, again barely audibly, pleaded not guilty. He was to be held in custody until his trial at Snaresbrook Crown Court.

In the meantime I continued to see Ann-Marie as often as I could. She was so lovely to be with, and for the first time in my life I felt truly loved and cherished. One of the things we had in common was our Jewish backgrounds. I would tell her about my Jewish grandparents and my great grandfather, Goodman Goodman, the father of my grandmother Miriam, who had left the Russian-occupied part of Poland in 1887 to escape persecution but ended up hanging himself in the toilets of a synagogue in Bethnal Green in the East End of London. I told her, too, of the anti-Semitism I suffered as a young boy, but discovered that this was nothing compared to what Ann-Marie endured as a girl living in Paris. She told me the story of the Germans occupying Paris in the early 1940s and her parents smuggling her out to family in Marseilles in the south of France, which at that time was not occupied. She never saw or heard from them again, and it was only years later that she discovered her parents were shipped out to a town in Germany and then on to the ghastly concentration camp at Auschwitz. Tears welled up in her eyes as she recounted this dreadful period of her life.

Eventually the trial at Snaresbrook Crown Court began, and I arrived early in the morning to ensure a seat in the public gallery, though there was no need because apart from a young reporter who was probably only there for work experience there were just two other people, who I suspect were either there out of passing interest, sheltering from the weather, or waiting for another case. I was nervous and felt very conspicuous. I still couldn't make my mind up as to whether it was manslaughter or a form of self-defence, but it certainly wasn't murder. After that first day, however, I was convinced he would be found guilty of the charge, and on the way home I felt riddled with guilt. I told myself that I must go forward and give my evidence.

I followed the case for a few days, and as a result I wasn't eating or sleeping. I was ashamed of myself. On the fourth day, the prosecution called their final witness, a long-distance lorry driver who had been upstairs on a double-decker bus that was parked across the road from the attack, awaiting a change of crew. He had only just been tracked down, and his account of what took place was identical to mine. The following day, to my relief, the defendant was found guilty not of murder but of manslaughter. Much was made of the continued kicking of his adversary's head after he was unconscious, but the foreman of the jury asked the judge to take into account that he was a much smaller man than his opponent and had recently lost his left hand in an accident and would have feared for his life. The judge clearly took this on board in sentencing him to only three years in prison. My nightmare was over.

I met Ann-Marie at noon that day at her apartment; I could smell the chicken soup cooking as I climbed the stairs. It was a beautiful summer's day, and as I embraced her I felt the trauma of the last three months finally leaving me.

'How long before lunch?' I asked.

'Oh, about an hour,' she replied. 'Why?'

'Well, it's a lovely day, let's go for a walk.' I wanted to breathe in the air and forget the case entirely.

We went for a walk in a local park just ten minutes away from the apartment, and I felt like I'd never felt before in my life. I wasn't even thinking about my business. All I could think about was Ann-Marie. She was a joy, and she made me feel special. I asked myself whether I should tell her that I loved her. But that made me think of that line in Frank and Nancy Sinatra's famous song, 'And then I go and spoil it all by saying something stupid like I love you.' I smiled to myself and decided to leave it until later.

We returned to the apartment, had lunch and spent the rest of the afternoon making love. As I was preparing to leave she suddenly told me she was going to Paris the following week. I asked how long for, untroubled. She went to Paris from time to time and the longest she had been away was only ten days. But she replied that it would be for three weeks. 'Oh, that's a long time,' I said, trying not to sound too disappointed.

In the past I had never asked her for her phone number in Paris as she always called me, but this time I asked if I would be able to contact her while she was away. 'No,' she said calmly. 'I'll call you as usual.' Placated, I embraced her, told her I would miss her and asked her to call me soon. With that, I left.

A week went by without her calling me, and I was missing her terribly. I knew now I was in love with her and I wished I had told her so. Another week passed with no call, and suddenly I realised I had no way of contacting her. I called the company she worked for and they advised me that her contract had expired over a month ago and she no longer worked with them. I made up some story and asked for her address, but of course it was the address in Commercial Road. I then asked if they had her Paris address, but they didn't. I put down the phone, and a wave of loneliness and terrible foreboding swept over me.

It was two weeks and four days after I had last seen her when my private line rang. It was Ann-Marie.

'God, Ann-Marie,' I spluttered, 'I've been frantic. Are you all right?'

'Yes, *chérie*, I'm OK. I've been busy with some serious personal issues.'

I tried to engage her in conversation but I could feel she was anxious to go. With a promise that she would call me next week and explain, she said goodbye, *chérie*, and she was gone.

A week later, as promised, she called. She was crying. 'I'm sorry, *chérie*,' she sobbed, 'my life is falling apart. I can't go on with this any more. I'm pregnant, and I can't see you again. I hate myself for doing this but I can't see any other way. I have to try and make this work.' She cried more as she spoke a few sentences of French before saying, 'The last year has been the most wonderful time in my life. I love you. Goodbye, *chérie*.' And then the phone went dead.

I was devastated. The phone call took only a few minutes and she told me for the first time she loved me, but I still hadn't told her. How I now wished again that I had done so when we were in the park. Questions spun around my head. Will she ring me? Will I ever see her again? How can I find her? Where would I start? And then it struck me what she had said: she was pregnant. Surely, I thought, the baby's not mine? I had always worn a condom … except just the once.

I went back to Commercial Road. There were two apartments at the address and I rang both bells, but sadly there was no reply from either. I rang the telephone number at Commercial Road a couple of times a day, every day, and I eventually got through. The woman on the end of the phone said it was a furnished apartment and she was kind enough to give me the telephone number of the letting agent. I immediately called the agency hoping that they would be able to give me Ann-Marie's forwarding address, but my hopes were shattered when they said that Ann-Marie had taken out a twelve-month agreement, had paid up front and had left no forwarding address. A dead end. I rang her old company again but got the same answer: no address other than the one in Commercial Road. My only hope now seemed to lie in the possibility that Ann-Marie would call me. The problem was that at the time we were moving from our Dock Street office to Whyteleafe in Surrey.

For a long time I thought the pain and sadness would never go, but the human spirit has the capacity to overcome most things in life. I never did discover what dramatic events had changed her life, or whose baby she was having. I can only hope she found as much happiness as I have with my lovely Lesley.

CHAPTER FOURTEEN

THE £3 MILLION LUNCH

The £3 million for the sale of the shops was, without doubt, the breakthrough for the Gold Brothers. Ralph and I were originally offered £2 million for our two shops in Tottenham Court Road by the investment arm of BICC bank, who wanted to develop the site, and it was a stunning moment for us. Ironically, years later the bank collapsed spectacularly. I gulped and instinctively wanted to take the cheque from the bank's representative there and then before he changed his mind, or I woke up. But then I realised that no one would come in and offer that sort of money unless the premises were worth more. So I said no and told him £3 million and he had a deal. He explained to me that the offer was already generous but I told him these stores were very valuable to us and I did not want to sell at his price. He came back several weeks later and told me they would never pay £3 million for our two shops.

And they didn't. But after ten months of serious negotiations we received a cheque for £2,999,999 – a pound short of my asking price! They had saved face. The purchaser had made such a public statement that he would never pay £3 million that he couldn't back down. (A few years later, Brian Clough bought Trevor Francis from Birmingham City, and rather than pay the million pounds he said no footballer was worth, he paid a million less a pound.) I never once believed in those ten months between the first offer and receiving the cheque that I would lose the deal by not accepting the £2 million, but it was still a stressful time. My common sense told me that when I was buying something I would always offer less than I intended to pay, as I did with the Hank Janson books: I offered ten old pence a book and finally paid twelve. I wasn't worried for long, though, as I quickly realised my stab in the dark was pretty accurate, especially after

Ralph and I did our homework, spending the time during the negotiations checking on how much the other ten shops on the site had been sold for. We have always said the man who does his homework is king. This was living proof!

My brother and I were solidly in tune as we fought our cause and we were prepared to take the pain for each other. We were sure the £2 million was in the bag, and when you know the backstop is in place you can gamble. Every time BICC bank came back with a bit extra, we knew that was in the bag as well. We had our two stores, and they were key to their project. Believe me, when they came back after some months saying they had recalculated their figures and upped their offer to £2.3 million we were really tempted because we could not wait to get the cheque in the bank, but this was serious money and we continued to negotiate in such a way that made them believe we were not going to budge from our price. All the while we monitored the activity of the company which had the project waiting for development. We did our homework again and decided that without our properties they could not proceed. So we held out, and eventually implied to one of their key negotiators that we had recalculated and thought the deal was now worth more than the £3 million quoted. Ralph and I believe that our threat of increasing is what accelerated their proposal. Indeed, the deal was completed a week later – and it was an enormous relief. I had lived on a knife-edge since turning down the original £2 million.

There was one thought, and one thought only: put the cheque in the bank, the same bank from which I borrowed my first £700 to set us up in the book trade. I gave the manager at our branch a call and told him I wanted to put a rather large cheque into our account. When I told him how much he was insistent I went to lunch with him and his senior manager, who turned out to be the very man who had given me the first loan! When I walked in I saw him waiting for us in the restaurant. I knew straight away it was David Witchall. I recognised him instantly, but he didn't recognise me at all. The obvious thing to have said was, 'I am David Gold and you set me on my way by lending me £700 ten years ago.' But I didn't. I couldn't.

I still held him in high regard for the way he treated a young cockney still wet behind the ears and with few skills. I recalled him at that first meeting using words like 'ramification' and telling me the loan was 'under my own cognisance', while I was saying all I wanted was a 'monkey' – 'you know, five hundred nicker'. Neither of us could understand a word the other said. He should have lent me nothing because I did not even have a business plan to show him; I didn't even know what a business plan was. I can only believe he thought that £500 was not enough to do what I wanted and he might as well take the gamble by giving me what he thought I needed. Or nothing! Now here I was sitting in a restaurant with him trying desperately to think of a sentence with the word 'ramification' in it. I couldn't. Was he a fool or a man of good judgement? Maybe it was a bit of both.

It is fascinating to consider why I was not up front with him when we met over that meal. Was it because when I went to him I was a 21-year-old scruffy East Ender? He called me Mr Gold, something I had never been called before. I was an out-and-out cockney and he was educated. It would have been the ideal moment to thank him again for his original kindness. Later, I wondered whether it was because I was ashamed of the original David Gold or whether I was so proud of the new David Gold. I have asked myself the same question many times since. Maybe it was a mixture of both.

It was certainly one of the best moments in my life, banking that £3 million cheque. For the first time I had serious money. The only time I had possessed any sort of real money before was when I lost my shop near Charing Cross station, but I used it all on deposits to purchase the freehold for those four new shops, two of which I had just sold for £3 million (the current collective value of the two premises we retained in Brewer Street and Wardour Street is estimated at £10 million). The sale of the buildings took us to another level. We were progressing nicely. Poverty was behind us, and this was easily the biggest single deal we had ever done. And this was when £3 million was an awful lot of money, far more than I had ever dreamed of. Some years later I was reminded of the exquisite feeling when Dudley Moore, in the film *Arthur*, having lost his inheritance a year earlier, said to a drunk, 'That was when nine hundred million dollars was a lot of money!'

So there I was, wealthy beyond my wildest ambitions. All my dreams had come true, so what else could possibly happen to me? I had been so fortunate as it all stemmed from a moment when fate turned against me and I thought I was unlucky. But which was the real turning point? Was it the landlord ending the lease at John Adam Street, or was it earlier, when Ralph's van broke down and I discovered for the first time how profitable late-night hours could be; or was it earlier than that, when David Witchall lent me £700 when I'd only asked for £500? A few years later we bought the name and leases of two Ann Summers shops for £10,000. Was that more important than the £3 million deal?

I am a great believer in loyalty, which is why I am still with the same bank, National Westminster in Shaftesbury Avenue, London, and they look after the Ann Summers business which turns over in excess of £150 million a year.

I think they were all special times. None of them was a defining moment on its own; rather, each was an important one among many.

CHAPTER FIFTEEN

CHEATED BY GODDY

Our dramatic success must have been a dagger in our father's heart, for he missed out on the windfall after trying to cheat us in our first business venture together. I have such a pain in my heart over Godfrey that I tend to write him out of my life, yet for a while the three of us were together in business and there was so much promise before the heartache and sorrow.

When he finally came out of prison Ralph and I gave him £200 – a fair sum of money in those days – and he went out, bought a grey van and started up in the book and magazine business. Eventually the three of us set up together. The shops required more products, and Ralph wanted more girlie magazines for his customers. Godfrey showed his daring by publishing his own pin-up magazines. The business started out as G. Gold and Sons, but Godfrey was fined £200 for publishing an indecent product so we changed the name to Ralph Gold Booksellers and my brother became the managing director. But then Ralph was convicted for importing obscene paperbacks, and he and the company were fined £1,750. We altered the name once more, this time to Gold Star Publications, and I became managing director. It was a tense time, however. Goddy was breaking up with my mother, which I hated to see after all he had put her through. Just as we were enjoying a bit of success, he was dumping her and using us. When we moved to Whyteleafe in Surrey we split up with my father. There was a short time when we felt we could all work together in one business, but the problem was that Goddy thought the business was run and owned by one man – himself.

The business was originally structured with the issuing of nine shares: three shares for Goddy, three for Ralph, and three for me. What Goddy did was extraordinary. He had Ralph sign papers which transferred two of my brother's three shares to him, leaving us with a total of four and Goddy with five. We did not know what he had done and my brother had no idea he had signed away control to Goddy. We were devastated when we discovered the duplicity. I had demanded a board meeting between the three of us to sort out the business problems, and this was when I discovered that Goddy had tried to steal two of Ralph's shares. The vote was 5–4 against Ralph and me before the meeting even started.

Ralph and I decided we had to break away from him as we couldn't work with a man who could steal from his own sons. We went to our accountant to seek advice and were told that the share transfer from Ralph to Goddy was illegal. The relief, the joy – we were still in business.

We went to our new premises in Whyteleafe while Goddy went off with a sixteen-year-old girl, Janet, who was heavily pregnant with his son, Mark. I have not spoken to him since, nearly 40 years ago. He went his way and I went mine. To his credit he went on to become a millionaire, manufacturing perfume for the street market traders – cheap contents in fancy packaging. Ever the chancer, he was the man who supplied the traders in the major cities. Everyone has come across them as they scoop up their wares when their 'watchers' spot an approaching trading officer. He sold the 40-year lease to our premises in Dock Street for a substantial sum of money. He even tried to set up in direct competition with us! He also became involved in the stamp business – pink stamps, a direct copy of the highly successful green stamps given away by the major stores. He and his partners made it work because Green Shield Stamps granted exclusivity in certain areas for the big conglomerates, which left the secondary supermarkets open for exploitation. Godfrey came in late and made a little money for a while before the entire stamp business collapsed.

He continued to make money from various ventures, and when he reached his 80th birthday he transferred all his money and his house to his son Mark. He was probably trying to be smart, to avoid death duty and to make sure Ralph and I couldn't claim anything, but it backfired on him. He is now penniless. His son is living in South Africa and cannot be contacted, leaving us to look after Goddy in his old age. Like my mother, Goddy is still alive and in his nineties. He wasted his money with increasingly bad business decisions in his latter years. The great irony is we are now caring for Goddy just as we did for Uncle Johnny.

For years I didn't know him. He was either away on the road, in prison, or philandering, and when he was at home he was only there for a short time. My mum would have horrendous arguments with him but they would invariably finish up in bed together. She adored him and forgave him for everything. I couldn't. I hated the experience of working with him and wrote it out of my life. For some time he managed to stay on the right side of the law, but he simply couldn't resist taking a chance because he lived on the edge, whether it was women, life or business. That meant further periods of time in jail.

Goddy must have kicked himself when he missed out on a share of that £3 million pot of gold. We had by then gone our separate ways and developed our own companies.

My father predicted we would be out of business in a year when we went off on our own, sick of his dishonesty. I must confess for a while I thought he would be proved right, especially as the vast majority of our assets went with him and the liabilities stayed with us.

But the two Gold brothers made a formidable and determined team, and I can say that with due modesty and deference. The balance sheet proves it. Ralph's skills in negotiations were formidable, and I quickly began to learn how to use the money we were making.

I can remember my pal David Tearle coming to me. He wanted to borrow £200,000 for a project he had been looking at for a while. I refused to lend him the money. Instead, I gave him the money, and we became partners. He was hoping to sell a property for £400,000. Six months later, however, he still had not sold it due to a slump in the market. Ingeniously, David rented some of the buildings to traders and set stalls up in the car park on short-term lets. The entire site was transformed into an indoor and outdoor Sunday market. It brought in sufficient income to pay the interest on the original £200,000 investment plus a handsome profit at the end of the first financial year. My brother and I, along with the Tearle family, still own the business to this day, having purchased a number of properties that added to the size of the site. The income pays for the interest of the original investment plus the subsequent acquisitions. The site, the Greenwich Market in London, is today valued at £15 million. David later came to me again for £1 million and doubled his money in less than a year. Again, we shared in the profit.

When I gave him the original £200,000 he told me how he envied my relationship with Ralph, how we could share our adversities and our successes. He clearly took it to heart and formed a strong partnership with

TOP LEFT: *Great-great grandparents Samuel Gold (b.1836) and Rachel Gold (b.1837). Both were born in the Polish sector of the Russian Empire.*

TOP RIGHT: *Great-grandfather Mark Gold (b.1863), enjoying his pipe.*

LEFT: *Wartime despair.*

BELOW: *An Anderson Shelter.*

My mum Rose, a gorgeous young lady.

Rose with her mother.

Granny Miriam.

Rosie as a teenager.

With Mum, Marie and Ralph.

Ralph, Rose and myself at 442 Green Street, West Ham.

Aged eight.

Rose and Aunty Joan.

Top left: With my brother Ralph.

Top right: At home with brother Ralph and next door neighbours Ann and Doreen. Note the fencing with the missing planks, which were used as cricket bats or for firewood!

Right: Mrs Green and her class – and how I wish she could see me now!

Below: The proud captain of Burke Secondary Modern School.

LEFT: Scoring for London Youth against Glasgow Youth at Selhurst Park.

MIDDLE LEFT: 18 years old, on my first and beloved motorbike, ready for a trip to Skegness.

MIDDLE RIGHT: Vick Phillips, Millie, Iris, Ken and me in the early days.

BOTTOM: My late wife Beryl with Count Vladimir on board the Queen Mary.

Proud young father with daughter Jacqueline.

Winning the Malta Air Rally in 1980.

My Cessna 337 that won the Malta Air Rally's Gozo Beacon in 1979.

With my helicopter in front of The Chalet.

ABOVE: With Norwich City chairman – and world famous chef – Delia Smith and her husband Mike.

LEFT: The brothers Gold prepare to let down their hair in the old fashioned way!

ABOVE: With Aston Villa chairman Doug Ellis.

RIGHT: Writing books seems to run in the family. Brother Ralph with his autobiography.

With Sir Bobby Charlton at the Football Museum in Preston.

The Chalet.

his two brothers, John and Andrew. The three of them established the hugely successful Up the Creek comedy club together. I guess he took on board the qualities Ralph and I had together because when the going got tough, as it often did, we stood side by side, supporting each other in word and deed. When you are on your own and things are going wrong, you really are on your own. I equate it with flying solo in an aeroplane: if you are alone any problem is magnified, but if there are two of you it is genuinely a problem halved. It was that strong relationship, born out of the East End of London, that got us through.

The relationship between Ralph and me was almost telepathic. I cannot recount the number of times when we have been in negotiations when I have gone to say something then felt Ralph saying silently, 'Leave this to me.' It also happens the other way round. We became almost like a long-term married couple in business. Sometimes we would even finish each other's sentences. My father's terrible act of treachery brought us even closer, as did our resolve when Godfrey left my mother just before she was diagnosed with lung cancer. The other thing which always bonded us was when the authorities sought us out, picking on our industry and in particular on Ralph and me.

There is no concrete medical evidence for this, but it is extraordinary how many people I have come across who have contracted cancer when there has been some personal tragedy. Ralph's second wife Annie, having broken up with her first husband, developed cancer, as did my mother when Goddy left for good and my cousin Ian was sent to prison for twelve months. His conviction – he was found guilty of selling the same books that were on sale on the shelves at WH Smith – was a travesty of justice. I am sure Ian contracted cancer because of the stress and trauma, and he died soon after. Cancer, I believe, can be triggered by tragedy. I think there are many people who would empathise with that point of view.

Ralph and I have never had a business argument in all our years. Of course we have had small disagreements, and he has always agreed in the end that he was wrong, which I thought was very nice of him! Somehow one of us had a strength in areas where the other one was weak. As well as the almost telepathic communication and understanding, our strong work ethic stood us in good stead in all our business activities. We have been pals right the way through, and still are. Most relationships seem to fail due to pressure of business, especially blood relationships, but we had great trust in each other and the stronger would always take up the baton. No pride was involved. The weaker one in any given situation would always take up a supporting role. It was like being side by side at Burke Secondary Modern when the bullies wanted to take on the two Jewish brothers.

A lot of women in our lives have been jealous of our relationship – certainly both of our first wives. That was always sad for us. Often, tiny things would become a problem. They never really appreciated just how close we were. Our relationship always survived those personal traumas; the marriages did not. If we'd had our way we would have lived next door to each other and shared a tennis court, swimming pool and snooker table. We would certainly have taken our rare holidays together. But we avoided those sorts of situations to placate our wives. We both lived a couple of miles from the office in Surrey, though, Ralph in Purley and me in Warlingham. If the traffic lights were green at the bottom of the hill I could be there in two and a half minutes. I remained close to the business until I moved to Caterham twelve years ago. I suddenly realised that if I didn't move then, I never would. I felt I ought to build a nice home, or buy one, to enjoy the autumn of my life.

My homes have tracked my life. I moved from an upstairs flat in Beckenham when I was first married into a two-bedroom bungalow in Orpington, then a four-bedroom house in Biggin Hill. After my divorce from Beryl I was in a flat in Croydon. Then I moved into the house in Warlingham – detached but modest, with a third of an acre and four bedrooms. It suited me to live there while I was building the business. Houses were not an issue for me at the time, and neither were cars. To this day the best car I ever had was a gleaming yellow and chrome Vauxhall Victor with flutes down the bonnet complete with power steering, heater and radio. Driving it was the best feeling I have ever had, much better than my first Bentley! The leap from my beloved motorbike to the Vauxhall Victor was incredible; the change from Daimler to Bentley was nothing by comparison. The car cost me £600 almost new – well, maybe not quite, as it had 20,000 miles on the clock. At the time I just needed to concentrate on the business. It was my life. The house was just somewhere I lived, the car a means of getting from the house to work and back again.

While I was living in Warlingham, Ralph was in Purley in a nice five-bedroom house complete with tennis court, snooker room and swimming pool. He had gone ahead of me in materialistic matters, but as I said, it didn't worry me because I was happy. I didn't need a pool or a tennis court.

When could I have used them? I was too tired by Sunday afternoon. The important thing to me at the time was the closeness of my house to the business.

The time for a change came in my fifties. I looked at myself in the mirror and thought it was time I found something nicer. I had worked hard, made plenty of money, and thought that at that stage of my life it was appropriate to have something special. I went to the local estate agent and told him to find me a house, and because I was still wedded to the business it had to be no further than five miles from the office. I wouldn't do that today, but then I felt it was still important. I still wanted to be in touch with the business every day and to know the hundreds of people who worked there by their Christian names.

When I bought my current house in Surrey, Ralph bought a house in Bayham with 50 acres and a lake, and kept his house in Purley, which he lived in with his second wife Annie before she died. He has just moved into a magnificent home in Godstone, also in Surrey, just ten minutes away from me. Ralph quickly realised that owning three houses meant problems, so he sold Purley. The need to be close is still something inherent in Ralph and me. He spends time away, but he knows this is where I will be for ever and he plays golf on my unique nineteen-hole course which I designed and built on the 50 acres around my home. It has one 610-yard hole, which I have made a par 6 (because I have never managed it in five). It is the longest hole in the south of England and doubles up as a runway for my four-seater Cessna aircraft and five-seater Gazelle helicopter. I learnt to fly the Gazelle in 2003 having been a fixed-wing pilot for 35 years. I cannot quite see Ralph's house from my window, but I certainly can as my helicopter gets airborne and clears the trees.

Ralph and I still do lots of things together as we have done since we were little urchins in the back streets of the East End slums. We are brothers and partners, and what is more we are best friends. That is the way it has always been and always will be. A classic example was when we used to drive into work together when we were based at Tower Bridge. We would spend the time in the traffic jams talking business. We would also put up a word for the day. The word might have been something simple like 'house', and we would have to put it into a sentence and avoid calling it an 'ouse. We went through hundreds and hundreds of words like this; even when we drove in separately we would still follow the routine. Sometimes it was words to be pronounced properly, at other times it would be new words –

something like 'ramification' – which we would have to use in a sentence. It was purely self-education. We were trying to improve ourselves, and the most important thing if we were to progress in the business world was to rid ourselves of the broad Cockney accent which made us almost unintelligible to others. You can have an accent and still speak well, but if you have an accent and speak badly it's a disadvantage in business. The exercises were designed to improve both ourselves and our business. We were dealing with business people and bank managers all the time, and we were convinced that to climb the ladder we needed to improve ourselves in every way. Goddy, now in his nineties, is still proud of his East End accent. He was proud of what he was, and he still made money even though he was never going to conform. But that was not our style. It wasn't solely the one-to-one meetings; we often had to stand up in front of a hundred or more people and welcome someone, or promote the business and ourselves. I often do a question-and-answer session at business conferences, something I would not have been able to accomplish without dramatically increasing my knowledge and my vocabulary. I still wish I could be really articulate, like Michael Parkinson for instance, whose command of the English language is wonderful and a source of envy.

I guess I have clawed my way up on my own, not through going to grammar school, public school or university. I did it in my car and in my spare time, and it has been hard work, but worth it, especially because of the bond between my brother and me. It all began, of course, as kids, but it has continued throughout our adult lives. I remember us buying new Ford Zodiacs early on when the business was growing. We both bought the same colour, and they were delivered on the same day. This reflected the equality of the brothers. We followed it up with two white Vauxhall Centurians, the first cars to be made with electric windows, and the pattern continued with our first Daimlers. We always bought the same colours, and have enjoyed Daimlers for the past 25 years. There was a year-long waiting list when they first came out at £2,000 each and we had to pay an extra 25 per cent to get hold of the cars we wanted ahead of the queue. We were always derided for having the same cars, like twins, and in the last few years we have begun to develop our own identities and gone for more individual choices.

We have always been known simply as the Gold Brothers. Ralph always used to say we were joined at the hip. I cut my hand, and he bleeds. We think and feel the same things. But, equally, I feel it is healthy at this stage in our lives to have our own identities. As our lives separate we focus on slightly different things. Ralph loves his golf and adores being in Portugal, whereas when we were both at work we were together in every respect. Ralph is competitive with his golf and is a regular on 'his' golf course in my back garden, but I have to say the love between us is undiminished, as is the camaraderie. Not that we are infallible, of course. We have made our mistakes in business and misjudgements with so-called friends.

A classic example was over a deal I did with Martin Banner, a friend who was doing some maintenance work on our villa in Portugal. He persuaded me to lend him some money and the deal was to buy a villa in a state of disrepair. We would pay for its renovation, he would do the work. While Martin was working on the renovations we paid him a salary. When it was sold, we would share the profits equally and recoup our original financing of the operation. Martin also owned a large piece of land with a local Portuguese man but had serious problems over the deal. We gave him the money he needed to buy the other man out.

A year later the villa was finished. I went down unannounced one weekend to have a look and was surprised to find that the house was occupied. It looked beautiful, set as it was in four acres of land with an orange grove and a stream at the end of the garden. I thought he had sold it already as it was clearly being lived in, but when I went round the side of the building I saw Martin and I realised he had moved into the house. I asked him why he hadn't put it up for sale and he told me he had fallen in love, married a local girl, and they had decided to move in as they had nowhere else to live. Now, because this was a 'friend' I played tennis with, we had no contract, only a handshake. We had done the second deal just as we did the first, on an act of faith, and with our money to finance the entire project. His solution was, 'When I sell the second property I will give you the money for the house.' I reminded him that we'd had a deal: the house would go up for sale on completion. But he had introduced new terms and broken the rules of friendship and business. He justified his actions by saying, 'You are rich and I am poor.' It was years down the line before we just about got our money back, with no profit.

A few years later I did similar deals with David Tearle. We had no agreements, just a handshake. He would call me about a project that needed investment and would give me a brief synopsis. If I liked it, and I usually did, I would give him the go-ahead. But that's the difference between the man you can trust and the man who is just using you and is not a true friend. For the one it is down to greed and envy and he is prepared to break agreements; for the other friendship is at stake and he would never let you down – and David made millions. I was asked recently, 'Whatever happened to Martin Banner?' My answer was, 'I don't care.'

CHAPTER SIXTEEN

DON'T TELL THE SERVANT

Without doubt, 1972 was the worst year of my life. They say good things come in threes. Well, let me tell you, bad things do as well. I found myself in court on three separate occasions, twice at the Old Bailey in consecutive months and once at Croydon Crown Court. And they were a far cry from my frequent visits to the magistrates' court when I was fined for keeping my shop open late and at weekends.

In January that year I was arrested and charged at Croydon Crown Court under Section Two – which meant a custodial sentence if found guilty – for the publication of a book entitled *Brutus*, which was about the games master at the Colosseum in Rome. The police had taken stocks of the book away from our warehouse in Whyteleafe a year earlier. We'd heard nothing more about it and assumed there would be no further action. How wrong I was. Defending the case was a most interesting man, John Mortimer QC. I did not know him at the time, and although he was already famous he was still on his way up. He is a remarkable man who strongly believed in our right to publish erotica and defended us with great zeal. He was a man I admired immensely, and the bonus was I knew he liked me. Later he became Sir John Mortimer, a top barrister who turned his talents to writing and enjoyed public acclaim for his plays and novels, particularly the much-loved television series *Rumpole of the Bailey*. He was firmly on our side and brilliant at what he did. The jury decided the book in question was not obscene and I was released from the dock.

Halfway through the case I realised that here was a very special man. He was delivering my case as if he had spent ten years preparing for it. He captivated the jury, the judge and everyone involved – totally the opposite to the disgraceful man who had defended Ralph in similar circumstances ten years earlier. Mortimer's summing up was outstanding. He stood there, his worry beads in hand, encompassing both the judge and the jury in his speech. He gave me great confidence just watching and listening to him. His clerk and number one was Geoffrey Robinson, a brilliant young man on his way up and now a top QC in his own right, and a great supporter of free speech.

Sadly, John was taken ill while we were preparing for the first Old Bailey case in September that year, when we were being prosecuted (or should that be persecuted?) for the publication of the magazines *New Direction* and *In Depth* as well as two paperback books, *Lesbian Lovers* and *A Woman's Look at Oral Love*, written by Ralph's former secretary Sue Caron. It was a great blow to lose someone who was as sympathetic and talented as John. He, like us, could not understand why we were being constantly attacked because of our products. He felt after hearing our story that there was a conspiracy – a theory substantiated by the fact that we were to be arrested on two further occasions. We were remarkably fortunate to have, at John's recommendation, the exceptional Montague Waters, along with Geoffrey Robinson who assisted him. Waters was largely unknown then but quickly achieved fame worthy of his ability (coincidentally, I have done business with his son since then).

I was very fortunate in having three eminent people defending me in those three cases. We won all three, but I lost a stone in weight – a lot for a small man like me – and I was feeling decidedly ill as I faced the prospect of prison. I felt like a criminal in the cells during the trial and in the court and I am still convinced there was a conspiracy. It was 'them' – the shadowy figures, the establishment – against us. Whether it was the Director of Public Prosecutions, who felt sex had to be suppressed, the head of the Vice Squad or the Home Secretary I never did discover.

The bitterness towards authority lasted for 30 years, and it was fewer than ten years ago that the directives were given that there would be no further prosecution against our products. The authorities had taken decades to come to an appropriate conclusion, but common sense prevailed, and we now have clear definitions. Law has to reflect life. Don't we all enjoy sex at some time or another? It drives the whole of human nature, though of course child sex and bestiality do not – there has to be a distinction. It has to be judged by the average person, and they must be on the side of right, whether it is sex, reading about sex or looking at sexy movies. It was rather like Adolf Hitler burning books he did not like on the streets of Berlin; here in Britain the authorities burned them in incinerators instead. I never once came across an ordinary policeman who thought our publications were obscene, and we entertained a number of them over cups of tea at our premises before they loaded their lorries up with our magazines and books.

The other question I ask myself is, why were we being picked on when others weren't? Was it because we said we would never capitulate to the blackmail, bribery and corruption of these bigots? Ralph and I swore to each other we would never look to bribe the police or anyone else at a time when we knew the practice was rife. On a number of occasions we were approached, and while nothing was ever offered directly, you didn't have to be bright to know how we could avoid being raided. I have asked myself since if I was being too moralistic. Maybe I should have faced up to the real world, as you do when you go into certain foreign countries where it is part of the culture to grease palms, not just those of individuals but well-established, respected companies too. You pay the piper and they play the tune. I have even found it in my travels as a pilot, stuck in places like Palermo and Catania in Sicily, and Bastia in Corsica, where I struggled for fuel or permission to leave because I hadn't paid the bribe. But we didn't succumb to the poison of the era, and I have to say I am glad. It is not part of our culture to pay off the police, blackmailers or anyone else. We were two honest men. If I had joined the others I would have avoided a lot of grief and saved a lot of money, but I am pleased and proud I did not. It is nice to come out of the end of three decades of conflict with the authorities without a criminal record.

Well, there was one conviction, for speeding – but does that count? I was seventeen years old, riding my motorbike down the Barking Road on my way to work when I saw out of the corner of my eye a man standing on the pavement with a white flag which he dropped as if he was starting a race. A couple of hundred yards on a policeman with a stopwatch in his hand raised his arm as I passed him. Fewer than a hundred yards after that another policeman jumped out into the road with his hand raised. I stopped, although I didn't know why I was being asked to.

'You have just been timed over a distance of one quarter of a mile in excess of thirty miles per hour,' he said. 'Do you have anything to say?'

'No, sir,' I replied. 'I'm sorry, but I'm late for work.'

I was found guilty at West Ham Crown Court and fined 30 shillings, with three months to pay. When I got to court the police officer read out to the magistrate my exact words. The magistrate banged his gavel and said, 'Guilty as charged.' I learnt an important lesson that day: we demand the truth from others, but beware when telling it. I am not saying anyone should lie, just to be wary when telling the whole truth. It is rather like when your wife asks you if her bum looks big in her new dress – beware of telling the truth!

If I had gone to prison over publishing or distributing pornographic material it would have been devastating for the business as well as for me personally. There is no saying what the police would have done had they been victorious. You could almost see them with their batons waiting to attack in ever-increasing numbers. It was all so wearing. You don't eat and you don't sleep when you are under siege and your liberty is being threatened. It wasn't just the ten-day trial in January 1972 but the months of preparation; by the time of the third trial there wasn't much to do because we had done it all before with the same arguments, witnesses and experts. The second trial at the Old Bailey was an exact replica of the first, but I could not hide my anger when the judge brought us all into his chambers and told everyone no reference could be made to the previous case. It was a disgusting decision, and when I listened to him I felt physically sick. To me it was like saying here is a picture of a man standing over his victim with a smoking gun and then not allowing the prosecution to use it; or having a picture of the accused in Australia holding up a newspaper with the date on it when his wife was murdered in Brixton on the same day and not being allowed to bring it to court as evidence.

Maybe I was becoming paranoid, but I was more convinced than ever that there were some serious people out there who wanted to make an example of us. Guilt and punishment must be achieved at any cost. Over thirty years on, after winning three major battles and being given a pittance towards costs, perhaps I am, but surely with some justification. How could the judge say we couldn't use anything from a previous trial when we had been found innocent of all charges? It was the worst case of someone being tried not twice but three times for the same crime. Double jeopardy, or should that be triple jeopardy? Still, we should not have been overly surprised after what they had done to the publishers of the Hank Janson books, which had less sex in than your average teen magazine of today, and certainly less than the *News of the World* every Sunday. How times have changed. The Reiter brothers, Julius and Kirk, who were imprisoned for publishing Hank Janson, should be posthumously pardoned, along with my cousin Ian Gold. Just a few months before my court cases at the Old Bailey, Harry Gorman and Ron Walker were sent to prison for eighteen months – the same sentence as Ian's – for selling girlie magazines that were deemed to be obscene. It was another travesty of justice. Harry and his wife Lynn are dear friends of mine to this day and I see them at most of the games at Birmingham City Football Club. I feel so bitter when I think of the likes of the Reiter Brothers, Harry Gorman and Ron Walker spending time in prison, while I was being dragged through the courts for selling erotica.

It is even more galling when the heads of cigarette and alcoholic drinks companies, who are responsible for killing and ruining the lives of millions of people, receive knighthoods and peerages. And while I am on the subject of government hypocrisy and stupidity, how can they honour someone who is a tax exile? I'm thinking of personalities such as Sean Connery, Mick Jagger, and many, many more. When they arrive at Buckingham Palace for their investitures they drive on our roads, through our new tunnels and over our magnificent bridges, and they are protected by our police, paid for by us, the taxpayers, yet they pay nothing. I could not do what they have done. I love my country. I hate paying tax as much as the next man, but we all do it because it is our responsibility – because we must, because we should. It's what makes the country work. Please don't honour those who avoid their responsibility to this great country.

I have high moral standards, the same as my brother and my mother. If I had gone to prison I would not have bowed. I would have come out and fought them down to my last penny because the people who were challenging us were evil, and were attacking good, law-abiding citizens. We were the honest people. We weren't hiding our product; we weren't doing anything illegal or selling under the counter. We were businessmen who advertised our presence in the magazines we published, printed with our own name and address on them. Mr Policeman, this is where we are if you have any questions. Did the real pornography have a return address? Of course not! They failed to stem the tide of real pornography and used the publishers of erotica as a scapegoat.

When Ralph and I sat down to talk about it we asked each other whether we were foolish making ourselves a target. But we always firmly believed in British justice, which we thought would prevail. In fact it stood up well to the test; our bitterness is directed at those who tried to corrupt it, the part of the establishment who attacked us. I like to see my enemy, but I couldn't see who was directly behind it. Those who wanted me in prison stayed in the shadows and left it to others.

If we'd been in the cigarette or alcohol business we could have found support in Parliament or the media. We had no one other than the marvellous John Mortimer and his legal team, plus Milton Schultz, an outstanding newspaper columnist, to stand up for us and lambast the judiciary for not giving us a fair deal and costs. But their voices were few. It was obviously harder to stand up in Parliament and say you were supporting the publishing of erotica rather than backing cigarette and alcohol manufacturers whose products were helping people to kill themselves and each other. The passing of time has clearly vindicated us but we are still held at arm's length while the cigarette barons and drink manufacturers earn their awards. I have nothing against alcohol, but just because some give financial support to the government, it seems they are rewarded.

In the first Old Bailey case it was Lord King-Hamilton who I will remember most. I am sure in his life he did many good things, but in those days he was ill advised. I would like him to read this, because I believe he should have declared an interest. Clearly he was a man so anti-sexuality he should have made it known during or before the case. You only have to read the transcripts to see how he was directing the jury, telling them they should disregard our experts and take their own counsel. What he didn't say in his summing up was that the prosecution did not bring one witness to prove their case that the material we published would deprave and corrupt. We could have brought a hundred witnesses to show it wasn't, but we settled for about a dozen, with doctors, psychiatrists and other notables. He tried to discredit these eminent professionals. He was so biased, and his handling of the case was nowhere near the normal standards expected of this country's judicial system. And in the end we were vindicated, he wasn't. This pious, bigoted, moralistic, pompous man should not have been allowed to preside over the case.

Why, I ask myself, was I having my fate decided by a judge who believed that masturbation was a sin and not a harmless common practice among young men? How come I got the one man in history who thought this way when my defence told him masturbation was practised by 97 per cent of the young male population? The judge answered, 'Do you expect me to believe that 97 per cent of the young male population have practised masturbation? Is this what you are saying to me?' My counsel reminded him that it was not an opinion but a matter of record from professional research. Judge King-Hamilton threw down his glasses theatrically, sighed, looked around the courtroom for effect and asked in a weary voice, 'Whatever happened to self-restraint?' That was the turning point in the case. The jury were looking at each other and wondering what planet he came from.

I wish I could have a debate with him now that I am articulate enough to express what I think and feel, and to see whether his ideas have altered. The sad thing is before the trial I looked up to him because he was a judge. But I lost my respect for him and everything he stood for. However, I didn't lose faith in our judicial system. I am sure he was selected to make sure I was found guilty. My QC and everyone else on the team were outstanding, but in the end the judge proved to be one of our greatest allies with his stupidity. We were found not guilty, but this judge, who believed young men should restrain themselves and that women didn't masturbate at all, carried on trying people with his bizarre views and his strange sense of the good, the bad and the ugly.

The High Court had earlier found the publishers of *Lady Chatterley's Lover* not guilty and the publishers of *Fanny Hill* guilty in a magistrates' court. They carried on publishing *Fanny Hill* anyway and the police never bothered to crack down because they knew it was now fruitless. I remember what the judge said in the *Lady Chatterley's Lover* case: 'Members of the jury, you have read the book, and now I ask you to ask yourselves, gentlemen, would you allow your wife to read this book? Would you allow your servant to read this book?' Astonishing! First of all, how dare he suggest that husbands should control what their wives read? That judge would be pilloried today. And as for servants, where was this man coming from? Was he a complete donkey? Was he totally divorced from what was going on in the society he was supposed to be judging? This was the law: one judge who believed no man should masturbate, and another who thought that everyone had servants when he was probably the only one in court who did. What is more, I bet his servant *had* read both *Fanny Hill* and *Lady Chatterley*!

In that first Old Bailey case there were twenty individual magazines and books for which we were found not guilty, yet still they refused to give us any costs at all, using the words, 'If you publish merchandise of this nature you must expect the consequences.' In other words, we were found not guilty by the twelve good men and true, but guilty by the judge. It took the jurors only a couple of hours to reach their verdict, and when I spoke to them afterwards there was just one man who held up the decision for one article that covered homosexuality and supported gay relationships. He explained he was concerned because he had a young son and these articles might influence him.

I was in the cells for two hours awaiting that verdict. I was convinced of my innocence and in the victory of my QC. In footballing terms we beat the prosecution 10–0 because they didn't have an argument, a victim or any evidence, while we showed that our magazines were harmless adult entertainment and subject to huge demand. My counsel proved that erotica was used in hospitals to induce sperm samples, and in psychiatric institutions, where the inmates had no other form of sexual release. Then there was, of course, prison and the armed forces. Do you deny these men erotic magazines when they are away from their wives and their girlfriends serving their country? We were only talking about erotica or soft porn, not the hardcore porn that is unacceptable to me and every other decent human being. Many of us in life will at some stage or another have enjoyed pornography or erotica in some form or other.

Victory was certainly sweet, even at such great personal and financial cost, but while there was no doubt in my mind about my innocence, I always hoped the judge might call a halt to the trial when he realised he was losing. Had I been found guilty, he would have sent me to prison. It would have been devastating, but we would have fought back because that is in the Golds' nature.

We thought it couldn't get any worse, indeed we expected the third case to be dropped, but it wasn't – and that meant facing Judge Bernard Gilis. He was no better than King-Hamilton. Indeed, we were warned before the trial that he was from the same club, but worse. Was he deliberately chosen? It is amazing that of all the judges who could have presided over these two cases, we got the two who were most emphatically against sexual freedom. It's as if the prosecution had selected the two judges most likely to earn them a conviction. Once again we were found not guilty on all counts, and this time the judge, begrudgingly, awarded us costs, though nowhere near the figure to cover our vast expenses: we were awarded only £6,000 to cover expenditure totalling nearly £100,000 for the third trial, and of course we hadn't received a penny from the first two trials. Moreover, I had spent another ten days of my life bound by the court, having to ask for bail every day and spending the breaks in the cells. When the jury were out considering their verdict I played chess with the warder. I won the game too, then sobbed with relief when the verdict was announced, hugging Ralph as we celebrated justice. I recovered by working harder than ever. We had to reinvent our business. I was worn out, but I knew if I didn't get back to work we would be back in Green Street in the East End selling buttons. A few weeks later we appealed at Old Street Crown Court against a decision to dispose of more than 50,000 copies of our magazines taken from our warehouse in Surrey. We won that one as well, as the magistrate declared them titillating but not obscene. An extraordinary chapter in my life – strangely enough the same year I separated from my wife Beryl. She was in court for the trials and was very supportive throughout that terrible time.

Perhaps I should sign this long chapter Mr Angry from Purley, and it serves no purpose to allow things like this to eat away at your soul so long after the event. But there are still questions that niggle. Like, how come Lord Lane, the chairman of Penguin Books, didn't have to stand in the box when he was defending *Lady Chatterley's Lover* while I had to stand in the box and go down to the cells during the breaks? The laws were mixed and muddled during that time, and the police were regular visitors to our premises. They arrived frequently to confiscate our product, and while one magistrate would instruct the police to return our magazines, another would tut-tut, shake his head and order them to be destroyed. There was a difference between the big cities and the provinces: in London we were invariably given our product back by magistrates who were used to dealing with real life; in the provinces, however, magistrates who were mainly dealing with parking offences agreed with the police and ordered our magazines to be destroyed. Remember, this went on for 30 years. We were a large organisation, and easy pickings. We weren't hiding, we weren't back-street, and we weren't selling pornography; we were selling erotica throughout the world, to Canada, America, Nigeria, Australia and New Zealand, and it was being accepted by customs in these countries. But the rules in our own country were so bizarre and so grey we didn't know when we were inside the law and when we weren't. There was no one we could go to and ask if this product was acceptable for the adult market, unlike the film industry, where each movie was certified. The extremely erotic film *Last Tango in Paris*, for example, was sent to the censors who recommended that certain scenes would have to come out for it to obtain a certificate. Then, there were A and X certificates to help the public judge what they wanted to see, but there was no one to certify magazines. For us, it was all hit and miss. We had to produce them under our own cognisance. Publish and be damned is what we did for three decades, and it cost us a fortune.

The Labour Prime Minister Harold Wilson used to tell Britain to export or die. His mantra was to buy British and sell overseas, and at the same time he devalued the pound. At the time I had two containers of girlie magazines that had been passed by the strict American Censorship Board and were ready for shipment when the police raided our premises. They asked what was in the containers. We told them honestly, they told us we couldn't export them, and they took the books out and burned them, even though they were not for sale in Britain and had been cleared by the US Customs. I had to ask myself, was I stupid? Was I missing something here? We were going to receive a considerable amount of American dollars for these containers of magazines, both for the country and ourselves, but the authorities proceeded to burn that money. Although according to them, they were burning filth.

I seem to have spent half my life battling authority, and not always in the name of erotica or girlie magazines. I had some success when I wanted a barrier constructed along the A22, a dual carriageway near my home that was divided by a hedge. Cars would come down the steep hill, lose control, career through the hedge and kill the occupants of oncoming vehicles. It was obvious to a child that a safety barrier between the two carriageways was desperately required. I campaigned for one to be built and even offered to loan the money to the council to do so until they could afford to repay me. I made this offer on a number of occasions but never received a response, probably delaying the project by two years. Four people were needlessly killed by accidents during this period. I also wanted the downhill lane reduced to 50mph, but leaving the uphill stretch at 70mph. But the law stupidly stated that the speed limit had to be the same on both sides of the carriageway, even though it was common sense to reduce the speed of the downhill lane and leave the uphill section untouched.

We wanted a barrier of some 600 metres erected on the downhill section. It was personal, because I used it, my daughters used it, my company personnel, company cars and lorries used it. I argued that there wasn't a motorway in the country without a central barrier, and this was a 70mph downhill chicane that dropped 300 feet in 1.6 miles. That, by any consideration, is steep and dangerous. In despair I instructed all my lorry drivers and company vehicles to avoid it and drive through Caterham village instead, in the process bringing the village to a standstill on many occasions. It made the point, and the council eventually erected the barrier, though not the 600 metres I'd requested but nearly five kilometres, which was just going from the ridiculous to the sublime. To this day the barrier has saved countless lives and has proved exactly why I was so determined to fight for it.

The law is an ass – or at least it can be. There was once a statute on the books that stated if you practised homosexuality you could go to prison. We now know the law was an ass in that regard. There are people who should be given pardons for the way they were treated over their sexuality.

I was hounded for three decades and never found guilty, and I believe to this day there was a conspiracy. I cannot put my finger on it, but I believe the police and Vice Squad were under pressure to seize impressive numbers of erotic magazines because they were so woefully incompetent and inefficient when it came to seizing hardcore pornography of the worst kind. How come no one was caught or imprisoned for that sort of hardcore pornography involving children, animals and depraved people while we, with girlie magazines, were continually harassed? Could it be bribery and corruption? Isn't it incredible that when the worst dens of iniquity in the West End were raided, there was nothing there? How come, when hours before it was flourishing? They were clearly tipped off. With this area closed to them the police needed numbers on their records, and we were the softest of touches because everything we did was transparent; we even helped them catalogue the magazines and load them on to their lorries. They knew too that they would be given tea and biscuits when they raided us – very civilised. Two days' work, half a million magazines, job done.

People asked us why we kept our product in our main warehouse rather than out of sight in a secret location. I didn't for some time because I believed I was right. Eventually, however, the relentless raids forced us to change our policy – but we felt like criminals. We were being persecuted and we were part of a hidden agenda. This was my business; I didn't want to hide. Thankfully, common sense eventually prevailed and the corruption was cleansed from the Vice Squad. Good juries made sensible decisions, and the authorities accepted the facts after a succession of surveys showed that erotica, or soft porn, was completely harmless.

So I ask again, where is the victim? What is the crime? When I was tried I was locked up with the worst kind of criminals, murderers and rapists. After a couple of days my lawyers asked if it was appropriate for me to be kept in the cells, and it was agreed I should be freed for lunch. But what was the danger of David Gold going out for lunch in the first place? When I was downstairs in the cells, I was invited to sit with the warders for lunch, and what was interesting to me was that they called me Mr Gold and were always polite. My cell was kept open as I waited for the call to return to court. One day a senior officer came along and, seeing that my cell was unlocked, went into a rage, causing panic among the ranks. From then on I was always locked in my cell. I was an enigma to everyone, all of whom wondered what I was doing there. But I was treated well. I was seen as harmless, even though as far as the chief inspector was concerned it was a case of 'Lock him up anyway. It's more than my job's worth.'

Yes, I am convinced the entire thing was a conspiracy, and I still believe that today. We beat the bigots from the establishment in that first Old Bailey trial, despite all their efforts, and it was a wonderful feeling. The family celebrated in our favourite restaurant Charco's in Caterham, where we booked a private room and invited all our closest friends. It would have been nice to say that was the end of it, but they had already taken away a second lot of magazines, virtually identical to the first, just different issues. I guess this was the first case where an innocent man was re-tried, even though British law states you cannot be tried for the same offence twice. There was no evidence for the second trial, never mind new evidence. The Crown prosecution brought exactly the same case. This was the authorities going for a retrial. We won again, of course, and this time the jury was out for less than an hour, but if I had been found guilty I would have been sent to prison, just like the Reiter brothers and my cousin Ian Gold. Ian had thousands of books going into his business every week, and they decided he was responsible for reading every one and was therefore held to account for those they considered unsuitable. He worked for my Uncle Dave, and we bought the business mainly because Ian was such a bright guy. He spent a year in prison for distributing erotica and the trauma of the experience I believe eventually killed him, so you can see why there is bitterness in the Gold family towards authority, especially when we have run our business so professionally.

I recall many years earlier when Ralph was in court for distributing a range of American paperbacks called Monarch Books. The police had raided the company and had taken the books, and he faced what was called a Section Two in front of a judge and a jury. Within fifteen minutes of meeting QC James Burge on the day of the trial, Ralph knew the barrister had not done his homework and was in big trouble. This arrogant man was picking up a huge fee without preparing for the case and told my brother he should plead guilty. He said he would go to the judge and plead guilty on Ralph's behalf and accept a fine instead of a custodial sentence. Because he did not represent my brother properly Ralph ended up with a criminal record he should never have had. Burge tried to plea-bargain instead of fighting for my brother. Ralph pleaded guilty because he was terrified he would go to prison.

Here was another Hank Janson situation, for these paperbacks were no worse (ten years later the same books were on sale in Woolworths!). Ralph came within a whisker of going to prison because of the stupidity of the establishment of the day trying desperately to curtail the growing popularity of modern icons such as rock and roll singers Elvis Presley and Mick Jagger as well as erotica. The establishment could see this uprising of the young and people wanting to do what made them feel good, and they thought it was bad for society. Victorians covered up the legs of tables and chairs for similar reasons. It is the same, in a bizarre way, with the religions that make their women cover up from head to toe so as not to inflame the young men. I think in a civilised society, you can trust most young men.

Lord Longford had labelled Ralph and me 'pornographers', but we were not the people he should have been talking to. He needed to be in the back streets of Soho, but not even the police could go there. So who was available? We were. We met up with Longford three times to discuss the situation. He was allied to the Wolverhampton housewife Mary Whitehouse, who was an ardent anti-pornography campaigner. I tried desperately to explain to Longford the difference between erotica and pornography and told him I would do anything to help him stamp out the hardcore variety because I despised it as much as he did. But I warned him I would defend erotica in the trenches. He insisted, however, that I sold pornography. I tried to explain how he was wrong to label the entire industry with one word, pornography, but he could not see how erotica plays a part in our everyday lives. I think I upset him when I told him I thought it was more pornographic to ask your wife to bear eight children for you, as he did, than to produce girlie magazines. We were talking about human nature, and I believe he wasted a great deal of energy in the wrong areas.

Lord Longford, sadly, had strong opinions without any great wisdom or skill; he only became a public figure and commanded a soapbox because he was titled and therefore made good newspaper copy. He certainly didn't gain the publicity because he was special or qualified. In fact, he ended up being ridiculed, the butt of nightclub jokes.

Mrs Whitehouse at least achieved something in terms of fighting against bad language in public and violence on television. She had my support for that, but not in her attempts to suppress erotica. The main complaint I had with Mrs Whitehouse was that she grouped sex and violence together as if it were all one entity. I was happy with sex, but I abhorred violence. I never met her, but I watched her whenever she was on television. She was a good woman. Her energies were misdirected in certain areas, but by no means in all of them.

We must have laws that people can relate to, understand and appreciate. Imagine if they introduced a speed limit of 30mph on the motorway. Make a law sensible and people will support it, but for 30 or 40 years they could not come to terms with the laws on pornography. The first magazine of this type, I remember, was called *Line and Form*. It was supposed to be for photographers, and to back this up on every page there were aperture and lens settings. In actual fact it was a girlie magazine showing nipples. Even this was a risk, and you had to have the courage of your convictions to sell such items. I stocked what sold and replenished it when needed. In business you have to have courage to fight ridiculous laws. I remember as a youngster of thirteen buying *Health and Efficiency*. Did it hurt me? Not as far as I know. If I had smoked, would it have hurt me? Yes. It certainly hurt my mum. Pubic hair was eventually accepted as the norm in the late sixties, but it nevertheless prompted police raids after *Penthouse* led the way, not to mention shows in the West End like *Hair*. Thankfully, we are now almost perfectly balanced in our society on this matter. An adult can read erotica or watch softcore pornography in the comfort of his or her own home without the fear that they, the newsagent or video shop owner are about to be arrested. I only wish such an acceptance had come a few decades earlier.

CHAPTER SEVENTEEN

ANN SUMMERS

It took ten years and the wisdom of my daughter Jacqueline to discover what a jewel in the crown Ann Summers really was.

We came upon the Ann Summers Marble Arch shop by chance on a wet November day in 1970. Ralph and I were returning from a meeting in north-west London when I pointed out the Ann Summers shop to him and we decided to go and have a look for ourselves at this well-publicised emporium of all things sexual. We were interested not only in what type of shop it was and the kind of customer it attracted, but also because the owner, Michael 'Dandy Kim' Waterfield, owed us money for some of the magazines we had supplied to him. The shop was busy, and we were surprised to see a number of women in the queue paying for underwear and sex aids. Previously, these kinds of items had been sent under plain wrapper through the post or purchased by men in shops in Soho. We soon became interested in the products on sale and even joined the lengthening queue to buy several items, which came to a little over £7. Add to that a £2 parking fine when we overran our meter time, but it was probably the best £9 we have ever invested! Ralph took the items home to research them further with his wife Joan, and we both began a lengthy and detailed investigation of the sex business, and the Ann Summers shops in particular – a business that at the time was thought of as quite shocking, selling as it did naughty undies, vibrators and the like.

The one thing we could not understand was why a shop taking £4,000 a week could not settle a £450 invoice on time. We soon discovered that Dandy Kim was a high flyer. He was also clearly a very clever talker, for we learnt that he had leased the property in Marble Arch from, of all people, the Church Commission. He owned a helicopter, a string of horses, was rumoured to be having a close relationship with Princess Margaret, and dressed and lived in the most extravagant style. He picked the name Ann Summers because it sounded like an English rose, and then persuaded his beautiful former mistress to change her name from Caroline Teague to Ann Summers in return for a directorship and an annual salary of £10,000 to front the entire enterprise. It was so successful that in 1971 the *London Evening Standard* named her Woman of the Year. Dandy Kim lived up to his nickname and used to arrive in his helicopter at Hyde Park, walk over to his shop on Edgware Road, pick up the day's takings and then fly off to the races. He was spending it faster than he was making it. Ann Summers was a star in her own right, but it was Dandy Kim who recognised her talent and nurtured her.

We eventually met Dandy Kim for lunch at the Waldorf Hotel where he explained that the long-running postal strike was the reason for the company's big losses, as much of his sales came through mail order. What he failed to tell us was how much he was paying himself. The company inevitably went bankrupt with debts of £78,000 and the entire Ann Summers business was put up for sale along with the leases for the shop in Marble Arch and another in Bristol. Ralph and I bought the company in 1972, and the Bristol shop is an Ann Summers outlet to this very day. We made a profit on the Marble Arch shop as our neighbours, the BICC bank, which eventually went bust in spectacular style, offered us an obscene amount of money for our 20-year lease. We sold it for £250,000 more than 25 years ago – a big sum of money. It was one of those deals where we were offered £150,000 and negotiated up because we knew there was nowhere else for them to go as we were next door to them on busy Edgware Road.

The Ann Summers shops were a copy of the highly successful Beate Uhse shops in Germany, a mail order and sex shop business which Dandy Kim had ripped off by pretending to be a magazine writer/photographer and going round their factory in Flensburg for four days, picking up and photographing all the information he needed. Ann was a wonderful front and a beautiful woman, and for a while she worked for us after we bought the company. We bought another freehold in the Queensway in London for £130,000 and we gave Ann the opportunity of running the three stores. Sadly she tried to turn them into an upmarket business, challenging the likes of Janet Reger, reducing the number of sex aids and increasing the lingerie. All these three stores began to lose money, and she left – by mutual consent. The shop in Queensway was losing the most, so we sold it for twice the amount we paid for it. The profit more than made up for the other losses she had incurred.

Dandy Kim Waterfield threatened to expose his relationship with a prominent royal by writing his autobiography, which must have shaken up the palace in those days. There was little about the royal family in the public domain then, even though it was rumoured that the national newspapers had thick files on the private lives of certain of its members. We also discovered he was looking to blackmail us. Dandy Kim returned to the scene a little more than ten years ago to write the 'real' history of Ann Summers, implying that he had a different story to tell and was ready to expose us. We met up with him three or four times and he told us if we bought the rights for £150,000 from him he would never publish the story. The threat went on for months as we tried to find out what he was up to, and to see a manuscript. We were baffled as to what he planned to expose. We could only guess it was envy at losing Ann Summers and disappointment at a failed business project with us involving sex phone lines. We funded the project, but unfortunately he picked the wrong system, and we decided to cut our losses and quit. It was rather like picking Betamax video machines when everyone else was going for VHS. He picked a system which, unfortunately for us all, didn't work. He was devastated when we pulled the plug, but we felt we were pouring money down a black hole. He made an insinuation that he had been beaten up by us after appearing in public battered and bruised. In truth he was probably mugged while drunk. As for his 'real history', we called Dandy Kim's bluff, and he never published.

We have been on the periphery of that sort of thing all our lives. Whether it was George Cornell with his threatening meeting, or the Krays coming to visit, we were always close to that dark area – not helped, of course, by our father's frequent dabbles in the criminal world. But it is right to be honest, as simple as that. All of my friends – Charlie Cross, Jimmy Brown and Vic Phillips – went out and made an honest living, and remarkably, all four of us started off as bricklayers. If one of them had been Jack-the-lad then we could all have gone the same way. I know because I have seen it happen to others.

By 1980 we were ticking over nicely, not making a fortune, when my daughter Jacqueline came to me with an idea to develop Ann Summers Party Plan. I told her to put together a business strategy – something I was not able to do when I approached my bank manager for a loan all those years earlier – and show it to me before taking it to the board.

She wanted an investment of £40,000 to put her project into operation and she came to the board and made her presentation. The board were split down the middle: two members said it wouldn't work and two, including Ralph, thought it would. Things were on a knife-edge from the moment the meeting began when director Ron Coleman said he didn't know why we were considering all-women parties. In one of the great statements of our time, he added that women were not interested in sex in that sort of way! As chairman of the meeting that day I had the casting vote. I deliberated for a moment, then said yes. In truth, I was always going to back her. I had enough confidence in her plan to have supported it with my own money. It was always important to me that people I worked with saw that there was no nepotism, but of course there was. I've had my arms around my daughters right through their lives, though I didn't want my accountant or my warehouse manager to see it. It was always important that they were seen to succeed through their own ability and hard work.

That particular day I was so proud of her. I knew she was nervous; I could see it when she walked into the boardroom. We had been discussing the plan before the meeting. 'Just present your scheme the way you presented it to me and you'll be fine,' I said. I was comfortable about the entire matter because I thought the vote was going to be overwhelming in her favour. The outcome certainly helped cement our relationship as father and daughter. Jacky married at quite an early age and we became friends when she came to work at the business. But even then we were not as close as we might have been because I was working hard and she was just eighteen years old and a junior clerk. All that changed when she came to me with her idea of developing the Ann Summers business through Party Plan. It is fascinating to ponder things all these years later, but I have no doubt at all it was an important day for both of us.

Jacky was given the money she wanted and within three months we knew this would be a successful business. The only thing we didn't know was just how big it would get. During the ten years of Ann Summers Party Plan development, my daughter was the driving force in the field and my brother was responsible for the buying side. I was always in the office by eight a.m. as I was in charge of logistics, and in the early days I even drove the forklift truck. When you have ten parcels a day going out, as we did at the start, you can write the name and address on the box yourself; but when you have 3,000 a day you can't, and if you don't deal with these issues on the warehousing side, the business will falter. It was teamwork. If any element had failed the entire thing would have collapsed. I was working flat out. While Ralph and Jacqueline could do their jobs in eight hours, my side was running from eight in the morning until ten at night. I was alternating between the office and the warehouse, working seven days a week. I worked four hours on Sunday morning, only taking the afternoon off. That is the work ethic, and without it we wouldn't have succeeded, certainly not at the level we achieved. Everyone in the company, and especially in the family, knew their responsibilities. They were clearly defined and everyone stuck to them.

It would have been hard to believe back in 1980 that this was to become the largest Party Plan in the country, but while others faded away Ann Summers just became bigger and bigger. It had a huge impact. Everyone, it seemed, wanted to work for Ann Summers, to hold a party in their front room or to purchase the merchandise. There was an army of female entrepreneurs out there. By becoming a Party Plan lady you actually got an opportunity to learn how to run a business, and thousands of women could sense that opportunity, offered in so few other areas. Housewives and mothers were able to look after husbands and families and still run a successful business. Female agents selling to a female clientele. The concept empowered countless women across the country. It even got royal approval of sorts, as the Queen's granddaughter Zara Phillips threw an Ann Summers party at Princess Anne's Gatcombe Estate. According to a newspaper report there were 25 girls present and they enjoyed every minute as they ate smoked salmon, drank champagne and purchased several items at the party at Aston Farm, where Zara's father Captain Mark Phillips lives. I believe that proves just how acceptable these events have become. Famous names are only too happy to be connected with Ann Summers. Actresses like Barbara Windsor, Dawn French and Patsy Kensit have admitted their interest in the products, and when Baby Spice Emma Bunton from the Spice Girls revealed that she wore red PVC knickers from Ann Summers we sold out our stock of them in two days!

Having achieved so much, you can understand why I am so disappointed with the establishment for not inviting Jacqueline to Buckingham Palace on 7 March 2004 to meet the Queen as one of the 200 most influential women in the country. I was thrilled that they invited Birmingham City director Karren Brady, but hugely disappointed for my daughter who has achieved so much in her life. In the 1960s the establishment could not come to terms with the business of erotica, and sadly it's still the case almost half a century later. Will the establishment ever change? Will it ever truly come of age? The business world has honoured Jacqueline time and time again, yet still the establishment refuse to give her the recognition she deserves.

It could have been a logistical nightmare if we had been setting up Ann Summers from scratch. But by using our existing infrastructure, Party Plan simply slotted in with our current business where directors, accountants, transport systems, tea ladies, telephone systems and the like were already in place. Indeed, many others have tried to compete with Ann Summers and have failed. The capital and infrastructure needed to make such a venture work makes it very difficult for a competitor, especially when our brand is so well established. Over the past 25 years people have spent millions trying to compete with us. Some came from a mail order base, so they had stock and some infrastructure but not enough. Those who started from scratch had no chance. Every time a competitor came in they would seduce our girls away for their experience, and for a few months our progress would falter. But inevitably the rival would fail and our success would continue.

I can plot the arrival of various competitors from our sales figures. I am able to pinpoint when Lovelace came in, and when Harmony tried their luck. In 2004 millionaire businessman Andrew Joseph invested over £8 million in a Hustler franchise, part of Larry Flint's American porn empire. The first store opened in Birmingham in October that year, and the second, in Brewer Street, in 2005. It was announced in February 2006 that Hustler had ceased trading. We recently fought off the huge German company Beate Uhse, whose idea Dandy Kim copied when he opened two Ann Summers shops all those years ago. They used their German name, and it went down like a lead Zeppelin. It sounded more like a German infantry corps than a sexy toys and lingerie shop. Despite successfully beating off our competitors for the last 30 years, we remain vigilant.

As my housekeeper Mary told me, 'An Ann Summers party is one of life's experiences.' Little girls get bigger every day, so there is always a new clientele. Party Plan is still growing, though obviously not at the rate it did initially. In the early years it grew at an extraordinary rate. We had to make a conscious effort to slow down the business while we brought in new computers, which were obsolete within a year, and improved our infrastructure. At that stage we had several thousand part-time girls out there working for the company, which only had 300 full-time employees working for it. A lot of the girls were not motivated primarily by the money.

We completed surveys, the results of which surprised us, as we discovered they liked the opportunity to socialise, to get out and to have fun. Unlike Tupperware and others, these parties had a fun element for those giving the parties as well as the guests. They had the opportunity to become actresses, stand-up comediennes; they would pose and tell jokes, and the hostess would provide drinks and some food in return for a percentage, a bonus and a free gift. That was the formula Jacky put together; Ralph provided the buying skills and I dealt with the logistics, as usual. As for the girls – they found us! It was a snowball effect. Someone would throw a party and a couple of those attending would want to do it themselves, and so it grew, the girls who introduced them being rewarded when the new girls held their first parties. It was a legal pyramid system with no losers, and the key factor was this sense of fun and the actress element, along with a new breed of lady entrepreneurs.

The managing director of Ann Summers, Julie Harris, was herself an original Party Plan girl. A remarkable woman, Julie attended her first party over sixteen years ago and since then has worked her way up through the ranks of the organisation, as organiser, unit organiser and area manager, to where she is today, Jacqueline's trusted right-hand person. She started at the very bottom and is now flown around the country by private plane as she launches the new catalogues and opens new shops.

After the remarkable success of Party Plan we decided to refurbish our six existing Ann Summers stores – including those in Brewer Street and Wardour Street, two of the four original shops we purchased before we sold the two in Tottenham Court Road for £3 million – which were still very male-orientated. We started refitting Charing Cross Road and Bristol, turning both into female-friendly stores. Within a week our turnover had increased by over 50 per cent. We renovated the other four as well, and all the turnovers increased dramatically. The following year like for like sales jumped by another 20 per cent. All of which further proves how right we were in our original court cases. The demand for erotica and not pornography was there. These were the women who weren't supposed to be interested in sex, the very people it was suggested should be protected from such things. Now here they were, going out buying crotchless panties, peek-a-boo bras and vibrators. They were, and are, sexy ladies who are looking to improve their marriages, their sex lives or just to feel good about themselves. You try to suppress the fact that sexuality is part of our very being at your peril.

But in those days it was difficult to open stores. Of the six, two we owned and four had very long leases. Some landlords didn't want us because we were seen to be opening sex stores, and local councillors and MPs were totally against us. We wanted to expand but we couldn't, as the establishment put up resistance. But there were other, more enlightened landlords who could see the potential and seized the opportunity. In 1993 we opened a brand-new store in Southampton, on Above Bar Street – not the best position, but the landlord supported us after seeing our refurbished Bristol store for himself. It was an instant success. It was significant because, despite its poor position, it was on the high street – our first one. Jacqueline then went on to promote the image. I remember the manager at Lakeside Shopping Centre off the M25 saying there would never ever be an Ann Summers in Lakeside while he was in charge. He is no longer there, but Ann Summers is thriving. That about sums it up. We have become increasingly acceptable. We are now a high-street brand driven by Jacqueline Gold, who is the face of Ann Summers. The empire has already passed 150 stores and is still growing.

The natural follow-up was the Internet. There were and still are lots of sex toy companies on the net, but none of them compares with Ann Summers because people trust us. The company has been built on quality and customer care, and we jealously guard our reputation. It is something we are very proud of.

We still came up against some bigots, of course. When we were ready to move into the Glades shopping centre in Bromley, we were told we couldn't use the Ann Summers name and we couldn't stock sex toys. They clearly did not understand the business or our customers. So we said, 'Thanks, but no thanks,' and opened a store on the high street just outside the Glades. Ten years on, they are now offering us a prominent position in their mall, with no conditions, to replace our store in the high street. We will eventually take them up on their offer because our successful Bromley store is only 800 square feet and we now need a minimum of 2,000 square feet, preferably 2,500, so that we can have a Knickerbox concession as well.

In 2003, we opened a store in Manchester's Trafford Centre, one of the biggest malls in the country. Our contractors were working on the new shop front, and the manager of the centre would pop round on a daily basis to check on our progress. Then, one day, we received a furious telephone call from him saying he couldn't believe we were putting up a Knickerbox sign when it was supposed to be Ann Summers. When we explained it was both he was relieved because he wanted an Ann Summers. What a turnaround. What a long way we had come, almost turning full circle. We seemed to be breaking down the taboos and barriers all over the country.

But to achieve this position, in addition to hard work we had needed to be firm in the face of intimidation. In the very early days when Jacqueline was at a business fair in Bristol recruiting girls for those first parties, she had a few items on display. Suddenly the police arrived and threatened to arrest her, saying she needed a sex shop licence. But she stood up to them and refused to be bullied by these two big, burly police officers – just like her dad had done all those years ago in the school playground.

Then, in 1994, we opened an Ann Summers store in Brighton and invited the local council's licensing officer to have a look around, who was clearly concerned about the significant percentage of sex items in the store. My daughter Vanessa, who deals with these issues, explained to the official that we did not consider PVC and see-through underwear as sex items. We were below the accepted percentage of sex items, but Vanessa was having trouble convincing him. Arrangements were made for a further meeting, but it was cancelled by the council officer and another one arranged for a few weeks later, to include a number of his colleagues. The official again cancelled this meeting. Vanessa made a number of attempts to agree a convenient time, and a date was finally agreed for twelve o'clock on a Monday afternoon. Vanessa arrived at ten a.m., briefed the staff, checked the stock and made sure the general appearance of the shop was to her satisfaction. The staff, dressed in their new uniforms, waited in anticipation. The meeting time came and went. Vanessa waited until three before calling the council office, to be advised that there must have been some mistake, despite Vanessa reading out the letter confirming the meeting.

Although disappointed, we were optimistic that this meant the officials must by and large be happy with the layout of the new Ann Summers store. Two weeks later, however, we were shocked to receive a summons ordering Jacqueline, as chief executive, to appear before the Brighton magistrates, charged with operating a sex shop without a licence. She was mortified the council could take this action despite all of our best efforts to resolve the problem. We employed the very best lawyers, but our greatest asset was Jacqueline's steely determination not to be bullied by the establishment. British justice again prevailed. The magistrate stated it was an 'abuse of power' by the council officials and dismissed the case. We have traded in

Brighton successfully ever since, and it is now the sixth most profitable store in the Ann Summers chain. In the not too distant future we are looking to open a superstore, complete with a Knickerbox concession, in the town.

There have been other challenges. Job Centres would not carry our adverts, and Jacqueline took the government to court over that, again refusing to be bullied. It all sounded a bit familiar to her old dad whenever she stood up against authority – all five feet two inches of her. The police backed off at that business fair in Bristol, and so did the government. In fact, those two policemen helped us along the way because as part of the compromise Jacky agreed to move the vibrators to a less prominent position near the back of her stand, and that is how we still operate. More personal items are positioned to the rear of what is a veritable Aladdin's Cave.

Jacqueline has come a long way since her £4,000-a-year wages, and of the two directors who were against her idea, one has passed away and the other left to set up a rival company. Unsuccessfully. As I said, anyone who tries to compete with Ann Summers finds us very resolute, especially when people leave our company to set up in opposition. All key staff, including our vital Party Plan girls, have contracts that preclude them from competing against us for two years if they decide to leave. They also know from well-documented history that those who leave and join the competition fail.

Perception can still be a hindrance. The launch of our exclusive airline, the family going into football in 1993, the positive articles and interviews, and especially Jacqueline on television – she was clearly not Miss Whiplash at all, but a petite, stunningly beautiful and articulate woman – all increased the profile of our company. Jacqueline continues to go from strength to strength and now commands £6,000 for her excellent after-dinner speaking. She talks for just shy of an hour and has been to China, Canada and all round Britain. She has brought mainly female audiences to their feet with her motivational speeches. Still, when people come to visit us at our headquarters they may be surprised when, instead of seeing a woman dressed in leather and carrying a whip, they are met by an attractive receptionist, and when they go into our warehouse or accounts or sales departments, instead of seeing girls in skimpy nursing outfits they see ordinary people going about their business. Perhaps, though, they are disappointed not to see scantily-clad women.

CHAPTER EIGHTEEN

COMBAT 18, GYPSIES AND HOOLIGANS

I seem to have been fighting wars for as long as I can remember. The first, of course, was poverty, and perhaps that gave me the strength for the other battles that followed: starting out in business (easy in comparison), taking on the establishment and the law courts, then trying to help Birmingham City football club become established in the Premier League.

But at least there the rules of engagement were clearly drawn. I always knew where I stood and I could see the enemy in front of me. Fighting both Combat 18 and itinerant gypsies is totally different. The rules become blurred, and often the opposition are like ghosts in old-fashioned smog.

Jewishness to one person is one thing and another to someone else. It's mainly a private and personal matter, but unfortunately not for everyone. However, I refuse to be intimidated and I have and will continue to confront these sick individuals because if we keep hiding their numbers will only increase. For those of you fortunate enough never to have come across Combat 18, they are a British neo-Nazi group formed in 1991 after meetings between the so-called Blood and Honour Group and football hooligans such as the Chelsea Headhunters (the '18' corresponds to the position in the alphabet of the letters A and H, the initials of Adolf Hitler). It is largely believed to be an offshoot of the British National Party. After a short and violent history it receded following a Panorama programme on television, flaring up briefly through the likes of David Copeland, who carried out nail bomb attacks on blacks, Asians and the gay community in 1999, and soon after that bombs were detonated in Brixton, Brick Lane and Soho, killing three people and injuring many more.

They were largely disorganised and something of a rabble but with enough clout to set up newspapers like *Redwatch* and *Stormer*, designed to intimidate Jews, ethnic minorities and police officers. They targeted high-profile celebrities, like the Olympic swimmer Sharron Davies, actress Vanessa Redgrave, the then Spurs owner Alan Sugar, MPs Paddy Ashdown and Peter Hain, even journalists Anna Ford and Bernard Levin. Former world heavyweight champion Frank Bruno's mother, Lynette, was a target in *Stormer*, which led to the imprisonment of its publisher, Mark Atkinson. The police did a pretty thorough job of infiltrating the group and jailing several of the ringleaders. It was a great joy to see them captured, especially those in Tooting, South London, close to where I live. Seven members of the gang were jailed for a total of 25 years at Kingston Crown Court in November 2002 after police discovered an arsenal of weapons in their van. Detective Inspector Magnus said after the verdict, 'There is no doubt that serious assaults were intended against a racial minority and extensive preparations had been undertaken.' Until then they were a shadowy organisation, a somewhat cowardly, slimy, evil outfit you never saw. You could tell the sort of person the group attracted by their methods: an anonymous telephone call where they put the receiver down before the call could be traced, or an illiterate missive cut out of newspaper headlines or printed on cheap, home-made printers.

Family and friends want me to keep quiet and to protect me, but I refuse to be silenced. I will not give in to these bullies. This evil has to be stopped, and the only way to do so is to stand up publicly against them.

I had only looked on them with disgust from afar when they first got their hooks into me. I received a letter through the post saying, 'We know who you are and where you are.' There have been many other letters and telephone calls since, all of them designed to terrorise me. It has been part of my life for almost a decade, and I am somewhat anaesthetised to it now, though it does galvanise you into taking precautions and paying attention to your personal safety. I cannot take anything for granted, and I have increased the security at my house. Every time they make contact I double-check everything and make the necessary alterations. My house is now secure. My bedroom suite has two doors and both are steel with steel frames, although it doesn't look like it. The room is something like one from the film *Panic Room* starring Jodie Foster. Watching that encouraged me to continue with my security. If anything happens I can be in the room inside ten seconds, where I can throw a switch and have all my security in place, plus a mobile telephone dedicated to the room. The ordinary telephone is divorced from the usual system, and I have a panic button in place, while the windows are all toughened, bulletproof glass. Of course I also have security in my grounds, staff living on the property, and surveillance cameras, but the real feeling of safety lies in having my own secure area within my house. All the outside doors to my house – ten or more doors open on to balconies and outside areas – open outwards rather than inwards. How often do you see in the movies the 'heavy' or the police officer putting his shoulder against the door and it bursts inwards? It cannot happen with mine. In addition, I follow a set routine when I get home that is designed to thwart an attack, not just because of Combat 18 but because there are bad people out there.

I was burgled at my last house, and it shakes you to return home from work and find your home almost empty. But that was before Combat 18, who are far more insidious than any cat burglar, professional or not. It terrorises you, but it also focuses you at the same time. There was an incident a few years ago when burglars handcuffed neighbours of mine to their staircase and shot their dog. The poor animal took eight hours to die. Can you imagine the horror of being unable to help your pet because you are imprisoned in your own home? Former football manager Ron Atkinson and his wife Maggie suffered similar problems in their home.

I am pleased to see that in the last year or so Combat 18 has gone quiet. My guess is it's because the police uncovered a serious cell when they caught those men in Tooting. It is a form of fascism, an extension of the Nazis, looking for the pure Aryan race. They are pro white; everything else to them is scum and filth. Of course, anti-Semitism rumbles on and has not gone away, although I am sure it will eventually when we become truly integrated. It will be like the Blue Mink pop song of the seventies about the world being a huge melting pot. We will all end up coffee-coloured, and hopefully the world will be a better place to live. The police have done a fantastic job, because when these criminals and lunatics are caught it stops their oxygen. Since Tooting I have not had a single telephone call, and I am not difficult to find as chairman of Birmingham City Football Club and of Gold Group International.

I am not going to hide. I might regret it, but it is vital we all make a stand. Combat 18 might have gone quiet, but they have not gone away. Even if they did, another group would spring up and take their place. If it is not the Jews who are targeted it will be the Asians or some other minority. You feel like saying, 'Hey, leave me alone, I'm not Jewish,' but the truth is, I am. I'm not Jewish from a religious point of view, but I am an East End Jewish cockney by birth and background.

My other long-running battle is with the gypsies who camp at the bottom of the lane where I live in Surrey, just half a mile from my house. Every Friday I send out one of my staff for two or three hours to clean the lane because they make such a mess of it, and I have been doing this for more than ten years. There is an ongoing campaign in the neighbourhood urging the gypsies to stop wrecking the local environment by dumping tons and tons of rubbish; we want them to live by the same rules as all the other residents. This campaign is not about victimising gypsies as people, it is purely their behaviour. Unfortunately, the gypsies on Tupwood Lane dump endless amounts of waste with no regard for the woodland, the wildlife or the local community. When you have a discussion with any of them, they will tell you, 'It's not me – it's the others.' But they will never name 'the others'. They stick together like a gang, or members of a clan.

I took the aggravation, the trespassing, the filth and the mess, not to mention the thieving, for a long time, but in the end I simply had enough of our friends the gypsies, who are hardly the romantics of yesteryear in their painted wagons. After having a load of rubbish dumped in front of my main gates, I took it upon myself to stir up the residents. My neighbours fear retribution. I do too – of course I am nervous at four a.m. when the gypsies buzz my intercom on the outside gate – but I still feel I have to stand up and be counted. I wrote a letter to the local newspaper. Eventually they published a heavily edited version of it, which infuriated me. When I tackled them about it, they claimed it wasn't balanced. Well of course it wasn't – it was my personal point of view! I was so angry at their weakness that I contacted the Press Council through Tony Livesey, the editor at the *Sport* newspaper, and the following week the letter was published in full with a 'balancing' response from Charles Smith, chairman of the Gypsy Council, which quite frankly was full of platitudes and had no substance. This is the unexpurgated version of my letter:

This has got to stop. The residents of the Downs Residential Site have responsibilities as well as rights.

Hundreds of tons of waste have recently been cleared from both the site and the surrounding countryside. I have personally been responsible for keeping the southern end of Tupwood Lane clear of rubbish for over ten years.

I feel I am fighting a losing battle.

The reason we do not speak out against this anti-social behaviour is for fear of reprisals. Normally when you confront a neighbour, it's a one-to-one confrontation, and as a rule you reach a compromise, but when you confront a traveller you find you're up against ten to twenty families.

It's time to stand up against them and to change the laws to give the authorities increased powers to deal with these anti-social problems.

Even their dogs are completely out of control. It's now impossible to walk down the southern end of Tupwood Lane or the footpaths that lead on to the Downs without fear of being attacked by the dogs. Even walking on my own land is a problem. The dogs have attacked and killed many of the creatures I have rescued, including ducks, geese, peacocks, guinea fowl, show chickens and many others. I have the right to shoot these dogs, but I cannot bring myself to do it.

For twenty years I've heard people say the police and the council should do something, but in fairness to them, European and human rights legislation ties their hands. Quite frankly, it's time for bold new initiatives.

What in actual fact we have done by giving travellers a permanent site is we have built a ghetto in the midst of our beautiful countryside surrounded by tons and tons of filth and waste. It's our own fault. Years ago we thought we could solve the problem of the travellers by helping them to establish homes on a permanent site supplied by us, the taxpayers. Clearly we were wrong. We made a mistake. It's failed.

The travellers claim they have an aversion to bricks and mortar and can't live in a house. Tough! I have an aversion to piles and piles of rubbish, rats, and being intimidated.

What can we do? To be honest, I'm not sure, but I do believe that doing nothing is not an option. I think we have to be brave and bold. I think it's vital that we break up these ghettos. I think the strength, the power, the belief they are above the law is born out of their clan-like environment.

No other minority in Britain has this status. Integration of the minorities into society surely must be our ultimate aim.

I know this will not be universally popular, but I believe we must be bold and at the same time retain the moral high ground. In exchange for abandoning the site I believe we should offer each and every resident of the site a council house. Then dismantle the site for ever. The council should then sell the site for a small development, say four to six homes. The income from the sale could fund the project. This would have the effect of dismantling the ghettos and integrating the travellers into society.

They believe that by intimidating me I will go away, but with the support of your readers, I won't.

Not one single letter was published by the newspaper in response to my article. However, I received five personal letters of support, though four of them were anonymous – further proof that people are frightened to speak out.

Contrast this with all the trouble I faced from the council just for sorting out a simple fence around my property. Having bought my home in Tupwood Lane with 30 acres of land, I purchased a further 25 acres adjacent to my property from Surrey County Council with the knowledge that the gypsies were using the land to graze their horses and had been doing so for many years. I successfully negotiated a deal with the gypsies to remove their horses from my newly acquired land. To make sure they did not return I erected a post-and-rail fence around the property, but first I had to remove 27 lorryloads of waste, including a dead horse, from the site. Some weeks later, when most of the fence was erected, I was visited by six officers of the local Tandridge Council who advised me that I needed planning permission for the fence.

'Surely not?' I said. 'It's a post-and-rail fence.'

'You need planning permission, Mr Gold, if the fence is over one metre high,' they replied.

'But it's not,' I said hopefully.

The seven of us went out into the grounds to measure the fence, post after post. Almost with glee the officer measuring it called out, 'One metre three centimetres, one metre two centimetres, one metre one and a half centimetres . . .' Another wrote down the measurements, and confirmed, 'You need retrospective planning permission, Mr Gold, for the existing fence and planning permission for the remainder of the fence you wish to erect.'

I could not believe it. It was like a Monty Python sketch. 'No problem,' I said. I just wanted them off my property. I was not concerned about the existing fence, but I was desperate to complete the rest as I was fearful the gypsies would return.

The council were obliged to give me a decision within 60 days. Bizarrely, 60 days passed and no planning permission arrived. Within their rules, it says that if you do not receive a reply within 60 days you can apply to the Secretary of State, which I duly did. Can you imagine that, my application for a 500-metre post-and-rail fence around the boundaries of my home lying on the desk of the Secretary of State alongside an application for a £500 million oil refinery, two skyscrapers at Canary Wharf or the QE2 Bridge over the Thames? How silly bureaucracy can be. And yet in the twelve years I have been here they have still failed to deal with the gypsy issue.

As big a problem in my life as Combat 18 and the local gypsies were football hooligans. The very words raise the hairs on the back of the neck of everyone who loves the game, especially those closely involved with it. My first close encounter happened some twenty years ago when Ralph and I were on our way home from Portugal. It all began when we were walking towards the check-in desk at the airport. We were followed in the queue by an elderly couple struggling with their luggage. I offered to help them and of course let them go ahead of me and Ralph, and the friend who was with us. They checked in, and we followed, only to be told that there was only one seat remaining. The other two exchanged glances without saying a word to me.

We were left with only one option of getting back that day: to catch a flight to Manchester instead of Gatwick. It was late when we finally arrived and we gave a taxi driver a £20 note – way above the odds at the time – to get us to Piccadilly station in time for the last train. There, we booked three first-class tickets, only to discover later that there was no first-class compartment and the man in the ticket office hadn't bothered to tell us. It was a milk train, as they called the slow stopping trains in those days, and there were no seats available as we walked through until we arrived at the far end and found three seats in a long, packed carriage.

We settled down when, all of a sudden, there came a loud, impassioned cry of 'Celtic, Celtic, Celtic!' from a huge band of Irish Celtic supporters, who had been to a game at Manchester United and after a night on the beer were heading back to London. We spent five hours on the train with them, and they were disgusting. A young couple, a beautiful black girl and her white boyfriend, walked through the carriage at one point looking for seats and were given the most filthy verbal abuse. Beer bottles were being thrown out of the windows on to platforms when we stopped, and the entire journey was a nightmare.

Worse was to follow when one of them lurched towards us and asked in a loud voice, 'Who do you support, Jimmy?' I know now I should have said either I wasn't interested in football or I supported my local team Whyteleafe, but I have always believed that everyone respects West Ham United, so I told the truth, despite my golden rule 'Beware of telling the whole truth!' stemming from years earlier when I was found guilty of speeding because I told the magistrate the truth ('Sorry, sir, but I was late for work'). In my naivety I thought even the most aggressive football fan would accept the Hammers, but the abuse was instantly turned on us. Ralph gave me a blaming look for the second time that evening. Happily the game has grown up a lot since then, although we realise the media are just waiting for the next incident on and off the terraces, whether it's at Birmingham or anywhere else.

I can remember the guys in the cloth caps and mufflers applauding the opposition when they did something exceptional. In those days people would pay to go and watch John Charles or Stanley Matthews against their local favourites. Even I would happily go down the Valley to watch Charlton if the opportunity arose, or to Leyton Orient, especially when I played for Leytonstone, when the Hammers weren't at home. Then came that period when violence erupted. It nearly killed the game, before the wonderful Taylor Report in 1990 was taken up and stadiums became all-seaters. The report's proposals led to football clubs taking responsibility through the chairmen for adequate policing and/or stewarding, CCTV cameras and the like, thus creating grounds where you'd be happy to take your wife and children. It almost certainly saved the game.

CHAPTER NINETEEN

TRIUMPH AND TRAGEDY

F lying has been my hobby and the passion in my life, perhaps the release valve from my business. There is no better way of blanking other matters out of the mind than by taking responsibility of an aircraft. It's also one of the most exhilarating experiences man can ever have. To be in control of your own plane or helicopter is to be in a separate world. But, as with all experiences, there are low moments as well as high.

There was a group of eight of us who revelled in the experience of flying, and in each other's company: Mark and Sue Campbell, David Tearle and his first wife Jacky, Stuart Paterson and his wife Liz, and my girlfriend Penny and me. I spent 25 years with Penny after the situation with my first wife Beryl and my lost love Ann-Marie, but it wasn't until I met Lesley that I found my soulmate. Penny was an extremely attractive lady but, sadly, we were always more friends than lovers. It had to be pretty good to stay with someone for so long, but it all went sour when we moved into the new house I live in now in Surrey. She gave up smoking after having a heavy habit for nearly 30 years. It dramatically changed her personality, we gradually grew apart, and eventually our relationship broke up. Before then, all eight of us were the closest of friends, although I didn't know at the time that Stuart was having an affair with Jacky. We would fly to Jersey in our own planes for long weekends.

Mark Campbell was killed in an air crash in Malta. Soon after that, Stuart Paterson also died in a flying accident. My closest friend David Tearle died a couple of years ago of cancer. Recently I stood by the side of a pool we had all used, remembering my friends, appreciating how vulnerable we all are, and realising that despite being the oldest among them I was the only one left. The tragedies of those deaths had a big impact on my life. In 1982 Mark and I were competing in the Malta Air Rally together when he went off on a flight with his friend Teddy White. I was sitting on the balcony of our hotel eating lunch with Mark's wife Sue, and as they flew past us no more than twenty feet away in a Harvard, a big, noisy, rotary-engine American plane, I thought, 'Bloody hell!' They were so close I could read the word Firestone on the tyres. Teddy, who was piloting, then took a very tight turn as he came round, the wing stalled, and the plane turned over just a couple of hundred feet above the ground, went into a spin, crashed into a nearby school that, thankfully, was empty for the weekend, and burst into flames. Sue was hysterical, understandably inconsolable. Her husband had just died violently in front of her eyes. We all thought Teddy would one day die like that because he was a devil-may-care pilot, wild, the only one who would have flown a former fighter plane, which he had restored himself and it was shattering to lose Mark in the same crash.

A year after Mark's death, Sue found happiness in a relationship with Stuart, who had left Jacky, David Tearle's ex-wife, some time earlier. Stuart owned his own Citation Jet and was a professional pilot. One jet-black night – no stars and no moon – he was descending into Stornoway airport having picked up six passengers from Paris. He had informed Stornoway tower that he had the runway lights in sight, but inexplicably he crashed into the sea. The plane and its occupants were recovered, and it was revealed that Stuart, the co-pilot and all the passengers had survived the impact but had drowned in the freezing Irish Sea. It was also discovered that the throttles were set at full power, suggesting that Stuart had selected full power at the very last moment before hitting the water. Two seconds earlier, and he and everybody on board would have survived. This tragic accident was caused by a visual phenomenon discovered only a few years earlier by the US Air Force. Sue, of course, had to take a telephone call telling her that she'd lost a second lover in a plane crash.

As for my closest friend, David Tearle, who I was in business with for fifteen years, he was my co-pilot when we won the Malta Air Rally in 1980. When I resumed flying again some years ago he promised that as soon as he had finished his current project, we would fly off on an adventure. One idea was to fly around the world in my Cessna 180. But then, sadly, at a time when we were doing great and our friendship was flourishing, he told me he had cancer, and just six months later he passed away. For me, life has been about great joys and great tragedies. It would be nice to have a clear line drawn between the two, but it does not happen like that. It seems the more joy you have, the more it is balanced with despair.

Malta also brought me great joy, and it was also a landmark for Ralph and me. Coming from the depths of poverty in East London and having realised that being side by side was the only way we were going to be successful, we followed that through into our flying. We had always experienced being telepathic in the way we lived our lives and did business, but it was never stronger than it was one day in 1980 when we flew back home from Malta in our separate planes.

The International Malta Air Rally was an extraordinary event. As the leading flying event in Europe it attracted all the top pilots. Aircraft leave from different destinations around Europe such as Iceland, Finland, Germany, Italy, France and Spain, and various airports from around England. Each pilot is given an arrival time over the Gozo Beacon, a small island off the west coast of Malta, and it is probably the most prestigious part of the rally to win. I had the good fortune of winning the Gozo Beacon in 1978, and it is the trophy I treasure the most. The competition is broken up into a number of events on the same day with points awarded for each position; the one with the most wins the Malta Air Rally. On arrival at the beacon there is another award for the most accurate elapsed time between the Gozo Beacon and the airport, and added to the two are the Concourse d'Elegance, where judges assess the quality of the aircraft, how it has been maintained, and all its safety equipment. We spent weeks before leaving getting the aircraft into pristine condition in the hope of gaining points. The final competition is the flight planning for the entire trip. All the elements come together with winners for each section and then an overall winner.

The first time I entered I came 36th out of 60 or so – a good result considering it was my first rally. The next time I competed I finished fifth, and over the next five years I followed this with second, second, first, first and second. After winning the Malta Air Rally in 1980, Ralph and I readied ourselves for our return to Blighty, with Ralph taking off before me. Our first leg was designated as Malta to Cannes on the south coast of France, where we were to refuel before flying on to Biggin Hill. It was a beautiful day, and the flight was mostly uneventful. I was on a private frequency over which I could chat to Ralph and talk to the control tower at Bastia as we overflew Corsica. I knew where Ralph was, some 40 miles ahead of me.

I was gaining on him when suddenly I had a call from him telling me he was having to put in right rudder to keep the aircraft straight and level. I was mildly concerned, but it hardly sounded serious and I told him to let me know if it got worse. He was flying a twin-engine six-seater Aztec PA 28, which I had previously owned, and wanted to know if it was anything I had come across before. I heard nothing from him for a while and assumed he had corrected the fault, whatever it was. I concentrated on getting my twin-engine Cessna 340 up with him for landing at Cannes, where we would have lunch together.

Ralph then got back to me and told me he appeared to be running lower on three of the four fuel tanks, while the fourth was completely full. I suggested that he select the cross-feed, which meant both engines would feed from all four tanks and they would find their own level. I still felt there was no serious problem or cause for concern – until he got back to me ten minutes later to tell me he was now convinced he could not get to the fuel on his left-hand outboard tank and was having to apply more and more rudder to keep the aircraft flying straight and level. I could not understand it and told him to recycle the cross-feed: the problem was probably a sticky valve, which normally clears itself by recycling. I also suggested he should reduce power and lean the mixture to conserve fuel.

We were still perhaps 60 miles from Cannes, and I was now beginning to get a bit twitchy. I was wondering whether Ralph could make the French coast if he couldn't get to that tank of fuel. I started working out the maths and came to the conclusion that without the fourth tank he was not going to make it. I was still trying to catch up with him and we were beyond the point of no return, so there was no turning back, and the nearest airport was our destination, Cannes.

Ralph came back to tell me he was convinced he was not going to be able to access the fuel in the rogue tank. I desperately racked my brains but couldn't come up with a solution, so I told him we should declare an emergency – not a full-blown Mayday, but an emergency – to let the authorities know we were having difficulties so they could be prepared. Ralph was reluctant as he could now see the coast of France. I couldn't yet see land, but I was now at full power, and eventually I reeled him in and we were flying side by side. My plan was that if Ralph ditched I would be in a position to guide in the emergency rescue service.

The situation deteriorated rather than improved, so we declared a full emergency. It was an unnerving moment. I was talking to Ralph over the radio, advising him what to do, even though in most instances he had already taken the action I was suggesting. A second voice can be a help in such circumstances, even if only confirming decisions. I was telling him to reduce power, maintain height, delay the descent and lean the mixture to reduce fuel consumption to make land. We were staying high because if he lost the engines he could then possibly glide in to land safely. We were at 10,000 feet and I was now alongside. We continued to talk. It was easier for me as I was OK, but Ralph was under stress. He had Annie, his lady, and Graham Balls, his co-pilot, in the plane with him. He was desperately trying not to show the stress, and telling Annie not to worry. One of the most difficult moments was for him to tell her to put on her lifejacket as a precaution without giving the full reason, which obviously upset her.

At last, Cannes airport came into view and we began our descent. But Ralph now faced another dilemma, because the landing runway was towards the sea which meant going over the town and coming in the other way. It would take a precious four minutes, time he perhaps didn't have, and if he did lose his engines he did not want to crash-land into the town. We agreed to land straight in downwind and not do the circuit. The tower agreed too, but just as we thought we would make it, Ralph told me one of his engines had started to splutter. In his efforts to try to get to the remaining fuel, he had turned off the cross-feed, selected the outboard tanks and used all the fuel. One engine began to shudder to a stop as Ralph relayed the news to the Cannes tower and to me.

I immediately started looking for the rescue helicopter as we had declared a full emergency. In all honesty I could not see him making it. I continued to pass on reassuring words, and to remind him that if the engines stopped he must get the cabin door open before he hit the water. The fear is once you hit the water it is hard to open the doors against the water pressure. I told him to open the storm window and to get his co-pilot Graham to be ready to open the door when he was a hundred feet from the water, and no sooner, as it would cause drag and there was always the chance he could make the beach. What you don't want is a heavy landing on water because the frame buckles, and if that happens, forget the pressure, you can't open the doors anyway. We also put on our landing lights so we could be easily spotted. Thinking back now, there was very little else we could have done in the circumstances. We had covered all the possibilities.

I could only imagine his stress as we went through these checks in readiness for a possible ditching. The only good thing was the high ambient temperature of the water and the fact that I would be directly over him.

Small comfort to Ralph and his passengers, though. Ralph reselected the cross-feed and thankfully the port engine burst back into life, but the situation was still dire: he was literally flying on fumes in the three accessible tanks by this time. We were taking calls from Cannes asking us how far we had to run, and then they told us they had us in sight. Fantastic news, but there was still no sign of the emergency helicopter, though I could see emergency vehicles by the side of the runway.

I was trying to calculate whether, if the engines cut out now, Ralph could make the runway from our present position – 4,000 feet high with ten miles to run. The answer was no, but if they kept going for a few more minutes he would make it. I have never prayed in my life, but I have to confess that at that moment I asked God to help my brother and keep those engines running for a few more minutes.

I could just make out a number of rallyists ready to take off, but they had been held back as the drama unfolded above them. They watched and listened in absolute silence to every word spoken by the control tower as Ralph and I, one of their number, struggled against the odds for survival. They, more than anyone, knew how critical the next few moments were going to be.

In the end it was nature alone that provided the key, for as we descended we entered a tailwind which was becoming more and more southerly. It gave Ralph just that extra little push he needed to reach the runway, which was right on the beach, leaving no room for error. But what had saved him could also have killed him. His relief was so overwhelming that he forgot he had a tailwind of 20 knots up his backside and he almost went through the fence at the end of the runway. I could see puffs of smoke coming up from his tyres as he touched down. Following Ralph down the runway were a number of fire engines and emergency vehicles. It was a wonderful moment. All protocol was abandoned and the calls came through from the tower saying, 'Well done, Mike Oscar [Ralph's call sign], well done, Mike Oscar.' Teddy White, who was to die in the crash with Mark Campbell, was at the end of the runway waiting to depart for Biggin Hill. 'Well done, Ralph,' he said. 'The beer is on me at Biggin.' Others were also calling out, 'The beer is on us at Biggin Hill, Ralph.' All this at a very serious and very busy international airport, while Ralph was tearing down the runway, struggling to stop before he smashed into Teddy's plane and the fence at the end of the runway. He eventually slowed down and taxied to his allocated parking bay, and as he arrived one engine died completely. That was how tight it was. When they checked the plane over, sure enough the outboard tank was full along with an empty tank outboard, an empty inboard and no more than a litre of fuel on the remaining inboard. How tight can you get? A milk bottle of fuel! Ralph jumped out of the plane and in true Hollywood style kissed the ground, left the aeroplane where it was, and got on a Boeing 737 back home.

Annie was oblivious to the real danger they were in until the very end, while Graham the co-pilot was brilliant throughout, remaining calm and in control. Ralph would have struggled had he had anyone panicking alongside him as he held the lives of three people in his hands. Later it was discovered that the problem lay with the cables to the cross-feed. All Aztecs in the world, something like a thousand of them, were told to check their cross-feeds within a week of the incident, and an AD (airworthiness directive) was then fired off advising owners to change this system because of a manufacturing fault. These planes had been flying for 30 years and the reason was almost certainly longevity wear, despite the constant checks and tests.

I once had an experience in the same Aztec, flying with a friend, Paul Carpenter. We were going to Rome and I had just fitted a transponder, which sends a signal to the radar controller so that he can identify you. I was really proud of my new modern piece of technology. When I reached the beacon over Sorrento we were asked for our identifying squawk, which I duly transmitted. The heading he gave us was Zero Zero Seven, but my co-pilot read it out as Zero Seven Zero and I mistakenly flew up a box canyon. Control was telling me to recycle my squawk as they did not have us on radar. I couldn't understand it. We were out of touch; I should have been able to see the majestic Seven Hills of Rome, but I saw nothing. We had lost contact with Rome altogether and were inside this box canyon. We had no radio contact, no radar, and there was nothing visual we recognised. We were simply on our own.

We eventually made contact with an American Airlines 707 which relayed messages between us and the tower. Control eventually picked us up again on radar without the help of my new facility and we were given new headings to get us out of the canyon and back on course. But it was very nasty for half an hour. It transpired that, apart from the human error, when they fitted the new equipment the connection had not been made properly. It could have been extremely unpleasant, and the engineers received a severe rap across the knuckles. Although we had taken up the wrong heading, the moment they received our squawk Rome would have seen our error and changed our heading.

In all the years I have flown that is the only time I was ever really in any sort of danger, and that was very early on in my flying career. Although I have to admit there was another nasty moment a few years ago. I was flying my four-seater Cessna 182 from my house in Surrey to the Birmingham City training ground the day before we were due to play Liverpool at Anfield in our first season in the Premier League. I had landed at the same place many, many times, but on this occasion I applied the brakes, skidded and crashed into a ten-foot earth bank at the end of the training ground. They had been cutting the grass, and it never occurred to me there would be fine, damp cuttings on the ground as our groundstaff maintained it like a bowling green. It was always kept short, and when it was cut it was no more than a shave. They acted like ball bearings, and when I braked it was like skidding on ice. I scrambled out in case the fuel tanks ignited. I was extremely relieved to be able to walk away from that one, though I did bite off the end of my tongue and the harness cracked my ribs. The first thing I did was to arrange for the dirt bank to be removed, then I ordered a new aircraft. But what I hurt most was my pride. Fortunately, training had finished and there were only a few people around, but the story quickly got into the press and around the dressing room.

But I have to say, flying has given me a great deal more pleasure than grief, and a little touch of glory. I even got a one-liner in *The Times*, saying that David Gold of Warlingham in Surrey won the International Malta Air Rally. But crash my Cessna, and it's in every newspaper across the country! One of the ironies in my life, especially once I lifted my head above the parapet and shed my very private life for the public exposure of professional football. Of course I talk to journalists, often as friends, but there is always the odd one who is only concerned with the sensational rather than the truth. Most are honest; they just want to do a good job for their newspaper or radio station. Those to be wary of are certain freelances who misrepresent you in order to provide the sports editor or editor with the story they have in mind. They never allow the facts to get in the way of a good story. It is a case of learning the business over the years, learning who to speak to and who to trust, not disliking journalists as an entity, just avoiding those who let you down. There is good and bad in all areas of life and you have to sort out the wheat from the chaff. Their industry in that respect is no different from any other.

I began to learn very quickly who could be trusted at both local and national level. There are journalists like Colin Tatum, Graham Hill, John Curtis of the Press Association, Russell Kempson and Alison Kervin of *The Times*, Janine Self of the *Sun*, Vince Ellis, Bob Hall, and Jim White of the *Daily Telegraph* and of course my friend Tom Ross, broadcaster and Head of Sport at Capital Gold, who are professional people and trustworthy. But I have not always got it right. I have made mistakes by trusting people who have let me down and caused me grief, but the ones who truly hurt are those who have written about me without even interviewing me. I have had that happen a number of times in my life. I have picked up an article and read insults and slurs by someone who is blessed with little or no knowledge of me. I knew I would be shot at, but the strength and volume of the venom still surprised me, especially when it comes from a writer you admire and respect like Patrick Collins of the *Mail on Sunday*. I simply don't know where his pieces came from because he certainly never spoke to me or anyone close to me. People tell me he is a very nice person. Whether he is anti the business I am involved in or simply just a columnist I do not know. These people who observe rather than interview have few contacts and therefore don't mind upsetting people. While it is distressing at the time, once I am past it I rarely hold a grudge, but I would say to anyone that I always prefer a face-to-face interview, even if their article turns out to be negative.

The only flying incident I have been involved in as a passenger was when returning home from Portugal one day. It was a normal scheduled flight with no problems, except for the fact that as I took my seat by the window, a truly huge woman sat next to me. Not only was she extremely overweight, she also needed a crutch to help her walk. My first thought, all those years ago when comfort on board short-haul flights was limited, was one of amazement: how had she managed to lever herself into the seat? Also on the plane was Henry Cotton the golfer; otherwise all was serene and normal. It was a route I had travelled many times, both by commercial airline and flying myself, and I knew the turns and the geography as well as driving on a motorway at home. I even knew the beacons, including Fifty North, the demarcation line in the Channel, which is called Ortec.

At this point I was aware of the pilot altering course and reducing power to begin his approach into Gatwick. I felt the change, then the power came back, and we heard the following announcement: 'This is an emergency, this is an emergency. We are about to land on water, we are about to land on water. Please remain calm, please remain calm. Put on your lifejackets and remain in your seats. Remain in your seats. Do not inflate your lifejackets.' I sat there wondering how I was going to get out of this and what the hell I was going to do. I was in the worst possible place. My girlfriend Penny had taken her normal travel pills and was fast asleep. She was in the middle seat, and the 25-stone disabled lady was in the aisle seat.

It also went through my mind that it was not an impossible situation. We were at 34,000 feet at Ortec and less than 50 miles from Bournemouth, Southampton, and a disused military airport on Thorney Island. I had landed on all these runways at some time in the past. I struggled to do the sums under pressure, but I believed it was possible to glide to safety at one of these airports. Descending at 3,000 feet per minute, it would take ten minutes to reach the water, and at, say, 300 miles an hour, the aircraft could travel 55 miles.

I was wrapped in total confusion as everyone around me scrambled into their life vests. My mind was full of contradictions. On the one hand I was telling myself there was no point struggling to put on the lifejacket because I wouldn't be able to get out anyway; on the other I still couldn't believe, as a pilot, what was happening. It simply did not add up. If the engines had failed, why couldn't we make it to one of the airports close by? Or even go back to Cherbourg on the French coast no more than 30 miles away with its massive 8,000-foot runway?

For ten minutes there was an eerie silence in the aircraft. A few passengers sobbed quietly and a number were praying, but there was no panic, just a heavy quietness. Then, to everybody's immense relief, we discovered that the stewardess had inserted the wrong tape. She had meant to put in the tape saying, 'Ladies and gentlemen, we are about to start our descent . . .' Not only had she played the wrong tape, she'd been in the cockpit with the captain when the tape was being played and hadn't heard it. I have to say I was stunned that, once she realised what was going on and she could see the distraught passengers in their lifejackets, there was no apology offered. Henry Cotton, being the personality he was, gave an interview to a newspaper which made the headlines. In it, he complained about the stress and, of course, the lack of apology from either the stewardess or the captain. We both found that appalling. It was so scary, especially knowing that if we had crashed I would have had absolutely no chance of survival.

One of my worst experiences, however, was not in the air but on water, with the sinking of the Townsend Thoresen *Herald of Free Enterprise* ferry outside the Belgian port of Zeebrugge on 6 March 1987. This time I was not directly involved, but – and this was worse – both of my daughters were on their way back home from a skiing trip and were due to be on the ferry. This was before the age of mobile telephones, so as soon as I saw what had happened on television I called the helpline and was passed on from person to person until I found someone to pass on the details. It was only halfway through when I realised I was giving descriptions that would have been used to identify the dead rather than the living. All I wanted to know was whether my daughters were on the ferry, while they were asking me about identifying marks.

I have never been so distressed in my entire life. I had a very heavy heart as I waited for the telephone to ring, and in between I was calling everybody I could think of, asking them if they had heard from the girls. It was a complete nightmare, sitting all on my own watching the television relaying the news and talking about the rescue operation and the ever-growing numbers of dead. Every ten minutes I rang their homes to see whether they had arrived. No answer.

Then that huge relief when the telephone rings at three a.m. and a voice says, 'Hello, Dad, just got your message to ring you.' Incredibly, they had missed the ferry that sank and decided to go on to Ostend to catch the next boat home. How many others were as lucky as that? And how many had missed the one before and caught the doomed boat? It was a roll-on-roll-off ferry, and when it left port not all the water had been pumped out of the bow ballast tanks, leaving the ship three feet down at the bow. The failure to close the bow vehicular door meant she capsized in about 90 seconds after leaving the harbour.

It resulted in the deaths of 193 people, most of the victims trapped inside the ship, which lay in shallow water, dying of hypothermia. It was the highest death toll of any British vessel in peacetime since the sinking of the Titanic 75 years earlier.

And for six hours I thought my daughters were among them.

CHAPTER TWENTY

DAVID SULLIVAN

The business acumen of David Sullivan was first demonstrated to Ralph and me nearly 25 years ago in a telephone call out of the blue which was both bizarre and brilliant. We were adversaries in business, and he was as ferocious as we were in maintaining our position in the marketplace, but what was typical of the man was that he was still able to pick up a telephone and propose a deal that made so much sense we could not turn it down. We both had a range of top-shelf magazines and we were fighting each other for space on the shelves. We were increasing production to flood the market and maximise the sales while David was doing the same, to disastrous effect. The day he telephoned and suggested he would hand over his distribution in return for us becoming joint publishers changed all that. It was a piece of genius, and we immediately asked ourselves why we hadn't thought of it first. We did the deal on the telephone with no official agreement, just a letter of heads of agreement, and it changed the nature of our business overnight. We were no longer in competition but in co-operation, thus changing both our businesses into substantial profit-making organisations.

That led to a business deal put forward by David Sullivan that involved Sport Newspapers and our partnership in owning shares in West Ham United. His brainchild, *Sunday Sport*, quickly became a cult newspaper selling in excess of 600,000 copies every Sunday before going to seven days a week. Everyone said it would fail, but it is still there fifteen years on. Then, of course, there is our joint venture in Birmingham City Football Club, a thirteen-year-old ongoing adventure.

I always thought my work ethic was high, but his was, and still is, quite amazing. He is relentless when it comes to pursuing his goals. His relationship with his newspaper editor Tony Livesey is unique. David's promotional genius, along with his persistence and his determination, makes him an exceptional man. I am delighted he is my partner and not my adversary, and my opinion has remained unaltered to this day. We have a special respect for each other as we bring different skills to the table, and our relationship has stood the test of time.

Before football we never once had dinner together; we were partners rather than friends. But when you are sharing in these great experiences, the ups and downs football throws at you, there is something else. There is a passion not there in business; there is excitement when you win, despair when you lose. We share these very emotional things.

We are business partners on the one hand and football colleagues on the other, and I find him interesting and challenging. He shoots from the hip, is very spontaneous, and can suddenly be at odds with the manager or whoever he has disagreed with. It does not happen very often, even though it was suggested he and Trevor Francis, the Birmingham manager between 1996 and 2001, had a rocky relationship. Not true. There was the odd spat that was blown up in the newspapers, just as he had the odd disagreement with Barry Fry, Birmingham's boss before Francis, with whom he is still a friend. He holds no grudge against Trevor Francis, as some may imagine.

These kinds of issues would leave David saying, 'Find me a buyer – I have had enough!' This happened a couple of times, and it was rumoured he was going to Manchester City, Spurs, or back to his hometown of Cardiff. When things are going wrong and you are being bombarded unfairly, it is an understandable reaction. He was once quoted as saying, 'I feel like General Custer with sixteen arrows in the back and up my backside.' Some will say David brought it upon himself because when he did interviews he would be brutally honest and tell it like it was with no thought of the consequences. David will always tell you the truth from his perspective. He accepts there have been times when he has put his foot in it. I have watched situations evolve as he has landed himself in trouble with the media, the fans and the manager, but David believes he has earned the right to speak his mind and everything he does is in the best interests of Birmingham City Football Club. He has even lambasted the team publicly because he thought it was a way of motivating them to perform. A kick up the backside for everyone, and if his outburst was followed by a victory then he would believe it was because of what he did and said.

David Sullivan is a great statistician, and lives and dies by the numbers. He is an extremely private and shy man but he is resolute in his beliefs and desires. He works from his mansion and rarely visits his various businesses. He had a normal upbringing in Cardiff. His father was a career man in the RAF, rising to the rank of wing commander. He was also awarded an MBE. David was never going to dig trenches – my euphemism for manual labour. He was always going to orchestrate businesses like Philip Green, the Croydon-born icon of British retailing. He is a motivator, driving people, as well as being an ideas man. His people don't have to come up with ideas; he does that, gives it to them, and they put it into operation. That is his real skill.

Here is a man who is a brilliant statistician, yet, like me, he stumbled into erotica. A lot of people think we 'went into' erotica, but what happens is you make the most of an opportunity, as I did when I ran my science fiction book shop. I realised girlie magazines and Hank Janson were making profits, this was what was selling, and I simply responded to demand. When I took over the bookshop it had not only science fiction but also a big range of Penguin books, reprints of the classics, like George Orwell. I would sell a Penguin and replace it with a Hank Janson. Those who are successful in erotica, like the Golds, David Sullivan, Paul Raymond and Richard Desmond, are also successful in other areas of business. Raymond was and still is in erotica, but he made an even bigger fortune out of property. The point is, these are quality, skilled people. It is not erotica that has made them wealthy so much as their business abilities. David Sullivan is a good example. He has a fantastic property portfolio and other businesses, as I do. I know dozens of names from the past who were in erotica and are now, metaphorically, digging trenches because they failed.

The perception that you just print the magazines, sell them and become a millionaire is arrant nonsense.

What I do know is that many would not go into this business for reasons of morality. But if the same people were offered shares and were told they would double their money within a year, they would buy them – this is the hypocrisy. It is a bit like an anti-smoker buying shares in a cigarette company because he knows the profits will be good. Both Ralph and I invested half a million pounds each to join forces with David Sullivan to launch the *Sunday Sport*. Apart from the *Racing Post*, it is the only national newspaper in 40 years to be launched, to survive and to make money. It will always be perceived as a downmarket newspaper pandering to the sexual side of journalism, but it is a success. Lord Stephenson, who was at the time chairman of Express Newspapers, bought 25 per cent of the shares in Sport Newspapers, but after being nicknamed 'Lord Porn' and constantly ribbed by the other tabloids he offered to sell his shares back to us. Ralph and I were invited to a meeting at the headquarters of Express Newspapers. We negotiated for over an hour in their vast oak-panelled boardroom complete with a butler serving coffee – the epitome of upper-class wealth and success. Here they were, trying to offload their shares in our 'downmarket' newspaper. You could almost smell the hypocrisy. The negotiations were all about them wanting money for their shares against us wanting recompense for their decision to pull out of the deal. The talks had reached stalemate when my brother said to Lord Stephenson, 'This deal is a bit like you leaving your wife for an eighteen-year-old girl, and when you got tired of her you wanted to return to your wife.' With that, Lord Stephenson got up from his chair and retorted, 'I really don't know what you are talking about,' and left the room. Four weeks later we received their 25 per cent share holding in Sport Newspapers and a substantial cheque.

A lot of people have their doubts about David Sullivan for one perceived reason or another, but as a businessman he is one of the sharpest I have ever met. He is astute, his work ethic is extraordinary, and his determination to succeed is unparalleled. He has often said it is sad to be in the girlie business because it has reached a certain level and can't go any further. He has boundless energy to achieve more, where others would say, 'I have done OK,' and rest on their laurels. David would be the first to agree that we missed an opportunity to acquire the *Daily Express* and the *Star* when he was ahead of Richard Desmond in the race to purchase the long-established national dailies. Had he been a bit more bullish he would have had the *Star* and *Express* as well as the *Sport*. That would have been a challenge I am sure he would have relished. Rupert Murdoch is probably the last of the great press barons, but watch out for Desmond. As a competitor he will go where angels fear to tread. In my opinion he could be, with a bit of luck, the new British press baron.

David is a truly amazing man, and time is very precious to him. He will not waste it with fools, and the hours he spends with his children are especially important to him. As long as I have known him, time has been the most precious commodity of all, as it is to all dynamic people. There is so much going on in their lives. I have experienced it myself. You have to make time because it is not readily available. We don't finish work at five p.m. and get home by six with dinner on the table by 6.30. Time has to be made; it doesn't just appear because there is so much going on and only twenty-four hours in a day. I remember when David was poorly and needed a quadruple bypass; he delayed the operation until the end of the football season so that he didn't miss any matches, once again planning his time to suit his life. His life-saving operation was planned around his life, not the other way around. Some say it is bizarre, and indeed he was very poorly and we were extremely worried for him. Shortly before his operation we went to his house and he could barely walk up the stairs. The bypass undoubtedly saved his life. After the operation he went into all the details and discovered that the average survival rate was ten years, and he could only have two bypasses in total. Some would then say they were going to enjoy the rest of their life in luxury and pamper themselves with the money they had made. Not David. He decided to speed up on the money-making process.

Just recently, though, he has been trying to slow down a little and be more philosophical. He wants to spend time with his children, whom he adores, and his partner Eve, who is such a joy. She is so perfect for David. She knows exactly how long the children should spend with him, and when it becomes too much they are whisked away. There are many women who couldn't survive life with David, but he and Eve are perfect for each other.

Another area where David and I have joined forces is horse racing. The sport of kings has become an enjoyable pastime. These sleek, wonderful animals could not be further away from the horses I knew as a child in Green Street, hauling coal carts and the like. We have now owned horses together for six years and it has been a lot of fun. The idea came originally from David, who has owned horses on and off for 30 years. He had come out of the game over ten years ago because he wasn't getting the pleasure or value he used to out of the 30 horses he had in training. But he then had the urge to get involved again, and asked me if I fancied going in with him to buy four horses for a total of US$400,000. I have to admit I had to think about it. It was, without question, an indulgence, and I had never been a horse person. But I have had some fantastic experiences thanks to this latest alliance. None more so than Royal Ascot, when I was in the enclosure with the Queen, with Barry Fry in top hat and tails saying, 'I never fought I'd be 'ere in the same ring as the flippin' Queen, 'ob-nobbing with the elite!'

We have sold horses for anything between US$100 and US$800,000. We have had lots of runners, some winners, and others that finished nowhere, and some that are apparently still trying to find their way home, but, incredibly, we are financially in the black. It could have been a lot more if we had sold our top horse, David Junior, named after David Sullivan's young son, for the US$4 million we have been offered. But we turned the money down, just as we did before then when we were offered US$2.5 million, when I said to David, 'I don't think two and a half million dollars will change our lives, but I do believe in the excitement of David Junior going on to greater things.' It is also David's judgement that this horse will go on to reach the very top, and his optimism led me to agree and see where it takes us. The following race after the offer it came eighth, then third in the next, and then, as we were beginning to wonder whether or not we had done the right thing, he won. In the third race, the Emirates Champion Stakes at Newmarket, a Group One race, he came in at 33–1 and we won £250,000 prize money. The following day was when the bid for US$4 million came in.

In March 2006, David Junior ran in the Dubai Duty Free race. Our horse was up against the best in the world. Ralph and David Sullivan had flown out to see the event. Sadly I couldn't join them as I had made the decision to go to Old Trafford where Birmingham were playing Manchester United. On the morning of the race, we were surprised to discover that David Junior was made the 5-1 favourite. The total prize money was US$5million, with US$3million for the winner. Brian Meehan, our trainer, had prepared the horse meticulously and was quietly optimistic. Lesley and I watched the race on TV and saw David Junior come out of the stalls and quickly settle down on the inside rail in sixth place with Tin Man in the lead. With 600 metres to go, David Junior had moved up to fifth with Tin Man still in the lead looking very comfortable. At this time I'm thinking that third place was achievable but with 400 metres to go David Junior had moved up into fourth place and looked the strongest of the contenders. With 300 metres to go, David Junior, three lengths behind Tin Man, had moved off the rail to the outside and it was clear that Jamie Spencer had given the horse his head and by the time he had reached the 200-metres marker, he was in the lead. He had passed Linngari, Seihali and Tin Man.

I was out of my seat. 'Come on my son', I shouted. The excitement was amazing, the adrenalin rush was like nothing I had ever experienced. God, how I'd wished I was there. David Junior crossed the line a clear winner by three and a half lengths.

My life is a roller-coaster. The highs are incredible, the thrill of winning and success is what drives me but you must have the strength and fortitude to cope with the downs, as they are inevitable … The following day, Lesley and I flew to Manchester in our private jet to watch Birmingham City lose 3-0 at old Trafford.

CHAPTER TWENTY-ONE

CLARET AND BLUES

It is no slight on Birmingham City to say that I would have jumped at the chance of owning West Ham United. It was only my failure at Upton Park that led me down a convoluted road to St Andrews.

The 'Ammers were my club, and had been from the moment I took an interest in why all that noise emanated on a Saturday afternoon from Upton Park down the road from the house I lived in. I was captivated, first as a spectator and then as a young hopeful with aspirations of playing for them. Ralph and I and David Sullivan showed just how serious we were in 1991 when we purchased 30 per cent of the club I adored. The purchase came about because somebody came to us knowing of our interest in football and my particular love affair with my local club. Indeed, I still have many contacts at the Hammers. Before I linked up with Birmingham City, I was a season ticket holder in the Premium Lounge where you paid a large amount of money and were given a ticket and a cup of coffee at half-time. I went every other Saturday, had lunch with my mother, and then went to the game. It was a ritual. The old Chicken Run – the wooden terraces opposite the main stand where from about the age of seven I used to bunk in at half-time when they opened the gates for the early leavers (who would leave a football match at half-time?) and edge my way to the front – had gone, but it hadn't yet been replaced by any special facilities. Not like they have now, with corporate boxes, hospitality lounges and the rest.

We paid the going price for the shares, willing buyers from willing sellers. But far from opening the boardroom door and having the welcome carpet rolled out, there was nothing. We had no contact with the board; they wouldn't consider inviting us to the boardroom. It was sad because we wanted to contribute to the club, join the board and be financial supporters. It wasn't to be. They simply did not want David Sullivan and the Golds at their football club, at least not within the inner sanctum. I can only guess they thought they were protecting the club from the perceived changes we might want to make. But what did they think we wanted to do? Dancing girls at half-time and bare-breasted models in the programme? I can only believe they felt threatened. If so, it was as a result of a misconception of what we wanted to do for West Ham. We tried a number of ways to break down the barriers, but the best they could come up with was half a dozen tickets for the boardroom on match days. There were no directorships on offer. These days, of course, any football club would want 30 per cent shareholders on the board, especially if they were offering the sort of financial support we had in mind. We tried clandestinely to build up our shareholding and again we found doors closed in our faces.

There was no specific individual we could challenge because there was no figurehead, as there is now in chairman Terry Brown. In fact it was Terry we sold our shares to when we finally gave up all hope of making a breakthrough. It was all extremely disheartening, and I hope that since then we have proved that our interest in football is right and proper. I have to say Terry was very businesslike and charming during the negotiations to buy our shares in West Ham. After protracted talks, we eventually sold to him at a profit.

It was a crossroads for us. One path could so easily have taken us to West Ham, but with that path blocked we went elsewhere. With the profit from our shares burning a hole in our pockets, there was still a collective desire to break into football, and David Sullivan was the driving force. He was not as devastated as I was at losing the chance to get into West Ham because I was a committed supporter; at the time it was Hammers or nothing for me. I had no yearning to own any other club. I was a fan, I'd lived in the area; all my hopes and dreams had been to play for them and then to own them and steer them to glory. Had it been just me I would probably have kept my shares, got on with my life and waited for an opportunity to come along. I was seriously disappointed, but there was no real bitterness. I felt I was so near, and to fail made it even more difficult to bear, especially after going so close to signing for the club as a young player. Twice, now, I had been denied.

But we almost succeeded, without the help of the board. We were negotiating with an elderly lady in Scotland for her West Ham shares. Had we done the deal, we would have gained control of the club. I don't know the truth of why suddenly and without warning she shut the door in our faces. I can only surmise it was something that came from within the club. The old board at Upton Park were very conservative, and perhaps that was the reason they did not want us to be involved, because of what they saw as our 'unusual' business. I still find it quite strange that we weren't welcomed with open arms when you consider we were Hammers fans, local people, with a third of the shares and money to invest. There simply had to be a hidden agenda.

Now, whenever there is talk of a takeover at West Ham United, my name seems to be mentioned. How times have changed! Not so many years ago, as an owner of 30 per cent of the club, the boardroom was effectively out of bounds which meant I used the guest room, or maybe one of the tea bars in the old stadium; these days I am welcomed by Terry Brown and his wife Jean, and indeed everyone else at Upton Park, and every time a new consortium emerges I am always called and asked if I am 'coming home'. People ask me this even though they know I am now completely committed to Birmingham City. In the thirteen years I have been involved at St Andrews, I have had numerous calls about this consortium or that consortium, three of them significant approaches asking me to join a West Ham takeover. For reasons of confidentiality I will not go into names and numbers, but the last approach came after West Ham drew 2–2 at home to Ipswich, having led 2–0, in the first leg of the 2005 play-offs. They thought they had missed their chance of returning to the Premier League, but the Hammers did make it back after getting past Ipswich at Portman Road and beating Preston 1–0 in the play-off final, at which point the calls stopped. The approach came from serious people with serious money. What do these consortiums believe I have to offer? I suppose that as well as money I have a West Ham background, plus the experience of being an owner and chairman of a Premiership football club. But despite yearning for West Ham in the first place, I would never have the urge to return while I am at Birmingham City. It is very flattering to be asked, but I have to do what is right. I have a job to do at St Andrews, and I am fully committed to Birmingham City Football Club.

CHAPTER TWENTY-TWO

A FIRST TASTE OF THE BLUES

My mother was never keen on losing sight of her three children, and as a consequence evacuation of us during the war was not top of her wish list. We went away now and again, but she would soon be racing up north to bring us back to the East End. The family we stayed with when we were evacuated would occasionally invite us back for holidays after the war, and in February 1947 Ralph and I went back for a week and had our first taste of something that became a major focus in our adult life – a football team called the Blues!

The family we stayed with were lifelong Birmingham fans, and Ralph and I were taken to watch the Blues play Manchester City in the fifth round of the FA Cup. Birmingham won handsomely, their big centre-forward Cyril Trigg scoring twice. I enjoyed watching the goals go in, and in my mind I've always thought it was 10–0 to the Blues. But that was a young boy's memory. When I looked it up it was only 5–0!

We went to the match with two adults: Mr Bill Tart, the man who had looked after us when we went to stay for the first time, and his brother. The train journey from Doncaster to Birmingham was a great adventure. It was considered a big treat as Mr Tart had managed to buy four tickets for the game watched by a huge crowd. I remember it so clearly because everyone was in the same uniform: grey suits, grey scarves and flat grey caps. Look at photographs of the time and the terraces were a mass of grey, everyone wearing those flat caps. All men; not a woman in sight. My brother was on the shoulders of Mr Tart while I, as the eldest, struggled to see from my standing position. I remember Ralph looking down at me and saying with wide eyes, 'There are a million people 'ere! I'm tellin' you, a million.'

'How do you know, Ralph?' I chided.

He responded cockily, 'Cause I've counted 'em!'

He was the undisputed king of the castle that afternoon, boss of all he surveyed from his perch above everyone, and he was going to take full advantage of his bigger brother.

In 1999 we relived those memories of our short stay up north when Ralph and I met up with Arthur, one of Mr and Mrs Tart's six children, for the first time in more than 50 years. The reunion was organised by Arthur's niece Anne, who took the task upon herself after hearing my daughter Jacky on the radio talking about Ann Summers. We invited Arthur and Anne to St Andrews for lunch in the luxury of the directors' dining room and spent hours talking about the old days.

From that day in February 1947 onwards I couldn't wait to get hold of the Saturday evening football newspapers – and there were a choice of three in London in those days; they also sold a single sheet with just the results and league tables for a halfpenny – to see how West Ham United, my local club, and Birmingham City had fared. I knew every team, English and Scottish. I could recite the league tables verbatim from top to bottom. As a kid, of course, my team was West Ham, the first side I had ever watched, from the Chicken Run, where I used to sneak in. I can still recall my heroes, players like Kenneth Tucker the outside-left, Eric Parsons the outside-right, and, later on, Ernie Gregory in goal. They were amazing times, but after going to that Blues match I developed a very strong affinity for Birmingham City as well. They were always the second result I wanted to know.

After the disappointment at West Ham, David Sullivan would have liked to own his hometown club, Cardiff City. Most of us dream, once our playing days are over, of joining the board of the team we supported, usually with little hope of achieving the ambition. But David just wanted a club, any club, but a club with potential. When Birmingham City became available they were the best of a number of clubs he had looked at, including Leeds United, Spurs and others. Leeds were discounted because of the distance, and Spurs because of their huge debt. Birmingham were in financial difficulties themselves, but he moved very quickly to purchase them. After he acquired the club, he realised he needed some help and called us to renew our partnership from the West Ham deal on a 50–50 basis.

There were two reasons why we found it irresistible. The first was that Ralph and I enjoyed working with David Sullivan. We already had a partnership with the newspapers and publishing businesses, and of all the clubs outside West Ham we had the strongest affinity with Birmingham City. I had always followed their results since that day in February 1947, even the week before we knew we were going to be co-owners. It was an easy decision in the end because I wanted to be involved in football, to have a say and have some sort of impact. When you think it was some thirteen years ago, you would be entitled to ask, 'What sort of impact?' My aim then was certainly not to be chairman, but definitely to share all the joy and heartache that goes with being a fan, but this time as a director, with a voice. I had no pretensions to be in the position I hold now because I did not know enough about the workings of a football club, which is like no other business.

St Andrews was in a dilapidated state when we arrived. It was, to be honest, a shock. I had a picture in my mind of what I was expecting, but it was in such a state of disrepair it was hard to comprehend. In those early days I had to ask myself whether I had spent my money wisely. The first game we attended as co-owners was on Tuesday evening, 16 March 1993, against Sunderland. Only two-thirds of the bulbs on the floodlights were working and the Football League had threatened action if we didn't do something to improve them. It was raining. It was a dour game. It was dark. It was dull. There were people standing in the rain looking extremely uncomfortable and unhappy. The only plus was we won 1–0, which meant we felt better leaving than we had done arriving.

To be frank, this First Division club was penniless and near to extinction. There were corrugated fences around the ground and it looked as though it hadn't seen a lick of paint since the Blues reached the FA Cup final way back in 1956. It was a club in decay. The average gates were falling. The crowds were miserable, in all senses. One league game early in that 1992/93 season against Grimsby, months before we became involved, had fewer than 7,000 fans present. Another game around the same time, a Coca-Cola Cup match against Exeter, who played in the division beneath Birmingham, attracted a pitiful crowd of 5,715, and what is worse Birmingham were humbled 4–1 on the night. In the fourteen league games in the season at St Andrews in the pre-buyout period, the average crowd size was down to 10,000 per match, which was a fall of some 2,000 from the previous year. If that was the direction in which crowd numbers were going, it was going to be tough to keep the club in existence. Things had not improved hugely by the time of the buy-out in March 1993, but in the nine games between the buy-out and the end of the season, the average crowd jumped to almost 15,500 per game, enough to boost the season's average to 12,328.

I recall quite clearly the moment when my commitment to the club was cemented. It was 4.50 p.m. on Saturday, 8 May 1993, give or a take a few seconds. Sorry I can't be more precise, but it was an extraordinary day. The flood of emotion that surged through me still remains vivid, as I'm sure it does for every Blues fan who was there to see it. The occasion was the final match of the 1992/93 season. We were at home, playing Charlton, and the league table before kick-off made for grim reading. The only cut-and-dried issue at the bottom end of the table was that Bristol Rovers were already relegated. We started the day in 23rd place, second from bottom and heading for the drop on 48 points. Cambridge United were in 22nd place, the third relegation spot, with 49 points – the same as the three clubs immediately above them. Another two clubs, Sunderland and Luton, with 50 and 51 points, were also still theoretically in danger. Seven clubs in peril, trying to avoid two relegation slots, one of which we occupied, and unfortunately for us we had scored fewer goals and conceded more than any of the clubs we needed to leapfrog to achieve safety. A draw and a battling last-day point was never going to be enough to keep us up. We had to win.

On that fateful afternoon against Charlton, the score was 0–0 as the game entered the final minutes. It seemed it was not going to be our day. We were down. That was the depressing, unavoidable conclusion. I don't know why, but even as that thought ran through my head, it just did not feel it should be that way. Then Paul Moulden, a 25-year-old striker we'd signed from Oldham only a couple of months before, let fly with a last-gasp shot propelled by magic. At least that's how it felt as the ball hit the back of the net. From 0–0 and down and out to 1–0 and safety. Cambridge went down with Bristol Rovers, and Brentford fell through the trapdoor at the last moment. One survived – Birmingham City. In an instant I felt like we were soaring upwards and onwards. I'm sure the vast majority of the 22,234 fans present felt the same. The crowd, which was appropriately our biggest of the entire season for its greatest moment, went wild. There was something completely magical about it all. The previous few months suddenly made sense. It felt right.

To put this in context, I have to admit that just a few months before that final match, before I knew I would become involved with Birmingham, I still considered myself a Hammer, emotionally, first and foremost. Indeed, a few weeks before I joined Birmingham I was watching a match at Upton Park and thinking to myself I couldn't change allegiance. Even when Ralph and I decided to join David Sullivan at St Andrews, I admit I planned to have some fun, spend some money restructuring the club, and then maybe sell it on for a profit. It was not about passion, not then. The fact that I had been to Birmingham as a boy and watched them win 5–0 in an amazing FA Cup match with my brother wasn't enough. It was just something we wanted to do, own a football club, and here was an opportunity for us to go and have a look and enjoy the challenge of taking a club on its knees to better days. But something special happened in those months of March, April and May, something that soared from possibility into certainty.

My first match at Birmingham as an investor was on 16 March 1993 against Sunderland, a 1–0 win I still find unmemorable. A few weeks later we beat Barnsley 3–0, but I would still have called myself a Hammer, emotionally, that day. Then on 3 April we actually played West Ham, and lost 2–1 through two extraordinary goals from Kenny Brown and Ian Bishop. In some ways maybe that defeat was the turning point. I was sad that Birmingham had lost rather than joyful that West Ham were on course to join the Premiership. I was pleased for them, of course, but sad for us. In the games between that West Ham tie and the Charlton match on 8 May we experienced something of a roller-coaster ride. We drew with Derby, won at Sunderland, then lost 6–4 at home to Swindon in an incredible game having been 4–1 up after an hour! I say 'we', and perhaps I was already starting to think in that way about Birmingham around then. But it wasn't until the Charlton game that it all became crystal clear in my own mind.

They say you cannot change your allegiance, it doesn't happen. I am living proof that it does. You can have a lifelong love affair with a woman or a football club and then suddenly you are somewhere else. My love and passion for the success of the Blues and all the people involved is incontrovertible. You are part of them, and they are part of you. It comes from sharing highs and lows. The Charlton match was the spark for me. You share it with your family, your loved ones, your pals, those who have worked tirelessly to achieve it, and those who have a passion equal to yours, the fans. It is why I have such an affinity with them, because we have travelled along the tough and dark road together from the beginning. I felt this great warmth and joy when the club stayed in the First Division. It was the start, and from that day it grew, and I became convinced we could do it. I was instilled with a passion and a commitment to achieve success.

The supporters, too, were getting excited at the prospect of something positive happening after years of decay and disappointment. It was all about the glamorous director Karren Brady and her boss David Sullivan. There was great hype, and they were publicly enthusiastic because they were trying to revive this sleeping giant. A lot of people thought the beautiful Karren was part of a gimmick, but as we have all discovered, Karren was and is no gimmick. She is a top-quality professional businesswoman, and it was the shrewd David Sullivan who chose her. He could see she had the quality and would give the club a profile. He had no fears about her facing and coping with the media or the fans, who needed encouraging back to St Andrews.

If gates had continued declining at the rate they seemed to be going before we bought the club, we were going to fail. But they didn't. First they stabilised, then they began to grow. In our first full season, 1993/94, average gates climbed to 14,506 – and in what turned out to be a relegation season! The next year, even in the Second Division, they were up again, to almost 17,000, as we won immediate promotion. By 1995/96 our average home crowd was 18,090. This was the hard evidence that we were doing something right. A decade after we arrived at Birmingham, crowds in the 2002/03 season averaged 28,813.

The support had been there all the time, waiting in anticipation, and slowly but significantly coming back to the football club. David and Karren were the driving force, handling the publicity and all it entails. The Golds were the figures in the background, as we have always been, working quietly away from the glare of the spotlight.

I knew we would need to put in more and more money, and I was suddenly doing it as an ambition. I had a desire to succeed for success's sake, not for profit. Selling was no longer in the psyche or in the equation. Success for Birmingham meant our commitment to rebuild, literally in those early years. The bulldozers moved in. The old stand was pulled down. The roof came off. When that happened it was as though Ralph and I were burning our bridges. There was no going back, no way out of Birmingham City for us.

All this is what Birmingham means to me, but actually, in the grand scheme of things, my own relationship with the club is far from the most important thing for the club itself. When people talk about the owner of a football club they are actually talking only about a guardian, a keeper of the keys for a period of time. The real owners of every club in the country are the fans, not because of the shares they own but because of their hearts and souls, the joy they feel and the tears they, their families and ancestors have shed, in many cases for a century and more. When this board goes and the next arrives, they will still be there, and if not them, then their sons and daughters, grandchildren, great-grandchildren and so on. It is their heritage. The club belongs to the Browns at 27 Linton Close rather than the Golds living in Surrey. But what was very evident to me when we arrived at St Andrews was that the soul of the football club had disappeared. It had been ripped out, torn away by our predecessors and by years of failure and neglect. Slowly we saw the heart of the football club begin to beat strongly again. I feel proud that we all played a part in helping Birmingham City's fans to hold their heads high once again, but Barry Fry was also a major contributor.

Back in 1993, I remember the face of the then manager of Birmingham City, Terry Cooper, the former Leeds United and England full-back. He had expectations of new owners who were prepared to put money into the club. He eventually resigned at the end of the year after keeping us up in Division One in our first season. There was a lot of pressure on him and his wife Rose, and he resigned in pain. There were times when it would have been easy for us to leave the club too, but when Barry Fry joined us as manager I knew there was no going back.

We were fans, and we knew about football as fans do, but we knew nothing about managers. David Sullivan is a statistician, and he decided the manager we wanted was one who could take an ailing club without large sums of money and push it forward. Barry fitted the bill perfectly because he had done just that at Southend. Everyone in football agreed he had done a remarkable job. He'd had little more than a single great player in Stan Collymore, a naughty boy from whom Barry coaxed the best football of his career before selling him for a handsome profit. Barry had Southend over-performing in the First Division. We liked the charisma he offered and felt we were taking on a manager who could take us forward and attract the fans back to St Andrews. Karren Brady had already shown that you could gain sponsorship if you were charismatic and successful, and bring the fans back through the turnstiles. Barry we knew would excite the fans, punching the air and running up the touchline with his drive and passion.

It was pure showbiz, and since then the game has lurched even further in that direction. The manager has to be good with the media because it is the media that drives the business. Fans and sponsorship are important parts of football, but the media should not be underestimated. We all knew changes were coming when the Premier League began in the 1992/93 season; the game had to become more charismatic, more showbiz and more fan-friendly. That was what was going to drive the moneymen and the sponsors: they would want to be linked with iconic people who turned clubs into more exciting, dynamic entities. So it was the right decision to appoint Barry Fry, though I had my doubts to start with. We thought he must be on drugs he was so hyper! He had so much energy and enthusiasm. He was like a rubber ball. I remember him saying to me, 'David, I will get you out of this poxy division.' And of course he was as good as his word, only I thought at the time that he meant into the Premier League rather than down to Division Two.

But we were in dire trouble when Barry arrived at St Andrews in December 1993. We were struggling near the foot of the table. For a while we carried on struggling, but towards the end of the season we began to win matches. We went to play Portsmouth at Fratton Park and beat them with a disputed goal, effectively ending their chances of reaching the play-offs. They were very upset with us. When we went to Tranmere on the last day of the season, we needed to win and for West Bromwich Albion not to win at Portsmouth for us to stay up. It looked impossible for the Baggies to win, but Portsmouth put out a near reserve side. We were winning 2–1 at Tranmere and I was sitting watching the game with my earpiece in, listening to the other results. We were beginning to celebrate our safety when they announced Albion's late goal – and we were down! Portsmouth had their revenge.

At one stage during that 1993/94 season, between early November and late March, we went through 23 league matches with only two victories. But by the end of that dreadful run Barry was beginning to have an effect, and in the desperate run-in at the end of the season we lost only once, at Oxford United, in our last ten games, taking 21 points but moving up only two places. In a bizarre way it was almost as if it was destined. We had to be relegated, we had to cleanse our soul, we had to set fire to the pyre and see the phoenix rise from the ashes …

In the beginning, I felt that with the money, our expertise in business and our determination we couldn't fail. It was a kind of arrogance, so when we were relegated it brought us down to earth. I was mortified. The despair I felt driving back from Tranmere all the way to Surrey was horrendous, especially as the night before we were relegated I had trouble with the bonuses. The players were just as mercenary then as they are now, and they were in dispute with Barry over what they should receive if they stayed up. But when I look back it proved to be a crucial time, not only to the football club but to us, the owners, who had to come to terms with the fact that this was never going to be easy. We had been successful in business, but this was a new, big learning curve. We could not apply the same principles to football as we had in our other companies. Relegation made that clear to us, and despite our ill fortune we were happy with Barry Fry. There was never any question of him being sacked in the summer of 1994.

As the new stand rose from the rubble, so the phoenix began to emerge. In 1994/95 we began to win matches. Crowds began to stream back through the turnstiles as we beat teams like Bristol Rovers, Cambridge and York. Life in the Second Division was not as bad as we had anticipated. However, at the first home game of the new season in the third tier of the English game, I was standing on the pitch looking at the new stand with Ralph by my side when a photographer came up to us. Why? To ask us to move out of the way so he could take a picture of the stand! We apologised and humbly moved out of his way. It was not the only time such things happened. Once we went to meet Mum in the old Trevor Francis suite. I told the doorman I was looking for Mrs Gold. He asked me if I had a pass. When I answered no, he said there was no way he could let me in. Fortunately, Jack Wiseman, the long-serving and popular chairman whose father had also been chairman, arrived in the nick of time, before it became embarrassing. He told the doorman it was Mr David and Mr Ralph Gold. It still meant nothing to the man, until it was explained that we were directors and the new owners. Later on in the same season we were doing well, sitting comfortably in the top two and almost certainly guaranteed promotion back to Division One. We were driving back south listening to Tom Ross, the local broadcaster, who answered a telephone caller who said he wanted to thank David Sullivan and 'those other two geezers' for what they had done for the club. We had been there almost two years by that time and we were still just 'those other two geezers'. We were in the background, financing, supporting and helping to transform the club. We were quietly getting on with our jobs, because this is the way we have always been.

It was an incredible season. Karren Brady confounded her doubters as she proved there was immense substance behind her obvious style. She handled the media superbly and earned the respect of people in the game. She raised the profile of the club, which in turn helped the corporate and financial side. Barry Fry was fantastic too, a hugely charismatic man who was pivotal in the resurgence of the Blues. Birmingham City were on the way back. I will never forget what Barry did for our football club. He might have started in Division One and finished in Division One, but in the interim he took us to the semi-finals of the League Cup and won the Auto Windscreens Shield at Wembley. We needed that. We needed to go and do something, and what Barry did was win the double, albeit the Second Division championship and the Auto Windscreens Shield. It was still hugely important for our supporters, for one simple reason: we were winning, not losing. The mentality of the club started to change.

Ralph and I went to see Barry in the dressing room before the game at Wembley. It was quicker to walk along the track from the dressing room to the royal box rather than go through the innards of the stadium. Imagine, the Gold brothers sitting in the plush red velvet chairs and using the royal toilet! As a schoolboy I was so close to making the England schoolboys team and playing at the famous stadium, only to miss out to a left-winger called Gerry Ward who went on to play for Arsenal. They tried to play me on the right but I wasn't good enough crossing the ball with my right; I was better at cutting in on my strong left foot. Barry had been to Wembley as a schoolboy and scored. But now here I was going back to watch my team. I had been there in 1975 and 1980 to see West Ham beat Fulham 2–0 and Arsenal 1–0 (with a Trevor Brooking header) to win two fantastic FA Cups, but to go to Wembley as a director was unbelievable.

We were playing Carlisle in the final, but it could have been Juventus. A couple of weeks before Wembley the hype was unbelievable. It was as though we were playing Manchester United in the FA Cup final. It was great not just for the fans but for ourselves as well. We filled the stadium, not only through our own ticket allocation but with all those tickets our opponents had returned. We could have sold another 20,000 if they had been available. Birmingham City fans filled Wembley that day. This is what Barry Fry had done, and if I had been him I would have claimed I had deliberately taken us down so that we could bounce back in glory. This was fairytale stuff, and I'm convinced it couldn't have happened without us being relegated to the Second Division. I remember cursing my luck when we were relegated, just as I had done when the landlord turfed me out of my small shop in John Adam Street all those years ago. Bad luck can sometimes turn out to be completely the opposite, even though at the time all seems lost.

Ralph and I were at St Andrews before the final and we were asked if we would do an interview. We had not done one before and had to debate whether or not to go ahead. We had to ask if we were going to make fools of ourselves, as we had done twenty years earlier when the BBC interviewed us: the *Daily Telegraph* had torn us apart for the gauche way in which we handled that interview. We talked over whether we should risk it. It was for a video to be shown on all the coaches and buses heading south to Wembley with our fans, with Barry Fry, David Sullivan and Karren Brady all starring. My feeling was we shouldn't do it, and Ralph agreed we should not take the risk. But when we arrived at St Andrews the cameras had already been set up and the technicians and interviewer were waiting for us. We didn't want to disappoint anyone, so we agreed to go ahead.

We were nervous. It was just like the day when I had to stand up in front of the school and read out my match report. I wasn't happy, but it turned out to be a success. It was a friendly interview, edited to enhance us. It was shown in the hospitality suites, on the trains, on the buses, in fact everywhere where our supporters were gathering for the big day. We realised its effect when we made that walk along the pitch track from the dressing rooms to the steps leading up to the royal box. We'd been into the dressing room to wish the lads good luck. Barry had persuaded us not to go along the corridors because we would miss the start of the match; instead, he sent his kit man, Gordon, to escort us back to our seats. We walked around the dog track and saw a sea of blue and white in this fantastic stadium, and suddenly there was a ripple of applause. It grew and grew until by the time we reached the first bend we were being clapped and cheered by all the Birmingham fans. Clearly the filmed interview had reached many of our supporters and they now recognised us and what we had done for the club. They were showing their appreciation. They even chanted our names. I still go cold just remembering it. The chants and applause came from nowhere. It was like turning on a switch, and suddenly we were no longer 'those other two geezers' but the Gold brothers. It was a hugely emotional moment, not only for us but also for our mother and all our friends who had come along to support the team.

We won that day, and on the final day of the season we travelled to Huddersfield where we won the championship in front of 4,000 of our travelling fans. They stayed on after the whistle chanting for Barry and the players. Barry persuaded Ralph and me to walk over to the fans, who were fantastic with their appreciation towards us. It was another emotional moment, and it further cemented our relationship with them.

I was not the chairman at the time, but Ralph and I had taken a significant step forward in our bond with the fans. I remember only too well the huge suspicion surrounding David Sullivan, the Golds and Karren Brady when we all arrived. At best, Ralph and I were seen as two ordinary businessmen, at worst as two cockney geezers viewed warily by the locals who wanted to know whether or not we were coming to rape and pillage their club. But in that early summer of 1995 we were finally recognised and accepted, more than two years after arriving and into our third season.

Some years later, on a wet and nasty night at Grimsby, I went into the crowd to meet some of our fans. I have always believed you can only take the fans with you if you are a fan yourself. It is easy when you are winning; when you really need them is when the going gets tough. No roller-coaster goes up and up. There are going to be bad seasons, even after being established in the Premiership like Charlton under Alan Curbishley. We have actually now caught up with Charlton because of our commitment and our investment, but we will not delude ourselves. We need to understand that bad seasons will happen, and when they do you need to carry your fans. They must see that you are honest and share everything with them, either with forums or through the media. When I talk to a reporter or face a camera I see our fans sitting on his shoulder, and that is who I try to talk to. Fans must respect you for what you are trying to do for their club. Someone like Terry Brown, who was devastated when Hammers were relegated, was not just a businessman, he was also a fan. It is sad that his fans could not see or understand his despair, as I did. He was one of them. He knew not only what it meant financially, but also to the supporters.

I have always related to the staff who have worked for me because as a bricklayer I was part of the staff, one of the men who rolled up his sleeves. My maxim in business is 'succeed or fail together'. The same applies to football and Birmingham City, because we know we cannot make it a success without the fans, and the fans alone cannot make the club successful. We need to do it together. The reason for our sudden burst of success was a unique moment in the club's history. The manager, the players, the fans and the board all became one, galvanised by a feeling of togetherness. It is rare, but it happens, as it did when Northampton went through the divisions, and more recently when Bradford City and Barnsley did so, however temporarily. Wigan are the latest team to surprise their fans, themselves and the rest of the football world with their performances in the Premier League in their first season, 2005/06. At one stage they reached the giddy position of second, just behind Chelsea and ahead of both Manchester United and Arsenal, and then went on to reach the final of the Carling Cup at the expense of the Gunners. It is the Wigans of this world who give everyone in the game in this country hope for the future, as Nottingham Forest did under Brian Clough in the past.

CHAPTER TWENTY-THREE

BUILDING AN AIRLINE

Our airline came about due to adversity. Having bought Birmingham City Football Club, we needed to get to games wherever they were played and be back home the same day. Driving up and down busy motorways, often with an overnight stay, was exhausting. We were far too busy, and suffered several poor experiences.

As a result we decided to hire a plane to fly us to a game at Newcastle, which cut out a particularly long drive. When we arrived at our local private airport at Biggin Hill, the captain of the plane, who looked all of fourteen years old, greeted us and asked us to sit down in a shed while the plane was being refuelled. We then got airborne in this ancient twin-engine Aztec, with Ralph and I sitting in the back – a position I instantly regretted. We were terrified, despite being experienced pilots. We bounced around and didn't see the ground from take-off to landing. There was only the one pilot and he chain-smoked the whole trip, much to Ralph's consternation. The experience was so horrendous that we seriously gave thought to coming back on the train the next day. We didn't, and the return flight was a little better, but as soon as we arrived home we both said in unison, 'Never again!'

But we still needed to fly, not only for football but for business as well, and a businessman does not want to battle the traffic to Heathrow, check in three hours before a flight, waste time in lounges and then find someone sitting next to him fiddling with his shoe, wondering what he has in the heel. So the very next day we ordered a King Air 200, a turbo jet, and hired two professional pilots with thousands of hours of experience. It was an instant success and a great asset to the business as we used it for all our needs, including picking up David Sullivan from Stansted on our way to football matches. In fact it was working so well that we felt we could not compromise, so we bought a hangar fully equipped with maintenance facilities, offices and reception areas. We were looking for safety, quality and service, and that is what we aimed to build for ourselves. The demands on the plane soon increased. David and other business contacts would also charter the aircraft for both business and pleasure. The day before we flew the pilot would ring to ask if there were any special requirements, even down to what newspapers we required. As a result of this demand we purchased another King Air 200, but even that was not sufficient. We required larger and faster aircraft. We now have eight jet aircraft, and it's just a short drive to Biggin Hill airport in Kent – cases from the car straight to the plane, airborne in minutes.

I am currently chairman of twelve businesses. It sounds excessive, but the crucial factor is they are all linked. Everything has, for me, been a natural progression once I departed the building trade and opened my bookshop. The synergy of our businesses has evolved. We bought our own printing works because of the difficulty we were facing getting our own magazines produced, and we were being held to ransom; the distribution was an add-on to the publishing, which came about because we needed more products for our shops; buying the biggest wholesaler added to our distribution services. The printing, publication, distribution and selling of books and magazines in turn led to the *Daily Sport* and the *Sunday Sport* newspapers. Even Ann Summers was an extension to the existing business because we were supplying them with product and they couldn't pay their bills; the owner went out of business, and we bought it. Party Plan came out of that. We had a warehouse full of stock, supplying wholesalers and retailers as well as Ann Summers, so when Party Plan began we simply used existing stock. Ann Summers Mail Order and Ann Summers Internet are only extensions of the original business with the same warehouse, offices, infrastructure, transport system and personnel. Just another add on. This was how our business evolved, adding bricks to the existing wall, not building separate ones. To start a new business without the right infrastructure in place is much more difficult, and if there is one key why we have grown as a group of businesses, it's that philosophy. Perhaps the only business that was not directly linked was Birmingham City Football Club, but that has gradually become entwined, and of course it led to us starting up Gold Air. All the shares of all these companies are held by the holding company, Gold Group International.

We now have six Lear Jets with four on order – one coming every six months – and two Hawker Siddeley 125s, plus the helicopter, the 182, which continues to give me great pleasure. To have Mark Parmenter – my driver and bodyguard, and manager of my house and grounds – pre-flighting it for me and starting it, for me to be able to step out of my back door, be airborne within five minutes, and get from my Surrey home to Birmingham City's training ground in 45 minutes is exciting. The helicopter is perceived as my aircraft, but it is part of Gold Air International. It is used for surveys and transporting pilots, as are the other small aircraft we own, such as the six-seater twin Aztec. It is not, however, all pop stars, footballers and the rich and famous, as we discovered in the middle of February 1998 when we received an emergency call to transport a heart transplant team from Birmingham to RAF Valley on Anglesey, off the Welsh coast. We were filming a corporate promotional video at the time at Gold Air House so we were well placed to get everything moving, and within 30 minutes Captain John Mason and his co-pilot James Aylett were taking off to collect the heart surgeons. Within minutes of their departure we received another call asking if could we provide a second aircraft to fly a liver transplant team to the same hospital. We were able to intercept a flight on its way to Prestwick with one of our staff on board. Captain Colin McClelland and Patrick Rogers were soon involved in the operation that took most of the night but resulted in two seriously ill people undergoing successful transplants. Two lives saved! How rewarding is that?

It has been fun developing from flying planes to helicopters and then to building an airline. I was recently on holiday in Jamaica with my daughters and our partners. On our way to the golf course one day on a minibus two young Americans spotted that I was wearing my Lear Jet cap. One of them apologised for intruding, pointed out my hat and asked me where I got it. Well, should I say 'I bought it in a shop', or should I tell them I had just placed an order for four more jets? In the end I told them I got it free with a Lear Jet. The American thought I was teasing, and laughed. I asked them why they were interested and it transpired they were two pilots who had flown a Lear Jet into Jamaica with their boss. We left it at that, and I changed the subject, which goes all the way back to scoring my first goal for West Ham Boys against Bermondsey Boys and trying not to smile because I didn't want people to think I was a swank and showing off.

It is a joy the way the airline business has developed from such relatively humble beginnings. It is quite amazing how Ken Bates became a customer, along with Peter Kenyon, David Beckham and a lot of other people in football, all using what is now the premier charter aircraft company in the country. Would Ken Bates, a fellow chairman, have hired a plane from me but for my sending him a package from Gold Air? Had he not known me he would probably have binned it without a second glance. Now his lovely wife Suzanne insists on Gold Air International because, as she says, 'It's the best, and the pilots treat me nicely.' I no longer get personally involved in Gold Air, but I now have such quality people running the business that once the deal is struck the people in place apply the Gold formula of 'The customer is king', and we continue our pursuit of excellence.

It is particularly special to me because of my great passion for flying. To own an airline, to have developed it from scratch, to be able to touch it, feel it and fly it, is a tremendous feeling. It was not a toys-for-boys situation, it was born out of a requirement, and at a stage in my life when I could afford it. Again, it is all to do with synergy. I was personally looking for safety, quality and service. It was what I desired, and it became a success because other similarly placed people were looking for the same thing. I wouldn't want people to think this is a David Gold indulgence. Gold Air is a business. It is there to make money, and it is making money. Hopefully it will make a lot more as the name gets around. I have to confess it gives me a great thrill when I board the aircraft and the pilot tells me Mr Bates or whoever was on board earlier and sends his regards. As the business becomes higher profile, you no longer have to go out and knock on doors because customers come to you. Being commissioned with a £1.5 million contract to photograph Great Britain from the air was great, and a good example of this. It is a form of recognition that these people come and seek you out – recognition that you are the best.

CHAPTER TWENTY-FOUR

THE SAD DEPARTURE
OF BARRY FRY

I take full responsibility for the ultimate demise of my dear friend Barry Fry at Birmingham City. I contributed by my inability to help him when he most needed it. I knew what I wanted to do, but I was reluctant to do it because I was aware he was a man steeped in football while I had only just arrived.

I was still not chairman at that time, but we had supported Barry financially, giving him money to spend to strengthen his team. He sometimes spent rashly. There was the £800,000 (a club record fee in 1994/95) for Hackney-born Ricky Otto from his old club Southend United – a boy with an extremely colourful past. But generally he made money in the transfer market. In the five and a half years that followed with Trevor Francis as manager we sold only one player for serious money, and that was Gary Rowett to Leicester for £3 million. By contrast, Barry Fry needed his own turnstile for the regular comings and goings of players, even needing an extra page in the *Rothman's Football Annual*! Otto was something else, almost worth the money for the fun he gave everyone. When we played Huddersfield on the final day of the 1994/95 season, a match we had to win to go up as champions, he was on top of the dugout in just his shorts, sunning himself. He was as mad as a hatter, and I am being restrained in my description. You could have been excused for thinking he was on drugs he was so eccentric, and never more so than on his debut against Leyton Orient when he came on as a substitute and scored – and then equalised for the opposition.

In contrast to Trevor, Barry was like a car dealer. He could buy one, give it a lick of paint, and sell it for twice the money. José Dominguez from Benfica was a stunning purchase for £50,000, and he soon returned to Portugal for £1.6 million. Barry also bought the big centre-back Liam Daish from Cambridge United for the same sort of money and sold him on for a million, and Gary Breen, originally from Peterborough, for £2 million. Steve Claridge was bought for £200,000, and we sold him to Leicester for £1.3 million. Tremendous deals from a remarkable man. He will always be remembered for his huge squad of players, but we should not forget some very astute buying and selling, and most of all his limitless enthusiasm.

But he made errors too. One of the biggest came on Boxing Day in 1995 when Ian Bennett, our first-team goalkeeper, was injured in a 1–1 draw at Sheffield United. Barry brought in a young player, Bart Griemink from Holland, to replace him. This six-foot-four-inch, fifteen-stone 23-year-old was a complete disaster. We were lying third in the First Division at the time, but Griemink was largely responsible for us tumbling eight places in the league. We finished the season in fifteenth place. Had we finished above halfway Barry would probably have kept his job. Had Benno stayed fit – we lost only six of 24 games he played in – I am sure we would have been close to promotion, and certainly Barry would then have kept his job. I still believe that had Trevor Francis not been available we would have kept Barry anyway, but word was out that Trevor, a former Birmingham hero who was seen as something of a Messiah, was ready to return should a vacancy occur. Barry went because of the slide down the table and the fact that Trevor was waiting in the wings making all the right noises.

Barry was a great optimist and motivator, and there is no doubt he will remain in the folklore of Birmingham for a hundred years. I and many others will never forget what he did for the club as he raised the morale and the profile. He was fan-friendly and the players adored him. They would go the extra mile for him. He could even lift the board when we were down. His rows with Karren Brady and David Sullivan were hugely exaggerated, but they continued to raise the profile of the club as we were being talked and written about all the time. Barry would use the press to get his way. One day, in one of his mad moments, he went to the local newspapers and maligned the board for their lack of commitment. Karren was so outraged at the subsequent article that she burst into the changing rooms after a training session determined to have it out with him.

'Where is Barry Fry?' she demanded. 'I want to see him right now!'

'He's in the shower, Karren,' she was told.

'I want him here, now!'

So out came Barry, wrapped in a towel big enough for most, but like a handkerchief around his ample girth.

Karren slammed into him. 'Barry, you have got to stop using the media to make your point to the board. It has *got* to stop.'

Barry lifted his hands above his head and said, 'Honest, Karren, I was misquoted, I swear to you.' Of course, as he stood with arms in the air in supplication, the towel slipped off his wet body. The sight of this roly-poly man, dripping water and dangling his bits in front of the glamorous Karren brought the house down and defused the situation completely.

The saddest day of all came towards the end of the 1995/96 season at a Midlands tournament, the Birmingham Senior Cup, for the professional clubs where the senior teams usually played their reserves until the final when they would attract 5,000 fans with a mix of first- and reserve-team players. The decision to sack Barry had already been made. David Sullivan felt very strongly that Barry had enjoyed his time and we needed to move on. David is very hot on statistics, and he'd become disillusioned as we slipped down the table. He was fearful that if we didn't do something drastic, staying as we were without showing ambition, season ticket sales would drop off. Emotion plays its part, but to be board members you cannot be fans and allow hearts to rule heads. Also, the fact that Trevor Francis was available meant there was a chance to bring back the Golden Boy of Birmingham City to St Andrews. It was just too good an opportunity to miss. Oddly, Ralph did not agree. He was all for Barry staying, but David's enthusiasm for a change carried all before him at the time. He felt Barry had not done enough in his last season, and he was worried that if we gave Barry another season we would miss out on the chance of bringing Birmingham's very own Roy of the Rovers back to the club. And there was I in the middle, vacillating over it, able to make a case for both arguments. In the end I came down on the side of David Sullivan, whose judgement I respected. While I respected Ralph's decisions in business, I thought David had the edge over him in football matters. My vote was the key, although I must say we debated and argued for a number of days before reaching a final decision.

The decision was taken on a Wednesday, and on the Saturday Birmingham were to play Aston Villa in the final of the Senior Cup at St Andrews at 7.30 p.m. That night Ralph and I were at the Burlington Hotel for the Midland Football Writers' Dinner, sitting on the top table with Villa chairman Doug Ellis, ITV's Gary Newbon and local broadcaster Tom Ross. It had been arranged for Jack Wiseman, still the Birmingham City chairman, to tell Barry the following week that his contract was being terminated.

Barry, unaware of what was happening, was at the final, which he took just as seriously as every match he was involved with. Afterwards, with a win under his belt and the trophy under his arm, he burst through the doors of the Burlington Suite in typical fashion. We were all in dinner jackets and bow ties while he was in his tracksuit, carrying the cup, which he put down in front of Ralph and me. 'I told you I would win you a trophy this season,' he said. 'We just beat the Villa 2–0.' He shook hands with both of us and left the room, leaving the trophy with us. I felt terrible. I really did. If only he could have lost that one match it would have been so much easier.

We finished dinner and went up to the bar, where we were joined by a now changed and refreshed Barry Fry, who launched into the story of how Birmingham had spanked the Villa. Everyone was delighted for Barry while Ralph and I sat for two hours with him knowing he was sacked. Here he was sharing all his enthusiasm and all his excitement with us, talking about how this was going to be a launch pad for the new season to come. I tried to match his enthusiasm, but I felt dreadful. I couldn't spoil his evening and tell him. At the end of the night we made our farewells and shook hands outside the hotel. He had no idea he was out of a job. I felt like a Judas. He was fired on the Monday. His parting words were bitingly accurate. He pointed out that neither David Sullivan, the Gold Brothers nor even his nemesis Karren Brady had had the balls to tell him he was sacked. He was right, of course. It was left to poor old Jack Wiseman to do the dirty work.

The remarkable thing is, we have stayed firm friends, I suppose as a result of him being such a charming human being, the only person you would forgive for his bad language, which was never malicious. I remember the first game for which Barry was in charge, a match at Crystal Palace which we lost 2–1. Barry burst into the boardroom and shouted at their chairman, Ron Noades, 'You lucky bastard!' I almost spilled my wine I was so shocked. Thankfully everybody burst out laughing, but there were a number who laughed nervously, including Noades, who wasn't sure about this bubbling little man who had bounded into the inner sanctum. I remember another occasion when we had been beaten 3–1 at Barry's old club, Southend. After the match, Barry burst into the Southend boardroom and said again in a very loud voice, 'You lucky bastards!' The room was full of ladies. Everybody broke into laughter, though I had mixed feelings. But what do you do? More often than not he knew the people he was ribbing, and they knew him. It happened again a couple of weeks later. We lost again, this time at Notts County, and were standing around congratulating the opposition board members and their ladies when in comes Barry, again bouncing like a rubber ball. 'You lucky bastards!' he said with gusto. 'That was a lucky goal!' And again everybody laughed because it was Barry, and anyway, we had been trounced and there was nothing lucky about it. I felt this had to stop, however, so I called him over and said, 'Barry, bursting into the boardroom like this and using such language is entirely inappropriate.' He looked at me, quite subdued, a look of disappointment on his face, and said, 'Sorry, chairman, you are absolutely right. It is inappropriate, and I'm out of order. I promise I will never ever use the word lucky again.' That's Barry Fry!

He is always the first man on my list when I have a dinner party, along with his delightful wife Kirsten; what is more, he is given the choice of bedrooms. We not only stayed in touch when he went to Peterborough, we also helped him out by loaning him players we wouldn't have loaned to anyone else. It was just because it was Baz. I think he has forgiven us. He will say it was a great experience, and I don't think he will ever forget that wonderful season in the Second Division when we won the championship and the Auto Windscreens Shield at Wembley. In return we had given him the best job he has ever had in football. But it was devastating for his young son Adam, who was a devoted Blue Nose, and his family. We had chosen him without knowing him because of his purple patch with Southend. Even that cost us money as we were fined for an illegal approach, but it was money well spent.

I suppose it is unusual for a chairman and a manager to carry on being friends after a sacking, but Barry is so hard not to be friends with. Everything he does is based on kindness. If he can do you a favour, he will go out of his way to do so. I suppose it was born out of those years he was with us as a manager. I liked him for the way he could lift you when you were down, particularly after a defeat. Usually it's the other way round, the chairman lifting the manager. He was so full of fun and energy, and he would cheer up the entire boardroom with his effervescent style. I used to go away with him the night before an away match, in the days before I flew myself to games, and spend the evening with Baz and the coaching staff. I found it a good way of getting closer to everyone, including the players, especially as I was in the background during most of his tenure, before becoming chairman.

Had I known what I know now, Barry would have been manager of Birmingham City a lot longer (I believe David Sullivan is now on record as saying that in retrospect we should have kept Barry for another year). He needed a chairman who knew the game and had knowledge of the business, not the David Gold of his time but the David Gold of today, with my greater confidence and experience. I believe I would have stopped him from making some of the mistakes he made. My lack of experience stopped me intervening, whereas now I would tell any manager if I thought he was wrong. Instead I thought he knew best when, quite frankly, I could see things he couldn't see. When he was the manager at Birmingham I would chat to him regularly, and at one stage I told him he should change his coaching staff, David Howell and Ed Stein, after we discovered them in the bar of a hotel with Vinny Samways, Barry's number one player who we were paying £6,000 per week, playing cards at two a.m. on the day of a game. I told him it was unacceptable. He eventually fired them. I had an impact in the decision, but what I didn't do was interfere in the replacements. That was up to him. I would have liked him to bring in experienced people like Jim Smith, Don Howe or Dave Sexton. Instead, Barry made a quick decision and we were no better off, jumping from the frying pan into the fire. Barry has the charisma and all of the qualities that drive people forward and enthuse the players and fans, but he needs someone with sophistication and planning and organisational skills alongside, which is what someone like Dave Sexton could have provided. He needed a sound man, someone to provide the sanity behind the insanity of Baz. But then, it was his insanity that made him the thrilling and exciting character he was.

Barry was still one of the best managers in the lower leagues, despite his problems with Peterborough, where he tried to be manager, chairman, owner and groundsman before stepping aside at the start of the 2005/06 season, remaining as the owner. He got himself in such a mess that he was calling us and asking what he should do next. He was spending his own money and discovering how tough it was to be an owner. If you just throw money around willy-nilly, blindly supporting the manager, it can all become a disaster. We did things to help him, like buying players from him and instead of making two payments over a twelve-month period we would make the whole payment up front to help his cash flow. There were other things we did too, not only because he was a nice man but also because of a twinge of guilt. And I know that if I became the owner of a non-league or League Two club, the first person I would employ would be Barry Fry. I'd start from there and aim for the top, and have a lot of fun in between. There is none better at wheeling and dealing at that level. How Barry has kept Peterborough afloat is down to making money in the transfer market every season, with a few miracles thrown in. Without him the club would have gone bust.

As I said, what Barry Fry did for Birmingham City Football Club should never be forgotten. He took us from an average gate of 12,328 to more than 18,000 in his final season in the First Division. He was undoubtedly the catalyst to raising our profile and starting the rebuilding, not only of the team but also of the stadium itself. He is, to use his own words, different class. To this day Barry will receive a standing ovation whenever he walks into St Andrew's. He still does forums with the fans, and even played Father Christmas for the players' children. He also attends as a guest at the Senior Citizens Club run by my mother Rose and Thelma, David Sullivan's mother. He is as much a part of Birmingham City as our theme song 'Keep Right On to the End of the Road', introduced by the Scots winger Alex Govan during the Blues' FA Cup final run way back in 1956. Barry is, without doubt, a folk hero at Birmingham, and is still adored.

CHAPTER TWENTY-FIVE

THE GOLDEN BOY

Trevor Francis was the Birmingham City Golden Boy, the fans' favourite, the fifteen-year-old who made it all the way to the very top. The Blues fans loved him; not even his move across the Midlands to join Brian Clough at Nottingham Forest had dented his popularity. In short, he was a god in royal blue, and his return to St Andrews as a manager was inevitable.

While Barry Fry was still in charge, Trevor had made it known through various sources that he wanted to come back to the club, and when we did eventually give him the bugle call he returned, still as the Golden Boy, though he brought with him an enormous burden of expectation. David Sullivan was proved right in his choice commercially because season ticket sales immediately rocketed 15 per cent, as he had projected. Finances play such a big role in the modern game. The more money you can generate through the turnstiles the better, and in theory you should become increasingly competitive, because the money is channelled into players' transfer fees and salaries. Every club at our level has a dozen or so competitors. Manchester United do not come into our category, and neither do Chelsea, Arsenal, Liverpool or Newcastle United. Our competitors would be the three promoted clubs plus about nine others, leaving out the top six and allowing for some fluctuation, as is the case with Newcastle in 2005/06. The target initially is 30 points by Christmas, and the belief then is that unless you commit suicide you will be safe. For our group of clubs, safety from relegation has to be the first priority, and generating more income than your competitors is crucial, essential if you are to move on to the next level.

As I said, Barry Fry had done a tremendous job in raising the profile of the club, and when Trevor arrived in the summer of 1996 it was truly amazing how much he was welcomed by almost everyone connected with the club. There was still a minor split with the disappointed Fry supporters, but such was Francis's popularity even the most disgruntled fan forgave us. Trevor was a different character to Barry, a fairly dour man who pursued organisation, respect and procedures. He was meticulous in all his preparations, and this was mixed with his enthusiasm on his return to the club where he made his name. He brought in systems, and his regime was completely different as he used his experience of the Italian football scene, where he had played for Sampdoria, and of international football, having won 52 England caps over a period of nine years. He made big changes behind the scenes, bringing in new players and backroom staff. Not all successful, it must be said.

Considering what Trevor spent in his first season, 1996/97, finishing tenth was disappointing. The club had languished in 20th place for far too long, and we needed a ten-game unbeaten run at the end of the season to stave off the threat of relegation and show the fans what might have been. One of the major problems was the signing of Mike Newell, which simply did not work out. Trevor signed him from Blackburn Rovers and stuck with him for a while before he became the focus of a row between Trevor and David Sullivan, which ended with the striker successfully suing David and Birmingham having to pay out £30,000 in compensation. Newell was dispatched on loan to West Ham and then Bradford City. There were, of course, lots of successes – Graham Hyde was an excellent purchase from Sheffield Wednesday, Paul Furlong from Chelsea, and Steve Bruce, the captain of Manchester United – but Newell's personality clash with Francis brought down the morale of the team. It was one unfortunate purchase through lack of chemistry between him and his manager. He simply did not fit in or score the goals we had hoped for. He was a bad buy, a poor decision by Trevor, even though we were excited when he and the others arrived. We paid out a great deal of money for them at the time and thought we were going to win promotion, but little went right for us, even in the cups. We were knocked out by Coventry City in the second round of the Coca-Cola Cup and by little Wrexham in the fifth round of the FA Cup – at St Andrews!

I became chairman in August 1997 and that season we finished seventh when Sheffield United pipped us on goals scored rather than goal difference, which is now the standard. We believed we had turned the corner when we got off to a flyer with four wins and a draw in our opening five league matches, but a dreadful run saw us slip to fourteenth, and by the time we recovered it was too late for promotion. In the cups we were put out by Arsenal (Coca-Cola Cup) and Leeds United (FA Cup), but the prize we were after and desperately needed was promotion. The season after that, 1998/99, Trevor took us to the play-offs; we finished fourth in the table after several times moving into second place and always being in the upper half of the top ten. The play-offs were our minimum requirement considering the money we'd spent, the people involved and the expectations of the club. The owners had done their part: we had rebuilt three quarters of the stadium and invested in the training facilities after the previous owners had sold off the crown jewels, leaving us to beg and borrow until we moved to a new centre at Wast Hills. Trevor was right to say that the training facilities were not good enough before our move, and while he made his stand we provided the funding and found the new facility.

In the first leg of the play-off semi-finals we lost 1–0 against Watford at Vicarage Road through a fifth-minute goal from Michel Ngonge. We thought this was a good result to take back to St Andrews, even though we had lost at home to Watford in the league. A place in the final against Bolton Wanderers beckoned. They had beaten Ipswich on away goals the night before and were heading to the final. Our hopes increased when we scored through Nigerian Dele Adebola in the first minute of the second leg at St Andrews in front of almost 30,000 fans. We bombarded Graham Taylor's team. We hit the post, hit the bar and had shots cleared off the line while they never looked like scoring. There is no doubt Watford goalkeeper Alec Chamberlain was Watford's hero and man of the match. It did not help when we were reduced to ten men in the 54th minute when David Holdsworth was sent off, but even then we were well on top and still looked to be the more likely winners.

It finished 1–1 over the two legs after extra time and we were into penalties. It was nail-biting. Paul Furlong, who had never missed a penalty for us, stepped up first and I would have put my house on him – but, unbelievably, he missed. I could not believe what I was seeing as penalty after penalty from Watford clipped the underside of our crossbar before hitting the back of the net. The score stood at Watford 7 Birmingham 6 when Chris Holland, who had been purchased by Trevor Francis for £600,000 against our better judgement, stepped up and Chamberlain made a simple save. The one miss was enough, and our dream had collapsed. It doesn't come much crueller than that. Imagine the tragedy of losing such a match, especially when we had scored so early. It really hurt to see Watford go storming on to win the play-off final, beating Bolton 2–0, and achieve what we had set our hearts on.

In Trevor's fourth season, 1999/2000, we scraped into the play-offs again and once more we were red-hot favourites to beat Barnsley over two legs. We went a goal behind to Neil Shipperley in the first half of the first leg, but at half-time we still fancied our chances very strongly. We came out for the second half and Trevor went with three at the back. Sitting in our directors' seats, we were mortified he should take such a gamble. And I am not saying this with the benefit of hindsight – I said it at the time. We sat in disbelief because the system had failed before. Trevor wanted to push up and thought they would protect their lead, but they hit us on the break, not once but three times, and while in terms of possession we were all over them, they beat us 4–0 at home. I was devastated. We went to Barnsley for the return but there was no heart in it. At four down we all knew there was no way back, even though we won the second game 2–1. Ipswich comfortably beat Barnsley in the Wembley final.

In 2001 Trevor made it a hat-trick as we took our place in the play-offs once more, again finishing off the pace in fifth place. We were challenging for one of the automatic places right up until the middle of March, but again we lost the plot and did not win in ten matches. The last two games of the season squeezed us into the play-offs. This time we faced Preston North End, a team we had already beaten twice in the regular season. We won the home leg, scoring just once through former Barnsley player Nicky Eaden. It was the only goal of the game when we should have won by more and given ourselves a cushion for the second leg.

At Deepdale for the return they equalised through David Healy to put the game back in the melting pot. Our supporters seemed to sense the worst, and at half-time Karren Brady, the comedian Jasper Carrott – a long-time Blue Nose – and I went over to join them. I don't know to this day what we were doing, but during the break Karren had commented on the fact that the fans weren't behind us and were deathly quiet, which is when we decided to walk to the other side of the ground and orchestrate the cheerleading – although it wasn't quite as memorable as Delia Smith and her wonderful cry to the Norwich City fans of 'Let's be 'avin' yer!'

We felt we had lifted the fans, but for some reason – most unlike them – they were sensing impending doom. We thought our efforts had been rewarded early in the second half when Geoff Horsfield put us into a 2–1 lead, but the supporters' apprehension was borne out when Mark Rankine tied it up with a last-gasp goal in the 90th minute. The League had changed the regulations and away goals no longer counted double in the event of a drawn tie, so once again we were facing extra time and the possibility of a penalty shoot-out. But not before an embarrassing row in front of the television cameras as we had the fiasco of the referee saying the penalties would be taken at the South End, where the Preston fans were, and not at the North End, where there were no fans because of rebuilding work. Trevor was furious as he believed he had an agreement with the referee before the match that in the event of a penalty shoot-out it would take place at the neutral end of the ground. In his anger, he twice took the players off the pitch. Eventually calm was restored, and up stepped Marcelo to take the first penalty. And once again we had a player miss a penalty for the first time not only of the season but of his life. Darren Purse also hit the bar, and we were out, having lost 4–2.

After the match we went back to the dressing room to console the players, though Karren stayed outside talking to the press about the poor refereeing decision. It was all very emotional, with everyone hanging on desperately for any excuse. The dressing room was like a morgue. The injured Jon McCarthy, whom we had bought for £1.5 million, was in tears having broken his leg for the third time. It was like being at a wake with 21 corpses, including Trevor and his assistants Mick Mills and Jim Barron. I never want to experience such a thing again, but it is part of being a chairman to share the downs as well as the ups. I tried to console a few of the players but it was futile, so I left.

We are not a club to sack managers, though we had sacked Barry Fry. We didn't sack Terry Cooper, and when Trevor Francis left it was by mutual agreement. Still, if you count Trevor Francis as a sacking, this is a grand total of only two sacked managers in thirteen years. That, I believe, shows everybody we are loyal, serious people. We are a board that keeps its cool under pressure and makes measured judgements. We pick our managers carefully and give them every opportunity to succeed – true in football, and also in life. I adopt the same principles in business and in my personal life. It is about backing your own judgement and standing by it through thick and thin. Chairmen and directors must accept the fact that managers are their choice and they have to share the blame when it goes wrong. You can have a good manager who fails because of various circumstances like injuries or lack of funds. Timing is an issue, but really you have to make the judgement of whether he is failing because he is incompetent, or because he has lost the plot, or the dressing room. Then you have to change before the situation worsens. The worst case is when a manager loses confidence in himself. Then there is absolutely no going back.

We supported Trevor all the way through. The only player we did not support him on was Ade Akinbiyi, and in the end, in fairness to Trevor, he eventually agreed that we were in a Dutch auction. Akinbiyi's price just went up and up. He was at Wolverhampton at the time, and we started off at £3.5 million. I remember agreeing with the rest of the board that we would go only as far as £4 million and no further. Trevor agreed he would not be held to ransom, and when Leicester went to £5 million Trevor backed down. At £4 million we were supporting the manager, even though at £3.5 million it was still a gamble – one that did not come off for Leicester. Five million pounds was a staggering sum for an unproven player. Akinbiyi had scored goals in the lower divisions, but for £4 million I wanted a red-hot certainty. It is hardly surprising he failed at the time with such a weight of expectation on his shoulders. I think he is one of the players who caused reluctance among Premiership clubs to bring in players from the lower divisions for big money. Twenty-five goals in Division One did not guarantee success in the Premiership, as was proven again by Bobby Zamora. He scored goals for fun with Brighton, then failed at Spurs before he was swapped as part of the deal for West Ham's Jermain Defoe after just half a season. Bobby is now back in the Premiership with West Ham, but the jury is still out. It is a risk to bring in a prolific scorer from the First Division, which is why so many clubs go abroad for proven internationals. Even then there is a catalogue of failed foreign stars, but it remains a greater risk to bring in an unproven player from the lower divisions, especially a striker who can only be measured in terms of goals.

Trevor survived the debacle of the 2001 play-offs, but not for long. No manager could have, after having a stand-up row for ten minutes that clearly had a detrimental effect on our penalty-takers. It was a sad conclusion to a season that had held so much promise, for not only were we challenging for automatic promotion, we also went within a whisker of beating the mighty Liverpool at the Millennium Stadium in the Worthington Cup final.

The odds were hugely stacked against us that late February day, and you probably couldn't have got a bet with any bookmaker when

Liverpool took the lead through Robbie Fowler. We equalised with a penalty by Darren Purse in the 90th minute, but Liverpool were still favourites. We gave them a game though, and with a minute remaining in extra time young Andy Johnson was brought down in the penalty area. It was the most obvious penalty of all time, but referee David Elleray, of all people, waved play on. The entire country watching on television and everyone in the stadium was convinced it was the most blatant penalty they had seen, but to the relief of every Liverpool fan the experienced Harrow schoolteacher just ignored it. We were into penalties once again, and this time we lost 5–4 as Sander Westerveld saved from the unfortunate Andy Johnson.

A few weeks later at a press conference I was asked what I thought of Elleray's decision. I felt it was the worst in history and I wondered how the directors of Liverpool Football Club could sleep in their beds knowing that they had stolen goods on their property. I went on to suggest that under the circumstances they should let us have the cup to display for six months. It was all tongue-in-cheek and no harm was meant, but the next time we played Liverpool – an FA Cup match in January 2002 – I received a frosty welcome in the boardroom from both the chairman, David Moores, and chief executive Rick Parry. I had meant the comment as a joke, but they clearly hadn't seen the funny side. After our promotion to the Premier League we played host to the Liverpool board in our non-smoking directors' dining room, and as a peace offering I gave David Moores permission to smoke – the only person ever to be given such a concession. We are now firm friends.

Once more poor old Trevor was so unlucky. Watford and Barnsley, now Liverpool and Preston. Remember, he had also lost two Wembley finals when he was the manager of Sheffield Wednesday. Was his luck ever going to change? Certainly his time was running out. We had gone so close, but at the beginning of the 2001/02 season we were still in Division One despite investing over £17 million in players.

In August 1997 we went to the market to raise money for the new stand at the Railway End at St Andrews. Jack Wiseman was by now in his eighties and nearing retirement. There is no doubt that he held the club together until we arrived and then nurtured us as novices through those early, difficult years, but it would have been unkind to ask him to carry on as chairman. We were going to the market and we needed a plc chairman, so we decided David Sullivan was perfect for the job while I would become chairman of the football club. David was the perfect appointment as he was the man with the energy and the financial skills to take the responsibility.

I took on my role with apprehension. Was I up to the job? It's not like being chairman of a company where you know the business inside out. Still, Karren ran the day-to-day operation and we were lucky to have a chief executive of her quality. My task was as a figurehead, pulling the strands together, putting an arm round drooping shoulders, motivating people, resolving problems, linking the fans closer to the club and dealing with the media, which was becoming increasingly important. 'No comment' simply meant journalists looked elsewhere for their stories. We had gone through that phase and discovered it to be a disaster. When it was going great it was all wonderful, but when it wasn't going well, the media side started to deteriorate into little slanging matches. Barry Fry would use the media to try and get his way, and David Sullivan would respond; Karren and Barry would fence, and then when Barry left, Karren and Trevor had their disagreements, all of them unfolding in the pages of the local and national press. Clearly there were problems to be dealt with. We all had our roles to play, with David the plc chairman, me as the club chairman, Karren as chief executive and Ralph as club president and director. Though by this time he had lost Annie and was concentrating on stabilising his personal life, he was still involved with the club.

I tried to do my best to mediate with Trevor when relationships deteriorated. I felt like Henry Kissinger, pouring oil on troubled political waters. There was quite a public row between Trevor on one side and Karren and David on the other over several issues. And always hovering over us was the threat of Trevor walking out, either because we weren't good enough for him or we weren't supportive enough. If he couldn't get his own way he would play us one against the other and use the media unashamedly. I believed, at the time, that it would be bad for the club if he left, so I spent my time placating as best I could.

Trevor had walked out for the first time over a problem that arose between a fan and his son Matthew after we had beaten QPR 1–0 in March 1998. I had left at the end of the game to drive back to London to attend a charity function, leaving Ralph and Jack Wiseman in the boardroom. They were amazed when Trevor walked in and told them he was resigning. Ralph did his best to calm Trevor down, but he would not have any of it and left. Trevor claimed the fans involved were abusive throughout the game and had barged their way into his private room where they verbally abused his wife Helen and his son Matthew as well as some of the players. Trevor also claimed that they had Matthew up against a car in the car park wanting to fight him. I got to hear of his resignation when I arrived at my hotel in London. I hadn't a clue why he had left and tried desperately to get hold of him. Karren, David and I tried to ring him on the Saturday night with no luck. My judgement was he was either in a sulk or considering what his plan was to be. Maybe he was even thinking he had overreacted to the situation. I eventually spoke to him on Sunday afternoon in an effort to resolve the problem and find out whether he wanted to go or to stay. I discovered that he had quit, he said, because a fan had an altercation with his son. It did not seem enough to me for him to quit, and sure enough it was as much to do with Karren Brady not consulting him over the sale of a corporate hospitality room as it was with his family being intimidated.

He felt it was inappropriate. He simply couldn't come to terms with the fact that a football club has different elements to it: the fans, the board, the footballing side, but most importantly the corporate and commercial part, which is fundamental to a modern football club. You have to compete with your rivals or you are doomed. He wanted the money to buy new players, and for his new car and the trappings of being the manager of a substantial football club. He felt the money should be there, and it was not his responsibility how it was raised. It was, of course, part of his responsibility. A manager must come to terms with the fact that the commercial and financial side of the football club is critical to his success and well-being. After all, it is fundamental to every businessman in the country in the same way. He has to balance the books, and the more income he generates the more successful he will be. What Trevor forgot when he got upset was that everything Karren did was in an effort to raise money for him to strengthen his squad. Trevor struggled with the concept, and said that if the club was so 'petty-minded' that it was looking to raise £2,000 from a corporate day, he was going to resign. That was the real issue, not his son being abused. The guy involved had been drinking, and when he was interviewed afterwards he admitted they were mucking about and was baffled as to why Trevor was so incensed. Trevor used it as an excuse to air his feelings on the 'petty approach' of the board and the club. His attitude was 'Why don't you just give me the money?' That's my cynical view on it anyway.

It was now a question of pride and what he could get out of the negotiations. He turned his anger from Karren to the corporate manager, Alan Robson, after he realised I would not accept criticism of our chief executive. I was now convinced he regretted his actions and was looking for a way back with his pride intact. The longer it went on the harder it would be to return from the brink. We agreed I would fly up to Birmingham airport on the Monday morning and we would meet at the Arden Hotel, as we had done on a number of occasions before. I tried throughout the day to resolve the problem over the phone, but he was insistent that we should meet face to face. However, as the day progressed I received more and more calls from reporters. The story was out, gathering momentum. I could sense a media frenzy if things were not resolved quickly. I called Trevor at around nine p.m. and explained that the situation had to be sorted out that very evening. But he still insisted on a face-to-face meeting. I told him I needed to know whether he wanted to put this behind him and get on with his job before I drove to see him, and he said he would provided certain conditions were met.

We eventually arranged to meet halfway between our two homes. I got dressed, had my driver bring round the Chevy, and I ended up in a lay-by just outside Oxford some time before eleven p.m. I was there until after one a.m. on Monday morning. (Over two hours in a lay-by outside Oxford in the early hours of the morning with another man! I deny all the rumours! Fortunately, so does Trevor.) Trevor was in a bullish mood and told me he wanted Alan Robson sacked, and assurances on all sorts of other things. He wanted a clearer definition between the football and commercial sides as he felt there were too many undefined areas. I could see quite clearly that he wanted to come back but that he saw this as an opportunity to negotiate his best terms, to get what he wanted out of the situation. I told him no one was looking to step into his area of responsibility, but other than assuring him I would look into his various other concerns, I remained resolute and determined. I did not capitulate to anything he demanded, especially on the commercial side. He also wanted a new contract, and strangely he wanted a clause stating that if I left the club it would free him. I guess he was saying he would only work under my protection, to hold off Karren and David. I told him I was flattered but I could not present the board with such an ultimatum. Ironically, Alan Robson left soon afterwards, but not because of Trevor's pressure. I never believed the commercial department were intruding on his area of responsibility, and he didn't have an argument. It was more Trevor being precious. We all wanted to do the best for the football club, and we all had our own ideas what that meant.

I admit management is a demanding job and little things can blow up and become very stressful. Clearly in this situation it would have been better had I been there and nipped it in the bud on the Saturday evening. It certainly would not have got into the media nor become so messy, but I couldn't be everywhere. Especially after a decent result, I feel it's OK for me to leave early and complete my other obligations.

During the time Trevor was manager there were numerous public arguments, with him threatening to leave over various issues. I always felt he knew we didn't want him to leave. He also knew he had the support of the fans and could use the fact to, in his opinion, improve the well-being of the club, whether in terms of infrastructure or procedures. But as far as I was concerned these things shouldn't be done on the basis of one man's opinion, but as the result of a consensus. It is fatal when a manager begins to believe he is more powerful than the owners. I have experienced this in business as well as football, and it always ends in tears. He was concerned the commercial side would impinge on his time by requiring him to attend presentations and corporate events. It all became such a big deal to him, but it could have been resolved with sensible dialogue. To me, it was part and parcel of doing the job.

He would often say, 'If you don't support me I may have to consider my position.' It was like having the sword of Damocles held over our heads. Despite getting to the final of the Worthington Cup and the semi-finals of the play-offs, I thought it was time for a change. I was worn out with Trevor, worn out with all the side issues, which detracted from the football. My view to the board was, reluctantly, it was time for a change. He had been given the time and the money and had still not achieved promotion. Not only was I worn out, more importantly I felt Trevor was too. I thought the only thing keeping him going was the near victory over Liverpool. Otherwise I felt he might well have walked into my office and resigned.

David Sullivan's loyalty to Trevor persuaded us to give him another season. Ralph was of a similar opinion, and against my better judgement I agreed. If I'd had my way we would have said our goodbyes during that summer of 2001. I felt we were all running on fumes. The romance with Trevor Francis was over, at least from my point of view. After we had an ordinary start to the 2001/02 season even David realised we had run out of steam and that Trevor no longer seemed to have the passion. It was a question of us all looking in the mirror and admitting it was the end.

In October, Karren and I asked Trevor to attend a meeting to discuss his future. I hadn't decided beforehand that we would sack him, but as soon as he walked into the boardroom and I looked into his eyes, I knew the chemistry had gone. At the time the club was twelfth having played eleven matches. In Trevor's final six games we had lost three successive matches, away to Manchester City and at home to Burnley and Preston; drawn with struggling Watford and Crewe; and recorded just one win, away at ailing Barnsley, who ended up getting relegated. We agreed a severance payoff, shook hands, and it was over. Five and a half years came to an end in twenty minutes, and all because I could see that the passion had gone.

It was big news, of course, and Karren asked me to attend the press conference with Trevor, fearing that he was angry and would take the opportunity to launch a verbal attack on the board. I told the media what a fantastic job Trevor had done for Birmingham City, how close we had come to promotion, and how the infrastructure and procedures had improved. After making my goodbye speech a reporter told me it sounded more like I was welcoming a new manager rather than saying goodbye to an old one, such was my praise. I didn't hold my breath waiting for Trevor to respond by talking of the support I had given him over the past five and a half years. All he said, somewhat mystically, was, 'Who knows? Some day I may return.'

To this day I don't know whether Trevor's words represented a serious plot to bring together a number of wealthy people to buy David Sullivan out. David's shares were up for sale because he was so fed up with the media and the fans blaming him for the demise of the Golden Boy, when in fact it was David who had saved Trevor at the beginning of the season. A lot of paper talk was fuelled by Trevor's parting remark. There were rumours that he would head a consortium to buy David out, and the fans were saying they would rather David Sullivan left than Trevor Francis. For a while there was great disruption, and the future of the club faltered. I made a public statement urging David to reconsider and stay so we could fulfil our dream of Premiership football together. He did.

After Trevor's departure by mutual agreement, David came out on record saying that Trevor never replied to telephone calls, didn't respond to messages, and had spent three months during which he didn't speak to David Gold, but apart from that he 'was good company at dinner'. It was completely true. Trevor is a nice man with a lovely family, and socially he is charming, but in our working relationship he pushed me to the end of my tether. I subsequently met Trevor at Jasper Carrott's inauguration, when he received his OBE. We were at a party at the Savoy Hotel, and Trevor was present with his wife Helen, and both were charming to me. But a couple of times when David and I were in Marbella for our annual few days' holiday, we always extended an invitation through his friends for them to join us, but he never took up the offer. There is no reason for him to hold a grudge against me as I supported him at every turn, but in the end I was just so worn out with his demands and his dour, uncompromising attitude, even after a remarkable season when we reached the Worthington Cup final. And our decision to replace Trevor was proved right as we were promoted that very season under our former captain and central defender Steve Bruce.

CHAPTER TWENTY-SIX

WELCOME HOME, STEVE

Steve Bruce was in our minds as a future manager long before he returned to St Andrews to replace Trevor Francis. When he left us to go to Sheffield United as player-manager I personally asked him to reconsider and stay with us one more year. I believe that with Steve at Birmingham we would have gained promotion that year. As it was we just missed out, as we always seemed to do under the unlucky Trevor Francis. When Steve left we lost not only a solid, rocklike central defender but also an inspirational and natural leader, someone who had all the potential to go on and become a top manager. I wished him good luck and told him I was sure we would see him again in the future. Ideally it would have suited us to squeeze one more season out of him, then he could have become a coach with a view to eventually being appointed the manager. The board was unified in its opinion, but when Trevor went, David Sullivan felt we should interview a number of candidates, despite the fact that Karren and I had already decided Steve Bruce was our man.

I know Steve always wanted to manage Birmingham from his days with us as a player. He liked the people at the club, especially the straight-talking David Sullivan. He saw passionate, quality people on and off the terraces and in the boardroom. When he was a player he had lots of contact with us, and we always told him he would one day return as our manager. When Trevor left, Steve knew he was in contention for the job. When I saw Steve for the first time, a planned 30-minute interview turned into a five-hour meeting as we discussed the future of the club, even though no appointment or agreement had been made at the time. It seemed it was as inevitable to him as it was to me. In fact, the meeting went on so long I sent a car to pick up his wife, Janet, who came over to

*TOP LEFT: With Steve
Bruce at St Andrews.*

*TOP RIGHT: Tommy
Gould VC.*

*LEFT: With Lesley and
my late friend Adam
Faith.*

*BELOW: With one
of the Gold Air
International jets.*

RIGHT: *The disgusting National Front flyer pushed through my door.*

MIDDLE: *My fight over the rubbish generated by the gypsies makes the local papers.*

Bottom: *Mum makes the papers!*

Gold blames travellers for pile of rubbish

THE multi-millionaire boss of Ann Summers has called for the travellers' camp 500 yards from his home to be closed down in a mounting row over rubbish.

The final straw for David Gold came in the early hours of Friday morning last week when a mountain of woodland waste was dumped outside the front gate of his Tupwood Lane mansion.

Mr Gold lays the blame at some of those from the Surrey County Council-owned travellers' site just up the road – he has been a long-standing critic of the constant rubbish dumping there and has taken aerial photographs of the site from his helicopter as evidence.

Mr Gold said he has been virtually under siege at times with packs of dogs roaming his land and killing his ducks and swans.

He also claims ornamental lights weighing 100lbs have been taken from his front gates and his intercom pressed several times at the dead of night.

He added: "We have had to put up with tons of filth and waste in a beautiful part of the countryside. Each resident there should be offered a council house and then the site should be dismantled forever."

The 16-plot site, which has been open for about 25 years, is owned by Surrey County Council and managed by Tandridge District Council.

Steve Evans, the county's principal engineer, said: "A number of travellers on the site have the right to recycle material that others bring to civic amenity sites.

"But over many years they have brought stuff back to the gipsy site and it has been mounting up. It included fridges, which can no longer be recycled, and various metals. We just could not stand back and do nothing."

Last autumn the rubbish was cleared at a cost of about £20,000, he said.

A new fence was also put around the site's boundary and the occupiers were reminded they must abide by the licensing conditions which include not causing noise and disturbance, and not accumulating rubbish.

Mr Evans said serious offenders could be removed from the site.

He said conditions on the site had "vastly improved" since then and a Tandridge council officer made daily checks there.

Rubbish: David Gold surveys the debris dumped outside his home   Photo: N0250D/1

Birmingham Evening Mail (Late Night Final)

Date: 13/07/2004
Type: General Consumer
Frequency: 240/Per year
Circulation: 127983 (ABC)

■ KEEP RIGHT ON: Rose Gold celebrates her 90th birthday at St Andrew's. Picture Tim Easthope

Golden years

BLUES HAIL QUEEN OF OAP FANS

TOP LEFT: *With the late and great Brian Clough.*

TOP RIGHT: *Friends! Barry Fry, David Sullivan and yours truly.*

ABOVE: *With my old friend Charlie Cross at St Andrews.*

RIGHT: *Lesley and the current FA Cup.*

TOP LEFT: With Reading chairman John Madejski.

TOP RIGHT: With local broadcaster Tom Ross in Birmingham.

RIGHT: David Dein, the Arsenal vice chairman, who made me so welcome on our debut in the Premiership.

BOTTOM: With Lesley and Portsmouth chairman Milan Mandaric.

A visit to St Andrews by Sven Goran Eriksson.

With Lesley and Karren Brady.

Working at home with my personal assistant Gio.

With Lesley at home.

Will Curtis' fly-past at The Chalet charity open day.

Jamie Spencer rides David Junior to win the Group One Dubai Duty Free race on 25th March 2006.

An example of the erotica in PEP magazine. Is this what all the fuss was about?

PEP *and* Carnival *magazines – would hardly make the top shelf these days!*

Daughters Jacky and Vanessa with Lesley.

ABOVE: With Mum and Lesley at home.

LEFT: The spot where I look in the mirror, straighten my tie, and remember who I am and where I came from.

join us in a glass of wine. They spent the rest of the evening with us.

The camaraderie between the two of us was fantastic. When he was a player I always gravitated towards him at functions, and in the dressing room. I was always comfortable with him, while I was rarely at ease with Trevor, particularly towards the end when I was always on tenterhooks waiting for him to promote his latest cause. There was rarely an ordinary conversation or exchange of views because I always knew there would be something on his mind. It was stressful waiting for the next demand, whether it was for new irrigation at the training ground, an upgrade of the changing rooms or improvements to his own personal facilities. There was always an agenda.

Steve had not been manager at Crystal Palace for very long, fewer than twenty games, and he had built an unfortunate reputation: he went to Sheffield United in 1998 and left in 1999, and he did the same at Huddersfield (1999 to 2000) and Wigan (2001), as well as his brief stay at Crystal Palace. All of this led to the belief that he was unreliable and flitted from club to club. It was said he left clubs because of a lack of integrity, but I know he left because of his integrity, not because of a lack of it. I knew then and have since confirmed to my own satisfaction that he is a gentleman, that he has respect, and that he is totally honourable. He had some nightmare scenarios to contend with, but he came out with his reputation intact. It is not for me to discuss his reasons, particularly for leaving Crystal Palace so soon after joining them, but he has my support and understanding. It is no secret people find it difficult working with Crystal Palace chairman and owner Simon Jordan. They were doing well in the handful of games Steve was there, but they were scraping the points thanks to Steve's motivation, and in those few matches they played with him at the helm they met a number of teams who finished in the bottom half. I don't believe they were anything more than a mid-table side. Clearly Steve wasn't comfortable at Palace or he would not have considered a move to us.

It was strange that Trevor should make the journey in the opposite direction, to Crystal Palace. Simon was outraged at losing Steve, as indeed I would have been in his position. I can see what was in his mind, having lost his manager to a so-called bigger club: what an irony it would be to take on the sacked Trevor Francis and win promotion to the Premiership while Birmingham stayed in the First Division! What a coup that would have been for Simon and Trevor; rarely could there have been a greater incentive. I am sure Simon was employing Trevor as manager of Crystal Palace in the hope that he could achieve promotion having failed in his five years with Birmingham. It would have been deeply satisfying to both Francis and Jordan, but they finished tenth and fourteenth under Trevor, proving points, I suppose, for both Steve Bruce and the Birmingham board.

But I was delighted when Palace gained promotion to the Premiership under Iain Dowie because it is the local club to where I live and a great many of my staff are Palace supporters, and I was disappointed when they went straight back down. My local paper is all Crystal Palace and my local restaurants are also Palace-friendly – I receive the usual comments when I dine there. I was equally pleased at the latest irony, when my old club West Ham United were promoted after a tough season and took Palace's place in the top division. It is all a great adventure. I may be a grown-up but I still feel like a schoolboy with my football fantasies woven around my first club West Ham, my neighbouring club Crystal Palace and my own club Birmingham City.

I saw Simon Jordan during the season when Palace were in the top flight and made a point of shaking his hand and welcoming him to the Premier League. But I feel he still holds a grudge. The next time I see him, I must tell him, 'Simon, move on, life's too short.' As chairman of a club fighting for its own Premiership survival, I was relieved it was Palace who had been promoted rather than West Ham, who would have been a greater threat to our position in the top flight (Palace beat West Ham 1–0 at Cardiff in the play-off final). At the time, watching the match, I felt Crystal Palace were more likely to be relegated than West Ham, and I was proved right as Palace and West Ham swapped places at the end of the following season.

I have always said beware judging a manager on one season. A manager can have a purple patch when luck goes with him, but there is more to it than that, especially his relationship with the fans, the board and the media. Steve Bruce won us promotion after just six months in charge, despite the fact that at one stage we were lying fourteenth in the table and as low as tenth on 9 March. He took us through to the play-off final after beating Millwall in the semi-final. In that game, it looked as though we were going to miss our chance yet again when the redoubtable on-loan Dion Dublin equalised a goal from Bryan Hughes ten minutes from the end of the first leg at St Andrews, but incredibly we went to the Den and did the same to them, only later, as Stern John scored the winner in the 90th minute to, at last, put us through to the final. That was some result after drawing the first leg, for not only did the team find the Den intimidating, I found their boardroom intimidating! Theo Paphitis, the then chairman, is a pleasant fellow and he had his close friend Simon Jordan with him at the match because, said Jordan, he had never been at the Den and seen Millwall lose. In other words, he was there to see us beaten because Simon was still carrying a chip on his shoulder.

It was an awesome place on the night, not only because of what the lunatic fringe did outside the ground but also because of the electric atmosphere inside the stadium. It was incredible, and the animosity in the boardroom was as powerful as I have ever encountered. Nevertheless I was sorry for the club when some of their supporters, or yobs masquerading as fans, torched two parked cars, and injured 47 police officers and, would you believe it, 26 police horses. As we drove away from the stadium in our Chevy people carrier, registration BCFC (doctored from 13 CFC), a team of riot officers were there to protect us from the yobs. As we accelerated away I saw that my son-in-law, Nick Young, who is married to my daughter Vanessa, was one of the officers shielding us. It was a frightening experience.

Beating Millwall was another amazing event in the adventure, and one of the most memorable, perhaps even more so than the penalty shoot-out in the play-off final against Norwich City at Cardiff's Millennium Stadium. I'd had six penalty shoot-outs in the nine years I'd been at the club, and that is the first we won, having lost all the previous ones under Barry Fry and Trevor Francis. I feared the worst, but I felt our luck must turn. The remarkable thing was we had come from so far behind. After all the wrangling following Trevor Francis's departure and trying to secure Steve Bruce, with Mick Mills and Jim Barron holding the fort in the meantime, at Christmas 2001 we were twenty points adrift of Wolves. But we reached those play-offs. The game, a tight one, was played in front of 71,597 spectators, and they had to wait until extra time for the first goal, when Iwan Roberts put Norwich in front after just one minute. Geoff Horsfield equalised eleven minutes later, and that is how it stayed. Penalties again – I couldn't believe it! But this time fortune was on our side, and we won the shoot-out 4–2. It was one of our academy youngsters, Darren Carter, who stepped up for the crucial penalty, and he hit it home like a veteran instead of the eighteen-year-old he was.

Steve Bruce had done all we had hoped, not only motivating his team but also integrating players he brought in shortly after he arrived. Steve Vickers, Jeff Kenna, Stern John, the Trinidad and Tobago international on a free transfer from Nottingham Forest, Olivier Tebily, Damien Johnson and Paul Devlin, the Scottish international right-winger from Sheffield United – they all came in and did a job for Steve and the club. And promotion could not have come at a better time: if we had stayed down in 2002 we would immediately have been burdened with the £3 million deficit left by the collapse of the ITV Digital deal. Instead, Birmingham City was back in the top division for the first time since 1986.

CHAPTER TWENTY-SEVEN

LOSER TAKES ALL

I felt for the Norwich City co-owner Delia Smith when she stood on the pitch and implored her supporters 'Let's be 'avin' yer!' in a bid to get them behind her struggling team. I will never forget the wonderful day when we got together before that play-off final at the Millennium Stadium and arranged a deal which was meant to soften the blow for the team not promoted to the Premiership. I knew and liked Delia long before we were due to meet in the play-off final, and we decided to put a proposition to her prior to a ball being kicked in Cardiff, suggesting that whoever lost the game should take all the gate money due to be split by both teams. We asked how she felt about the winner going to the Premiership and the loser taking the cash windfall. She said yes, and it somewhat softened the blow of not making it into the Premier League.

I found her an absolutely joyous person in the most disappointing moment of her footballing life, losing on penalties in the final. She was so gracious in defeat. My experience of the rich and famous is that many of them are unpleasant people, while the most pleasant are the ordinary people you meet in the street or at football matches. Once people become rich and famous they seem to have no time for others; they seek out their peers and want only to be with other rich and famous people, strutting like the peacocks I have in my garden. But Delia is a charming lady, and I was so delighted when Norwich were promoted in 2004, even if they stayed up only for a season. When we lost to them in the Premiership that season playing with ten men and after murdering them, in football parlance, it was softened by the fact that it was Delia's team, especially as it gave them a chance of staying up before they froze at Fulham in the final game of the season, and were slaughtered.

Our little deal has been kept under wraps ever since we signed our names to the contract, because at the time, when we presented it to the Football League and the Football Association, they were opposed to it and we had to have it legalled out. But it's something I recommend to every club in the final because the winner does take it all by the very nature of the payments in the Premiership, while the losers just have their share of the gate money. How civilised to be able to share good fortune with people you like.

Gaining promotion to the Premiership was one of the great moments of my life. The excitement, the thrill of it all; going through the city in the open-top bus; the pageantry . . . it was just an extraordinary experience. I couldn't resist being on the celebratory bus ride and I loved every minute of it as we drove through the city where the police had closed all the approach roads to the town hall. It was just wonderful. Tens of thousands of people turned out just wanting to be a part of this tremendous achievement. You could feel the warmth of the ovation from the people watching as every person involved was mentioned. It was truly a great thrill, and sharing it with my brother, the players and the fans was special. There were so many memorable moments, especially seeing my mum in tears. Suddenly we were up there with the big clubs, looking forward to trips to places like Old Trafford, St James's Park, Villa Park, Anfield, Goodison, and our very first match of the 2002/03 season, away to Arsenal at Highbury.

We were beaten 2–0 with first-half goals by Thierry Henry and Sylvain Wiltord. Arsenal vice chairman David Dein was charming, and he made a presentation to us in the boardroom commemorating Birmingham City FC's return to the top flight. I was on the television that morning at the BBC, and when I arrived at Highbury I was on Sky with David Dein showing off the FA Cup, the Premiership trophy and the Charity Shield. David welcomed us to the Premier League, while I was asked about the day and our expectations. I looked at the three magnificent trophies behind us and told them I'd forgotten to bring the Auto Windscreens trophy we won in 1995. It was a joke, but it put it all in perspective. It was a touch of humility because we were and are Birmingham City, not Juventus, AC Milan or Real Madrid, but we had a part to play nonetheless and we were going to do our utmost to enjoy it, at the same time keeping a sense of proportion.

Suddenly I was finding myself receiving a number of calls a day from the media. I had my calls screened by Giovanna Wallace, my personal assistant, who was able to arrange for me to call back when time permitted.

I wasn't shirking my responsibilities, it's just that there were some difficult moments when questions were being asked about our French striker Christophe Dugarry. Was he really injured? Was he on the way out? Dugarry had had a knee injury, and although he had recovered his form was terrible and critics were asking, was it the end of a great player? I was saying no, even though I was unsure of his future myself. I did not want to spend my day being negative and repeating things I only half believed. When we were in the First Division it was just the local press with the occasional national newspaper or television station coming in. It was different now. You only have to look at national newspapers to see how many pages they devote to Premier League football. The hours on Sky, Talk Sport radio or Radio Five – they are insatiable. Local radio and television were still there, but now there were all the rest of them as well.

It required a huge effort, that first season in the Premiership, especially after losing both of our opening games. Playing Arsenal away, no one expected any different, but everyone had great hopes of beating Blackburn Rovers at St Andrews, and when we lost 1–0 people were ready to write us off as no-hopers. But we had great faith in Steve Bruce. After promotion he'd brought in Kenny Cunningham from Wimbledon, an outstanding buy and a superb skipper, Aliou Cisse, Robbie Savage from Leicester and Clinton Morrison from Crystal Palace – with, sadly, Andrew Johnson going to Palace as part of the deal. When the window opened in January 2003 we purchased six new players including the Polish captain Piotr Swierczewski, who played only ten minutes of football for us, and Ferdinand Coly, who was a complete disaster. You win some and you lose some. We also brought in Jamie Clapham from Ipswich, Steven Clemence from Tottenham, Matthew Upson from Arsenal, who went on to play for England, and, most importantly, the extrovert Frenchman Christophe Dugarry, who, it turned out, almost single-handedly kept us in the top division. He played the last fifteen league games for us and scored five goals in a spell of four games which brought us a total of twelve points. When at the end of April a header from Stan Lazaridis went past Mark Schwarzer in the Middlesbrough goal to make it 3–0 and four wins on the trot, we knew we were safe. It was all too close for comfort, but without us putting up our own money to bring these players in we would probably have been relegated.

Time for celebration; time to recall how the great fight was fought. Cunningham and Jeff Kenna battling through injury; Geoff Horsfield playing as an emergency centre-half against Manchester United and Leeds

United; young Matt Sadler playing left-back and marking David Beckham at Old Trafford. Last but far from least was Dugarry, who was genuinely world class when he was being written off on both sides of the Channel.

But the real joy and agony of football is its unpredictability. Just when you think you have it right, the game gets up and kicks you in the teeth. We finished our second season in the Premiership, 2003/04, in tenth place with 50 points. Despite slipping to twelfth having scored five fewer points by the end of 2004/05, there was a terrific finale to the season as we beat Arsenal 2–1 and subsequently spent a lot of money bringing in quality players. At the start of the 2005/06 season I was convinced ours was the best squad the Blues had enjoyed for 25 years. I looked at the fixtures and honestly believed we could be in the top six by Christmas, but instead we found ourselves struggling at the foot of the division, fighting against relegation instead of challenging for a place in Europe. Newly promoted teams like Wigan and West Ham, instead of floundering like Sunderland, were in the top half of the table, leaving us with a dark cloud hanging over our heads.

Immediately the media were naming Steve Bruce as the manager most likely to be sacked, but as our record proves, we are not the sort of board to rush into these things. Still, I had to make a statement saying we would not be sacking our manager. It is not blind loyalty; it is a measured judgement by a sensible and loyal board. You pick your man, and he does not suddenly stop being the manager you selected. Of course managers do run past their sell-by date at clubs, as Trevor Francis did with us. He was worn out after five and a half years of trying to get into the Premier League. But Bruce is a younger, vibrant man; he has a great will to win, and this was a time when we all needed to pull together. I have seen managers at other clubs I would have fired. An example was Glenn Roeder at West Ham. A nice man, but this is not to do with personality, this is business, and when it comes to a club manager in the senior divisions he needs to be charismatic as he not only has to carry the players but the board, the media and the fans as well. No matter what we chairmen think of ourselves, it is still the manager who is seen as the figurehead, and it will be his job on the line if the team fails. But Steve Bruce ticks all the important boxes, and more. You can't get away with losing the media, you have to keep the fans and the players onside, not to mention the people who employ you.

Luck ran away from us in 2005/06. During the first half of the season we had six penalties awarded against us, all of them dubious, while not winning one. We had six sendings-off too, and not one of the opposition sent off. It begins to appear to be an imbalance. In addition we lost virtually all of our midfield. Robbie Savage had left for Blackburn, but the big problem was injuries: a number of our big-name players were absent with long-term problems, and in the mix were short-term absentees. We had an excessive injury list way beyond what you would normally expect. We lost Mehdi Nafti for virtually the entire season; we saw only a fleeting sight of David Dunne; Muzzy Izzet had been out for a year, and was outstanding when he came back against Newcastle when we produced our best performance of the season to that point, only to get injured again; Mikael Forssell, who had been injured for the whole of the 2004/05 season, did not return to fitness until Christmas 2005; Damien Johnson was suspended for the first three games of the season; Neil Kilkenny, a young central midfielder for whom I have great hopes, also suffered an injury; Julian Gray, Stan Lazaridis ... so it went on. Every time I went to the training ground I would go to the treatment room to meet the players rather than the dressing room or the practice pitch. We had to throw people in before they were ready because we were so short of numbers. Muzzy was a classic example: when I went into the dressing room at Newcastle he was stretched out on the floor having treatment. (St James's Park is a magnificent ground, but the away team dressing rooms are a bit Spartan and small, and as there was no treatment table available he had to lie on the floor with ice packs on both legs and blood everywhere from a cut on his head.) Of course everyone has penalties given against them, players sent off, suspensions plus injuries and other problems, but we seemed to have them all come at once instead of being sprinkled through a season. There just seemed no way during the early part of this critical season when Steve could get anywhere near his best eleven out on to the field. Sometimes the eleven in the treatment room were a lot stronger than the eleven we were sending out on to the pitch!

It's amazing how much the game has changed in a few years. It's not so long ago that Liverpool won the title with only about sixteen players used all season, and here we were struggling to cover with a staff of 40! I don't know what the answer is, but it is a growing problem because of the greater intensity of the game. Maybe it is only 5 per cent more intense, but that small percentage is enough to take players over the edge and into the red alert area. Look at Newcastle United: they had virtually an entire team out in 2005/06 with hamstring injuries. They blamed the training pitch and moved to where the colts were practising, but when you think of the bleak windswept hill they used to train on, it seems very odd. I am told it was cold up there when the wind blew during pre-season training in the summer. There is certainly an unusual amount of injuries in the modern game, which has meant the bigger clubs have had to take on more and more players. Bladed studs may be one reason, but nothing has been proved. We do need a lot more research into the current malaise.

It hurts me to say it, but we have to admit that we missed Robbie Savage, and we did not replace him. I supported him and did everything to hold on to him and persuade him to stay at St Andrews. His move to Blackburn Rovers left a sour taste in the mouths of all of us at the Blues. There were so many reasons and so many excuses and all the sob stories about him wanting to be nearer his home because he was worried about his family, but they failed to stand up. What he was really doing was reneging on a four-year contract offered and signed, we thought, in good faith. He signed that contract when he was due to go into hospital for surgery at the end of the 2003/04 season, with his future as a professional footballer in doubt. He had realised the back/neck operation was not as simple as he had thought and he rushed in to sign the contract out of fear for his playing career.

He was outstanding when he came back, but as we moved towards the transfer window through Christmas 2004 he organised and worked out his own move. He made himself intolerable to work with and orchestrated his own demise. He had made up his mind he was going to Blackburn, and nothing was going to change his mind. He told the press it was closer to his parents' house and it was important to him to be near them. Needless to say, the press do not believe everything they are told. They measured the distances involved and found that his parents' house was closer to Birmingham than it was to Blackburn. The truth was he wanted a new challenge, and he just abandoned Birmingham City. He had an excellent contract with us but he moved because of the money and because he wanted to be with his former Welsh coaching team of Mark Bowen and Mark Hughes, both of whom had moved to Blackburn. Had he had the courage to come out and say as much we would have accepted it much more readily. But he was childlike in his approach. It was as good as saying, 'I want that – giss it!'

I loved Robbie Savage. I thought he was a fantastic character, and he was great for Birmingham City. I also believe people who sign contracts should honour them. It might be said we got more than decent money for him, but that wasn't the issue. I wanted the man who was playing for me for the first two and a half years in the Premiership. Having given so much to us, he let both Birmingham City and me down by his attitude, and I find it hard to forgive. There are loyal players in football, such as our Australian Stan Lazaridis. They are not all mercenaries after the extra pound, as Stan has proved over and over again. The one who really stands out for me is Steve Bull at Wolverhampton Wanderers, who turned down all sorts of moves to all sorts of top clubs to stay with his local team through hell and high water, and was rewarded with an England cap by Sir Bobby Robson when out of the top division. Stan stands out as the same sort of person, as does our skipper Kenny Cunningham, who will play through the pain barrier for his manager and club. Robbie's problem was it was always someone else's fault and never his.

On the face of it, we swapped one problem for another when we took on the young winger Jermaine Pennant after he had suffered problems at Arsenal and was in danger of missing out on what promised to be a glittering career in the game. Here is a young man with amazing potential but also with the baggage of personal problems. I can empathise with the man as the problems he has brought upon himself come from his impoverished background. It is a classic case of too much, too soon. It took me twenty years to claw my way out of poverty, but he was pulled out almost overnight and was given money beyond his wildest dreams. He has subsequently struggled to adjust, but I am convinced he will. The football club has done its best for him, but he is not going to take too kindly to being nannied 24 hours a day, seven days a week. All we can do is make sure he knows we are available to help him whenever he needs us. He has the skill to play for England, and better judges of footballers than me believe that to be the case. I sincerely hope he does, because he is such a charming young man. He has the opportunity because he will improve under Steve Bruce. When you are an attacking winger you have to have loads of self-belief, and he has this quality in abundance.

Jermaine knows I am always available to him. I have, in the past, flown up to see him and other players when they have needed it. I will sit and have lunch and an informal chat with them, and listen to their problems. After the latest episode there was only so much I dared do; I cannot become his father. I have to pace things and judge what part I am going to play. I am there for every match, in the dressing room before and after the game; I am there to pat him on the back after a game, and at the training ground. But, I repeat, I am not his father. After this latest issue the club made itself available to help him, though of course much of what we did must remain private. He wrote to Karren Brady saying how sorry he was for having a drink too many and suffering because of it. Nothing too unusual for a 21-year-old, except when you are under the spotlight, as he is and always will be as long as he is in football. He was suitably sorry and embarrassed, and that is what makes him durable and endurable. I could not cope with arrogance. If he had said, 'So what?' there would have been little we could have done. At least he gave himself a chance, and it has to be said he bounced back brilliantly during our fight to stave off relegation.

George Best may have been the same under Sir Matt Busby; he is a great example for Pennant to look at and see how talent and popularity can be wasted. I was with George during the season at Portsmouth, when we arrived at Fratton Park for lunch. George was at the bar and I felt so sad and sorry for this fallen idol, standing with a glass of wine in a different world to the rest of us, with no one talking to him. I watched him out of the corner of my eye for fifteen minutes or so as I talked to the Pompey chairman Milan Mandaric, and before lunch was called I walked over to him at the bar, shook hands and found myself saying, 'How are you, George?' I kicked myself for such a banality, for it was obvious from just looking at him how bad he was. He was just weeks away from being whipped into intensive care. You could see the sadness and loneliness in his eyes, and as I shook his hand I could almost hear him answer, 'How the f*** do you think I am?' I chatted for a while with this man I idolised, this handsome young Irishman with the charismatic personality, a man who had bewitched me with his wizardry and stunning skills. I envied his talent, his adulation from the female population, and here I was talking to him, trying to raise his spirits, trying to encourage him. But he seemed to have accepted the inevitability of his plight, which was depressing for me. Milan was hugely loyal to him and should be commended for that, but George himself had little to say in ordinary conversation. It was as if he was saying we had all seen him at his best at football grounds around the country, and now we were seeing him at his worst. I shook his hand for the last time and wished him luck, though I realised it was not luck he wanted, but peace. I knew I would never see him again.

It seems we all lived his life with him through intensive media coverage, from the footballing heights, through the nightclubs, the girls, the high society and down into the depths of alcoholism. When I was close to the man, shaking his hand and gazing into his glazed eyes, I could see how far he had been dragged under. It was a sad experience. I wish I'd had young Jermaine Pennant with me at the time because the sight of George Best that day, a couple of months before he passed away, spoke more words than Jermaine's advisers or I could spout in a lifetime.

CHAPTER TWENTY-EIGHT

SEXY BUSINESS

I am always associated with 'sexy business', and I am glad that's the case. But my definition of it probably differs from most people's. Detractors prefer to use the term in a negative sense. For example, they might point to the Ann Summers range of goods, which are literally the sexiest items available from the Gold empire. Some critics sneer, priggishly in my view, and take the view that 'sexy business' is always bad business, shady business, business to be judgemental about. But when I think about 'sexy business', it's not skimpy underwear, or sex toys, or the Kama Sutra that come to mind first. It's football. It's Birmingham City making a jaw-dropping signing. It's flying aeroplanes, or it's Gold Air. It's Sport Newspapers. It's opening a new Ann Summers shop and seeing Jacqueline arrive on a Lear Jet to cut the tape. And beyond that, it's the whole dynamic buzz that goes into building, sustaining and growing a business empire, and that includes aspects most people wouldn't find 'sexy'. You can try to tell me wholesale and retail distribution is dull until you're blue in the face, but not in my book! It's the engine driving the sexy motor. Print works and plate making not sexy? How do you think your daily newspaper gets made? Without these cogs in the machine there wouldn't be any business, let alone just sexy business. The whole machinery of what we do is sexy to me.

Of course there are aspects of my work and businesses that carry a special joy. Football, let's face it, is a sexy business, and nothing is sexier for the manager, the chairman or the fans than signing a top international player. There was no greater thrill for me than when we signed England centre-forward Emile Heskey from Liverpool in May 2004. Like romancing when you are young, it is often the chase that is the most breathtaking. Once we had made up our minds who we wanted, David Sullivan and Steve Bruce pursued that deal, and then pursued it some more. And more. When they pulled it off we were all ecstatic. It was a great feeling.

The key to the deal was Steve Bruce. Players want to play for him. They will join Birmingham City because of him. He was a quality player and he remains a quality man, with experience on the pitch at the top level and the respect of current players to match. He is very convincing when you meet him, and it is all part of the package encouraging the stars to come to St Andrews. Karren Brady, David Sullivan, Ralph and I now all have high enough profiles to add to the package too. It all helps in encouraging players to join us, and Steve Bruce's transfer dealings excite us.

Trevor Francis's first tranche of transfers after his 'homecoming' as manager in 1996 also thrilled us. He brought in the likes of Steve Bruce himself, direct from Manchester United, the most successful club in the land at the time. They'd just completed their second Double in three years. Steve was their captain and a mainstay, and he left Old Trafford for St Andrews. How sexy is that? In the same period, Trevor also brought in Paul Furlong from Chelsea and Mike Newell from Blackburn, who'd also won the Premier League in recent years. Sadly, of course, Newell didn't work out. Had he done so, had he fitted in, who knows what might have happened? But after Newell, Trevor brought in too many players who didn't enhance the squad or improve the team. We couldn't see the difference they would make, and sometimes players actually made the situation worse. Trevor's pride made him stick with a player. Chris Holland was a classic example. When Trevor bought him he'd played just three league games for Newcastle, and even those had been a few years earlier, as a teenager. Trevor played him, and while we were saying he was not good enough, he stuck with him. I'm the first man to admire loyalty and promote it as a virtue, but this wasn't loyalty, I felt, it was more an error of judgement. I can only believe that Trevor had seen Chris on occasions when he had played above himself, and he was waiting to see if he could reproduce the same form. But if it can't be done after a dozen games, or if a player does it for only half a game, what good is he to the team?

When Steve brings in players, you can see the improvement. Not with every single player of course because no one gets it right all the time. Even Sir Alex Ferguson, Arsène Wenger and Sir Bobby Robson have been known to make mistakes. But Steve has made fewer than most.

Every player you buy has to improve the team. Eventually, even players who have done that will have to move on when better players replace them. Clinton Morrison was a classic example. He was bought in 2002, a good player with a good attitude who made us a better team, and he was eventually squeezed out, in 2005, by the arrival of even better players. Onwards and upwards is the only attitude to have, in football and in any other business. That is why I relish being involved with all my companies. I'm delighted to be a part of so many sexy businesses: Ann Summers, Birmingham City, Sport Newspapers, Gold Air International. They all support each other in their own ways.

When we open a big Ann Summers store, our whole publicity machine – our entire business machine – kicks in. You can read about it in our newspapers, and a lot of other newspapers too! You can see it happening on our websites. You can watch as Jacqueline gets out of one of our Lear Jets to open a store in Cork or Edinburgh or Valencia. If some mall owner somewhere is still unwilling to accept sexy business – and I mean thriving, dynamic, popular, mainstream business – then more fool him. The detractors can gripe, but we'll keep doing what we're good at, and enjoying it.

I feel privileged to be in a position to do so. How many people have the opportunity to watch a stunt display team fly over their garden for fun? Will Curtis, the managing director of Gold Air, is the up-and-coming pilot in aerobatics. He has won several awards, and his display is quite stunning. He did a ten-minute display for me when I had a charity open day at my house in Surrey, and he has performed a similar routine at one of my business meetings. It is breathtaking, especially at a private venue – rather like having your own firework display instead of going to a public one.

Then, of course, we have our shareholding in the *Daily Sport* and the *Sunday Sport* – successful, profitable newspapers that sell on the newsstands. In recent decades there have been any number of newspaper launches, like *Today*, a national title, and a clutch of Sunday newspapers, regional and national, that have failed to live up to their publicity and expired. *The Sport* newspaper is a remarkable success story. We fill a gap in the market. There are a great many newspaper people prepared to look down their noses at us, but they are little more than hypocrites, just as they were when the great Bobby Moore, captain of the World Cup-winning team in 1966 and one of England's greatest ever footballers, came to work for the *Sport*. I was so angry when I read an article soon after his tragic early death from cancer in 1993, at the age of 51, which stated that Bobby had had to 'resort to' working for the downmarket rag *Sunday Sport*. How dare they? First of all, where were all the big shots when he was out of work? How come they didn't start a campaign for the great Bobby Moore, either to raise money for him, give him work or help him make a living? All they could do was deride him after he was dead by saying he had fallen on hard times and had to earn a living by working for the *Sport*. I loved him, as did everyone on the paper. He was a proper gent, and I am proud that when Bobby told our editor, Mike Gabbett, he was looking for work, Mike brought him on board immediately. You might ask, 'Who wouldn't?' The fact is he wanted work and we were the ones who offered it. It wasn't a grace-and-favour appointment because people read him, especially the older fans who had watched him play or knew him. He was an asset who added to our circulation. I am very cynical when it comes to the kind of things said after his death. Where were those 'friends' when he really needed them? Who wouldn't have Bobby Moore heading their promotions now football has become king of all it surveys? If I achieve nothing else, I will always be thrilled that I was given the opportunity to work with and help such a gentleman and such an icon in our footballing history.

David Sullivan, of course, was the man with the idea of launching the *Sport*, and he brought the project to Ralph and me. Not bad, considering that years earlier we had been business adversaries. We used to have meetings halfway between our offices, at the Tower Hotel, where we would have lunch. It was there that David came up with the idea of a saucy, fun, Sunday sports paper. He felt our customers would be young football followers, and he was rightly convinced that there was a huge market for a combination of sport and page three girls. A number had tried and failed before, but David was determined to pursue his idea. He wanted to bring out a newspaper called the *Sunday Sport*. If we wanted in, he told us, we would have to commit to a million pounds each – a lot of money then and now.

Because of our relationship, having come together after years of conflict, and because we were making money from our top-shelf magazines, both Ralph and I felt a commitment to support this man and back his idea. We were already aware of David's editorial skills, his determination and his work ethic. So we agreed to put our money in, and *Sunday Sport* was born.

From small beginnings came headlines like the hilarious 'World War II Bomber Found On Moon', and the classic follow-up, 'World War II Bomber

Found On Moon Disappears'. Other memorable and obviously tongue-in-cheek headlines included 'I Found Face Of Jesus On My Fish Finger', 'Double Decker Bus Found In Iceberg At South Pole' and 'Aliens Have Eaten My Son'. It soon became a cult, fun newspaper and was quickly making money.

What we were discovering was that David Sullivan was a genius when it came to promotion. He cleverly used the paper to promote other products – each of the various businesses working together as a force to a greater effect than the sum of their individual parts. That continues to be the case. We have a couple of television channels too and use the paper to promote them, increasing profits for the business. Later, we brought out a Wednesday and a Friday paper, so we were publishing three days a week. We discovered that the Friday paper was still selling on Saturday, so we ended up calling it the *Friday-Saturday Sport*, which increased sales even further. It did so well we eventually decided to bring out a Saturday paper in its own right. This might be considered odd in comparison to other publications, but we were like no other publication. There were no rules for us because there was nothing else like it on the market, and we were in competition with no one else. Eventually we ended up with a seven-day newspaper.

We are not deluding ourselves. We know it is very much the paper for the young male, a niche market, but it is a profitable business and it is now in its fourteenth year. The circulation of the newspapers is around 1.5 million copies per week, in net sales, with a massive readership because it is handed around from mate to mate at work. In the early years both Ralph and I tried to contribute to the *Sport*, but it soon became clear that David was in his element and he demanded more and more control of the day-to-day decision-making for the newspaper. We were happy to agree as the newspaper became increasingly successful. Moreover, from our relationship with David Sullivan has grown our business with Sport Newspapers, Birmingham City Football Club and Sport TV.

David is involved in everything. He is a remarkable man who is often misunderstood, and he remains one of my best friends. All credit to him for what he has achieved.

CHAPTER TWENTY-NINE

MONEY, MONEY, MONEY

Floating companies on the stock market is always something of a gamble, even more so when a football club is concerned, because it survives and thrives on different factors compared with other businesses. There was a period when the men in the City jumped on the football bandwagon because of the vast amount of television money expected in from Sky, but they didn't anticipate football chairmen and their boards using the cash to compete with each other to attract the best players by offering bigger wages. We are now hearing of wages of £125,000 a week for top players like Rio Ferdinand. If you are Roman Abramovic you just sign a cheque because it is little more than pin money for a multi-billionaire. But that's not the case with the vast majority of clubs and their chairmen. It was interesting how virtually everyone had it wrong. It was not only the City that thought money was going to flow into the football clubs without realising that no sooner would it come in than it would all go out again in ever upward-spiralling transfer fees and wages.

Over a hundred years clubs and their finances have evolved very slowly. There have been few major changes in all that time. The first serious change was the removal of the maximum wage in 1961. This was no great problem because it was right and sensible and was quickly built into the finances of every club. After the abolition of the maximum wage there was a balance, with shareholders getting a return on their investments and players earning a decent salary. The top players were earning around £100 a week, they were able to drive to work in their own car instead of riding in on a bike or walking, and they could afford to buy a house and become elitist, while the fans had value for money. There was no question of the board and the chairmen taking large dividends. I guess at the time dividends to them were, by and large, secondary as they enjoyed the status of their positions and being able to watch their football from the equivalent of the royal box at the opera. This was more fun, and they could conduct their business from their exalted positions.

Subsequently, football has completely changed with the Bosman ruling. A different sort of person now populates boardrooms as well as dressing rooms. In 1990, Jean-Marc Bosman, a rather ordinary player with Belgian club FC Liege, changed the face of football finances when he sought the human right of freedom of movement in employment in order to join French club Dunkirk – hardly an earth-shattering move in the transfer market by any standards. In 1995 the European Court ruled in favour of Bosman, deciding that existing transfer rules were in breach of European law. This of course led to free movement of players in the Union of Member States once a contract expired. Small and large clubs suffered alike, and it was the superstar players who benefited most because they could command huge signing-on fees and wages if they moved for nothing when out of contract. Wages throughout football grew, and many lesser players were lost because clubs cut their squads.

During the times when we had Stanley Matthews playing for Blackpool, Tom Finney for Preston North End and Nat Lofthouse for Bolton Wanderers, there was very little movement between clubs because they were all paid roughly the same. It promoted great loyalty among players. Often the players had been born in the town they played for and were usually within a walk or a bicycle ride of the ground. Bosman changed that position of power, allowing out-of-contract players to offer their services to the highest bidder. I believe the Bosman decision was bad for the fans and bad for football clubs. A compromise would have been so much better. Bosman was a step too far and did more harm than good. Clearly it was right and proper for Jean-Marc Bosman, but this does not mean it was right for the rest of football.

At the same time there was a huge influx of TV money into the game. Some clubs continued to manage their budgets sensibly while others believed they could buy their way into the big time. But that takes more than money, unless you have an obscene amount that makes mistakes irrelevant. It takes planning, time, balance and common sense as well as the money for transfers and wages to make a club successful. I remember during the end-of-season Asian Cup in Malaysia in July 2003 we held a press conference and I said in front of Ken Bates, who was then still chairman of Chelsea under the new ownership of Roman Abramovic, that I had believed common sense was returning to football – until Mr Abramovic came on to the scene and inflated the transfer market and expectations once again. I don't condemn it, and had he come to Birmingham with his roubles I would have welcomed him with open arms, but it has undoubtedly had an effect on the rest of English football, and in particular the Premiership, because everyone was suddenly under pressure again. Chelsea were able to raise their bids for players until the target club and player cracked, and there are winners and losers. The winners have been West Ham, who received huge sums for Joe Cole and Frank Lampard; Blackburn for Damien Duff; and Manchester City for Shaun Wright-Phillips. The money enabled these clubs to secure other players, including Blackburn buying Robbie Savage from Birmingham City, so a number of clubs have benefited from Roman's money. The losers, for the moment, are Arsenal and Manchester United, who have dominated the English game for a number of years. You can see Chelsea winning the Premiership for several years to come. But nothing is for ever. No one can project what might change, but change it will. I can remember years ago when people were saying Manchester United, with its huge fan base, large corporate income and wealthy sponsors, would dominate English football for years to come. They did for a while, but I repeat, nothing is for ever.

The money that came from Sky helped make the Premiership the finest league in the world. Prior to that the Italians, Spanish and Germans would all want to have claimed the title, but I have no doubt now that it is ours. Without Sky money we would not have got great players from around the world – the likes of Gianfranco Zola, for example, who we enjoyed for years at Chelsea before the Russian Revolution. Thierry Henry, Ruud van Nistelrooy and many more great players now represent our clubs and play on our own grounds; we have the sort of international quality that could previously only have been seen on television. I am a great supporter of the Premier League and all it is attempting to achieve.

Sadly, the Championship had a tremendous setback when they lost their income after the collapse of the ITV Digital deal. It damaged many clubs and led to a lot of them getting into serious financial difficulties – they had spent the money before they received it. A lot of the clubs that struggled had recently been relegated from the Premiership; they saw an opportunity to regain their lost and valuable status and were badly hurt. It meant the gap between the Premiership and the rest grew alarmingly. There will be difficulties for years to come, as we can see in the way most promoted clubs from the Championship struggle to keep pace in the top division. But then along comes Wigan and everyone has hope again.

While I am in the Premiership I would support a reduction from three clubs relegated to two, but such would be the shrieks from the Championship it is unlikely ever to happen. Personally I am for the status quo, but from a Birmingham City Football Club perspective I would be happy to see a return to two up, two down. Five years ago, though, when I was a chairman in Division One, as it was then, I would have fought them in the trenches to keep three up, three down.

Still, there is little doubt football is becoming healthier as the clubs come to terms with the new financial realities. Things are now levelling out and there is more stability, but we still have a serious problem in terms of the gap in income between the Championship and the Premier League. Championship clubs still need to find a way to increase their income. They must somehow find a way to make themselves more attractive to the TV companies. Originally I urged the lower divisions to accept the 20 per cent of TV income which was offered by the Premier League, but many of the chairmen of the remaining 70 clubs felt they could do better, and of course when ITV Digital came along and offered £350 million over a three-year contract they felt they had made the right decision. After the collapse they were proved wrong.

I must admit I saw considerable stupidity in my time from individual chairmen in the lower leagues – the disgraced and discredited former Darlington chairman George Reynolds, for example, who attended his first League meeting in 1999. I listened to him expound the virtues of a plan for his football club, and I thought he was going to have to learn and learn fast. He didn't, went bust, and went to prison in 2005 for tax evasion. It was the safe cracker's fourth prison term. He was a classic example, banging his fist on the table and trying to apply normal business practices to something as intangible as football. But how many other businesses are dramatically affected by one of their workers tearing a cruciate ligament and being unable to play for a year, another demanding to leave to be nearer to his parents having just signed a four-year contract, and yet another exposed in the papers for sniffing cocaine? How many other businesses are there where the staff earn more than their managers, and where a seventeen-year-old boy can become a millionaire overnight?

There are others among the chairmen (and they know who they are) who are responsible for not taking the 20 per cent deal and not aligning themselves with the Premier League, which would have maintained a stronger relationship between the Premiership and the lower divisions. The break-up of the Football League, when the top 22 clubs formed the new Premiership and separated themselves from the original 92 clubs, was a bad day for the lower divisions, perhaps even worse than Bosman. The smaller clubs were still smarting from the break-up. It could happen again, with the Championship breaking away – and that, of course, would be a disaster for the smaller clubs. I can remember Douglas Craig, the chairman of York City, pontificating on how important it was that the smaller clubs had an equal vote, and that they should stand firm and not capitulate to the bullies at the larger clubs. It was like watching King Canute trying to hold back the tide! The lower divisions made a big mistake and should have stayed with the Premiership. It was the smaller clubs who broke up the league, not the other way round. How can you have Darlington with one vote and Arsenal with one vote? The smaller clubs were intransigent, believing the breakaway was a veiled threat and would not happen. Inevitably, it happened.

Fortunately, a wave of common sense then swept over the remaining divisions, and I was involved with the restructuring of the voting system. The previous arrangement meant that each division had a representative on the board, enabling Divisions Two and Three to outvote the larger clubs in Division One by two votes to one. It was this structure that forced the Premier League to break away in the first place. Had this format remained, the First Division would have been forced to follow suit. Things had to change, and they did. Three positions on the board were given to the First Division, two to the Second and one to the Third, with the chairman receiving the casting vote. A proposal by the First Division to split television revenue giving the First Division 80 per cent, the Second 12 per cent and the Third 8 per cent was carried by the board. In the Premiership, a lot of the money is distributed equally among the clubs; then they are guaranteed a minimum of three matches on television, which give the clubs involved £1.4 million while Arsenal, Manchester United and Chelsea may earn £10 million or more. Then there is the ladder payment for where you finish in the table, worth around £450,000 per place. The idea that the payments should be reversed, with the bottom clubs getting the most, as was suggested in some quarters, is absolute nonsense.

The Premier League has stood the test of time and is an amazing institution contributing millions to grass-roots football and good causes. Clubs have good grounds and big attendances week in, week out, while Italian football is now struggling with half-empty grounds and small income from their individual television rights. We can only look and avoid other people's mistakes. The European Commission was fearful that collective bargaining was unconstitutional, but they have come to the conclusion that it is in the best interests of all clubs, the fans and the viewing public at large. I must say that Premier League chief executive Richard Scudamore and the board have done an excellent job. I am a great admirer of both Richard and chairman David Richards who I believe will be with the Premier League for a long time to come. Their understanding of the clubs' requirements, their negotiations with the television companies and their dealings with the European Commission have been outstanding.

I have no doubt that the Premiership is the greatest football league in the world, setting the pace in style and communication. America have their big sports that take up the airwaves, but they are fighting against the tide as football sweeps in. They pay a pittance at the moment, but that will change because wherever you go around the world there are kids playing football, which is certainly not true of American football, ice hockey and basketball. Once the sport really gets going in the States – and it will – imagine what it will do for the world game.

CHAPTER THIRTY

THE WONDERFUL WORLD
OF FOOTBALL

Football to me in my early days was my whole life. From my place in poverty across the road in Green Street I could see this wonderful, wonderful world of football. As I've said, one of my great pleasures in those early days was sneaking into the Chicken Run, where the hardy Hammers fans stood, at half-time. I became mesmerised by it all. I recall seeing Stanley Matthews playing for Blackpool. I was less than ten yards away from this wizard, this star . . . fantastic. I then stood outside to try and get his autograph, looking through the railings, ignoring all the other players for an hour until he came out – and climbed straight into the coach. I was devastated.

Many years later he ended up back at his old club, Stoke City, where he'd played as a 50-year-old and where he was now serving as a life vice president. I was in the boardroom before a match against Stoke City in the old First Division talking to Peter Coates, the then chairman, when I was asked from behind, 'Can I get you a drink, chairman?'

I turned round, and there was Sir Stanley Matthews. Shaking his hand, I replied, 'No thank you, Sir Stanley, I'm fine, but would you mind signing my programme for my son?'

'No problem,' he replied. 'What's his name?'

'David,' I lied. I have no son! I just wanted the autograph for myself after all those years. I still have the programme to this day.

Then there was the equally legendary Tom Finney. I went over to him and confessed he was my boyhood hero, and we chatted. What a thrill. Another was the Lion of Vienna, Nat Lofthouse, of Bolton Wanderers. To me, Matthews, Finney and Lofthouse were true gods of the game, and all were charming, polite and communicative, humble in their greatness. I was in awe of them.

Going to each football club has broadened my horizons, and meeting the chairmen is a great experience. But I will not go where I am not wanted. I said that about West Ham when I gave up on them after putting in so much effort. The last straw was when a West Ham supporter abused David Sullivan in a restaurant during the period when we held shares in the club. It was different at Birmingham City, where we were treated with respect after we had quelled the initial suspicion of why David Sullivan and a couple of cockneys from the East End of London wanted to take over the Blues.

In the Premiership, I have only been treated badly by three people. One was Mohamed Al Fayed, the Fulham chairman, who invited me to lunch with him at Harrods. He treated me very well and we had a pleasant afternoon, but he left me unimpressed by not going to away matches with Fulham, and at Craven Cottage he segregates you in a separate room, arrives like royalty, shakes your hand and immediately leaves for his own private room. In my opinion that is not in the spirit of this amazing institution called the Premier League. I find it sad when chairmen do not adhere to the protocol. Respect for and the provision of hospitality to our guests in the boardroom at Birmingham City is fundamental to everything the club represents. David Dein at Arsenal sets the example. His guests are treated in exactly the way you would expect from a great football club, but it would not be the same were he not there. His charm and hospitality make the difference.

Ken Bates had a fierce reputation, but his hospitality remains unquestioned, whether it was at Chelsea or at his new club Leeds United.

I remember, in my second year in the Premier League, returning to our boardroom after completing my pre-match duties and seeing an unshaven man in jeans and not wearing a tie. I turned to Michael Wiseman, one of our directors who takes responsibility for welcoming guests and ensuring that protocol is maintained, and said, 'Michael, you know how important I consider standards to be in our boardroom, and we shouldn't compromise.'

'Yes, chairman,' he replied, puzzled.

'So, who allowed that man over there who is unshaven, wearing jeans and no tie into the boardroom?'

'Well, I did, chairman. I thought you'd make an exception.'

'No, Michael, I don't think we should. It's important we maintain standards. Anyway, who is he?'

'It's Roman Abramovic, chairman,' Michael replied, smiling.

Before Roman and his family arrived his security officers asked to survey our facilities. They required four of his bodyguards to be in attendance at all times during his stay. We agreed with their request but with one exception: we would not allow any bodyguards in the boardroom. However, after some negotiations and in an effort to accommodate our illustrious guest, we reached a compromise and allowed one member of the security team to accompany the family in the boardroom with three others remaining outside. After the match my brother Ralph was talking to Roman's wife, Irina, and her young son. When Ralph innocently asked the young boy where he went to school, Roman's bodyguard interjected telling him not to answer the question! Irina and her son just took it in their stride, leaving Ralph feeling extremely uncomfortable.

That day we treated Roman, who does not speak but understands English, his lovely wife Irina, their children and his entourage with our usual hospitality. However, this was not personally reciprocated on our return to the boardroom at Chelsea. Of course we were treated well by the charismatic Peter Kenyon and his lovely partner Louise, but where was Roman Abramovic? About half an hour after the end of the match he entered the boardroom with an aide who spoke to Peter for a few moments then left, ignoring the directors and owners of Birmingham City FC. It isn't difficult, Roman. Let me help you: instruct your interpreter to go over to the visiting directors and owners and say, 'Roman apologises for not being able to spend time with you but he has been extremely busy with corporate guests and he has asked me to thank you for coming and hopes, despite the fact that we gave your football team a thoroughly good thrashing, you enjoyed our hospitality and wishes you a safe journey home.' You could have done something similar when you visited Birmingham. Your interpreter could have come over and said, 'Roman has asked me to thank you for treating him, his family and entourage with warm hospitality and consideration and looks forward to seeing you when you next visit Chelsea.'

He must make a greater effort to integrate. He is not God, he just has a bit more money than the rest of us, with a substitutes' bench worth more than most of his rival's teams. When we played Chelsea at Stamford Bridge in December 2005 – they comfortably beat us 2–0 – they had a subs' bench costing £70 million while ours cost £1 million. He might not be the chairman, but he is the owner of the football club, and that is all the more reason to be welcoming and magnanimous towards visiting chairmen and directors. He should also be gracious when he visits other clubs, and, petty as it sounds, he should wear a tie when he visits away teams' boardrooms. He must remember that these clubs have over a hundred years of tradition that should be respected. If he was invited to the Palace – Buckingham, that is, not Crystal – I am sure he would wear a tie, so why not in the boardrooms around the country? Sir Bobby Charlton has more reason than most to be on a pedestal, but he is always charming and pleasant whenever we go to Old Trafford. Martin Edwards too, when he was chairman, was an absolute gentleman with charm and humour, despite his colourful reputation.

The hospitality of David Dein at Arsenal, Richard Murray at Charlton, Milan Mandaric at Portsmouth, Jeremy Peace at West Bromwich Albion, Terry Brown at West Ham, Doug Ellis at Aston Villa and many others is outstanding, providing me with special memories of people who go out of their way to be welcoming. Freddy Shepherd from Newcastle puts on probably the best lunch in the Premier League, served by the butler, Graham Peters. Despite the fact that he tried to steal my manager, I like Freddy very much. He is down-to-earth and forthright, as he displayed after we beat them 1–0 at St James's Park in August 2003. We were preparing to leave when Freddy asked me if I'd enjoyed the food and hospitality. I replied, 'Yes, Freddy, it was superb.' His response was, 'Good. You've got your three points, now f*** off!' I also recall going to White Hart Lane and being treated particularly well by one of their directors over some guests I had joining me. Spurs have a remarkable hospitality area spread over a huge space where their guests are looked after superbly. All Premier League clubs are different, with varying standards; some have huge boardrooms, like Bolton Wanderers, and others are small and friendly, like Everton. Sir Philip and Lady Carter at Goodison Park are always most courteous and welcoming. It gives the Premiership its dignity and style.

The third person to treat us badly we have met before – Simon Jordan, still embittered at losing Steve Bruce to us. He also arrived at Birmingham City without a tie, and our stewards explained the rule and offered him a tie to wear. Simon's response was, 'F*** off', and he went and sat with his friends in the directors' guest lounge. I know Simon was aware of the rule and was being antagonistic. However, under the circumstances, had I been there I would have made an exception and invited Simon into the boardroom. I regret the incident, but he had his revenge. That day, against the odds, Crystal Palace beat us 1–0 with a goal from Andrew Johnson, whom we'd sold to Crystal Palace as part of the deal to bring Clinton Morrison to St Andrews. The return match at Palace a few months later was no better. Simon was curt and unfriendly, clearly still carrying a chip on his shoulder. But again he had his revenge: Palace won comfortably with two goals from Andrew Johnson, both from the penalty spot.

I penned an article just before this match in the local Crystal Palace newspaper, the *Croydon Advertiser*, saying how lucky Simon was that we took Steve Bruce as he now had in exchange substantial financial compensation for Steve, a fantastic manager in Iain Dowie, millions for Clinton Morrison, Andrew Johnson, who is now an England international and is reported to be worth at least £6 million, and £20 million in extra income for returning to the Premier League – all arguably because we took Steve Bruce from Crystal Palace! So Simon, as I said before, forgive and forget, move on, life's too short.

CHAPTER THIRTY-ONE

THE MOST CONTROVERSIAL
MAN IN FOOTBALL

Ken Bates, former chairman of Chelsea and now chairman and major shareholder at Leeds United, is a man who seems to bring out the passion in everyone. He is either loved or hated, with no half measures. I can recall my first visit to Stamford Bridge and coming face to face with him, someone I had held in high regard for many years, a colossus in his sphere as chairman of a top football club who to me was as interesting as managers and players are to the fans. I wanted to see these chairmen in action, how they operated and how they coped. His enthusiasm and blunt talking attracted me, and I readily confess I am a fan of this larger-than-life character. He seems to have the ability of an India rubber man to work his way out of difficult positions in which others would just throw up their hands in despair.

I was thrilled in the summer of 2002 as I loaded my helicopter with my briefcase and overnight bag for a two-day stay among football's elite at Stapleford Park, a beautiful hotel in the rolling Leicestershire countryside. All of a sudden I was chairman of a Premiership club of some size and stature. I was due at my first Premiership meeting, scheduled for 7 June, and I was to arrive early the evening before for dinner with Ken Bates. As I landed my helicopter in the grounds of Stapleford Park, I felt apprehensive but excited.

At dinner I met, for the first time, the very affable David Richards, chairman of the Premier League, and chief executive Richard Scudamore, who I had met previously when he was the chief executive of the Football League. I remember when, after handing in his resignation to the Football

League, a number of chairmen expressed their annoyance to Richard for leaving them for the Premiership. Richard silenced the dissenters brilliantly by saying, 'I'm only doing what every chairman in this room dreams of every day – promotion to the Premier League.' I have always held Richard in the highest regard, from the first day I saw him give his inaugural presentation to the chairmen of the Football League. I found him very impressive. It was indeed a sad day for the Football League when he left to join the Premier League. Among others joining us for dinner was Roz Donnelly, executive assistant to the board, Brian Phillpotts, director of FAPL Enterprises, Mike Foster, the company secretary, and one other person to whom I had been introduced but didn't know and couldn't place.

Before dinner, Ken Bates ordered a number of bottles of his favourite wine, Pouilly-Fuissé, a rich white Burgundy which I have to say was delicious. Ken, for all his fearsome reputation, made me very welcome, insisting I sit next to him. However, he is a demanding character. He always insists, for instance, that his Pouilly-Fuissé is available, often having his secretary telephone in advance to ensure there is sufficient in stock.

It was an enthralling evening to a newcomer like me. As the wine flowed, so did the stories, particularly from Ken who sat at the head of the table like the chairman of the board in the hotel's magnificent private dining room. The food was scrumptious, and towards the end of the evening I was asked about the play-off final against Norwich at the Millennium Stadium a few weeks earlier. I explained to the assembled company that it was a fantastic day, one of the most thrilling of my life, and that after the game I went on to the pitch to congratulate the players and the manager and to enjoy the celebrations. I was then taken to the press room, and one of the first questions was, 'Is Steve Bruce the next Alex Ferguson?' I have to say that I was on a bit of a high at the time and feeling mischievous. 'I hope not!' I replied to the stunned reporters. What? I could hear them thinking. Are you mad? 'Yes,' I added, 'I hope Steve is going to be as successful as Alex, but I would be disappointed if he became as belligerent, charmless and arrogant, never to see an incident but to have X-ray eyes when it suits him. The problem with Alex,' I continued, warming to my theme, 'is that he is not magnanimous in victory and he's not gracious in defeat.' This is how millions of us see him on television every week.

Most of the guests found this story amusing and were grinning hugely, and I was soon to find out why. Ken Bates was filling my glass with more Pouilly-Fuissé when a voice from the other end of the table, the man I didn't recognise, said, 'David, have you ever met Sir Alex personally?' With a strong emphasis on the 'sir'.

'No,' I replied sheepishly.

'Well, let me tell you I know him very well, and I can assure you he is the opposite to all of the things you have accused him of.'

'Oh my God!' I thought to myself. 'Who is this man?' I turned to Ken and whispered, 'Who have I upset? Ken, what's his name?'

'Maurice,' came the simple reply.

'Maurice,' I said, 'I assure you I meant no offence. It was a light-hearted response to a question I quite frankly found amusing. It was never meant to be taken seriously.'

The following morning, while I was sitting in the lounge having coffee with Karren Brady, Maurice walked into the room and joined Martin Edwards, the then chairman and major shareholder of Manchester United. I asked Karren who the chap was.

'Oh, that's Maurice Watkins, a solicitor and a shareholder of Manchester United and a very influential man at Old Trafford,' she replied immediately.

This was my introduction to the Premier League, dropping a major faux pas. But at least I meant it, and the story was supposed to explain the fact that my manager did have charm and grace and I could see him as a future England manager with all the necessary qualities that are so important in football today. You have to be an ambassador, not the type who slams the door in the face of the media, because they are your link with your fans. Every club, through its manager, must have a rapport with its supporters. It always rebounds on the angry manager, because if the press cannot speak to him they will look elsewhere for stories, especially when it is a club the size of United, and sports editors demand a daily story from the Reds. Too often the anger leads to the manager not facing the press or sending a member of his coaching staff to the after-match press conference, which leaves the fans feeling cheated. I would say to Sir Alex, 'Don't take everything so seriously. Take criticism with a smile and move on. After all, you are one of the greatest and most successful managers of all time.'

Manchester United regularly beat us, and we rarely score a goal against them. I have always spoken to Sir Alex and shaken hands after games; in return I have received a grunt or two. After one game against United I went into Steve Bruce's room, next door to the dressing room, as I usually do on match days. In there on this occasion was Sir Alex, and once again I went over and congratulated him on a magnificent victory. I was given another handshake and another grunt as I tried to engage him in conversation, only to find he was looking over my shoulder at his interview on the television. He was, once again, charmless and rude, and I guessed he was ignoring me as a result of the comments I had made two years earlier. But come on, this isn't life-threatening. He'd had his revenge several times on the pitch, but still he could not be bothered to be civil. I made my excuses and left. There was no way I was going to stay in the room with him; I even sent someone back in to get my coat rather than collect it myself.

The story, however, has a happy ending. Either Sir Alex is mellowing in his latter years or he has decided I am not such a bad chap after all. We had a 30-minute conversation at Barry Fry's testimonial match when Sir Alex kindly took a team to Peterborough and won 6–0. I saw the other side of this stern Glaswegian, and I must say I liked it, as I did the next time we met when again he was charm personified. The words 'water under the bridge' spring to mind. I believe there are two Sir Alex Fergusons: the one we see being interviewed after a match – curt, charmless, businesslike and sometimes rude, but also a man under great pressure with huge responsibilities – and the one outside the pressure of competitive football, the one I met in a relaxed atmosphere at Barry Fry's testimonial, who is charming, approachable and interesting, with a great sense of humour. I have met him a number of times since the testimonial, and I must say he has been exactly the same. And more recently, at Old Trafford after beating us 3–0 with two goals from Ryan Giggs and one from Wayne Rooney, Sir Alex invited me along with Steve Bruce to his private room after the match for drinks. I congratulated him on his victory against us and he reciprocated by congratulating me on David Junior's victory in Dubai the previous day. He was charming, humorous and told us a number of great stories … of which I have been sworn to secrecy! Sorry, Sir Alex, for judging you on TV appearances. It was a pleasure meeting the real you.

I suppose it is difficult because he spends his life surrounded by acolytes, smarming around him and treating him like a god. There are many successful managers who think they can walk on water, and who eventually get themselves very, very wet. Some say Brian Clough was that sort of personality, but when I met him I found him to be a man with considerable humility, charm and humour. He didn't see himself as someone who could walk on water any more, although there was clearly a time when he did. He was making a speech at a dinner, and he made time to come over and talk to me. We spent some time chatting and I enjoyed his company immensely. We made arrangements to have lunch together, but sadly, before that could happen he became ill, and later died. A great loss.

The day after the contentious dinner at Stapleford Park, there was a roll-call of the Premiership clubs. It was the most wonderful 'Here' I've ever said. It took me back to my days at Creden Road School when the register was called out by Mrs Green, but what a difference! How the years had changed the circumstances! Here I was now with all these remarkable chairmen and important people in the world's biggest sport. Just recently a local newspaper asked me who I would most like to invite to dinner, living or dead. My choices were Margaret Thatcher, who restored Britain's pride; Charles Lindbergh, because of my huge interest in flying; Isambard Kingdom Brunel, who, apart from being a great British engineer, simply had the most wonderful name ever (just imagine introducing him); and Mrs Green, who said to me after I had failed my eleven-plus, 'Gold, you will never amount to anything!' Bless her heart, she is long gone, but I would have loved to show her, in the nicest way, how wrong she was. On the day, Ken Bates made sure I was looked after. Whether he was offering a helping hand to a new boy or whether it was because we both came from similar backgrounds, I do not know.

The following year, Birmingham City Football Club were invited to a tournament in Kuala Lumpur to play against the Malaysian national side, Newcastle United and Chelsea. While we were there, Ken, his fiancée Suzanne, and Lesley and I were invited by the Prince to lunch (after Chelsea had won the tournament). When the Prince was served the waiters were on their knees, and we were given a brief lesson on the protocols to be observed. The Prince, fortunately, was a charming man, and we exchanged the usual banalities, asking him if he played polo, to which he replied he did, with Prince Charles and other members of royalty and aristocracy from around the globe. He also said he was looking forward to becoming king. He then started to relate a story as we sat listening, holding him in high regard and being careful not to interrupt. Only Ken could do so, and sure enough he turned to the Prince mid-story and asked him, 'Are we going to chat all day or are we going to eat?' We were stunned. Lesley and I looked at each other, shaking our heads in amazement. Ken was treating the Prince in the same way he treated the top people in football; only he could do it and get away with it. What is more, the Prince took it in his stride: he finished his story before signalling for a waiter to start serving. Ken Bates gets away with murder all the time.

The controversial and larger-than-life Freddy Shepherd was also on the trip, but he had to turn down the invitation to lunch with the Prince because he had to leave that same morning for Las Vegas, where he was exploring the possibility of convincing a big casino company to build a casino at St James's Park. It was a pity Freddy could not be with us as it would have made a wonderful table with the two most outspoken, almost brash chairmen in football. I have a great affinity with both of them, especially Ken, who comes from an East End background while Freddy came from a northern background. With the Prince in the middle it would have been fun listening to these two chairmen swapping stories and insults. There would have been these two great icons of the game, the outspoken Bates and the bluff Shepherd, in this serene, almost surreal atmosphere; the future king of Malaysia with his charm, poise and posture sitting between two rough diamonds. It was an amusing enough experience to watch Ken in action; to have had the two of them would have been hugely entertaining. After the lunch I telephoned my old school chum Charlie Cross and told him the entire story. David Gold having dinner with the future king of Malaysia – and, of course, Ken Bates. I think he was more impressed with the fact that I'd dined with Ken. During the lunch, Ken's fiancée Suzanne had told the Prince how much she loved his horses. It is a tradition over there that if you say you like something they will more often than not give it to you. Sure enough, the next morning the Prince presented her with two horses. Lesley joked to me about how much she loved the ring on his finger, and was close to telling him. We would never have got it through customs!

Ken is already being missed in the Premiership for his character and the discussions he provokes. A lot of people inside and outside the game don't like him because of his outspokenness, some say rudeness, but there are lots who miss him for the many good things he offered. I personally cannot wait for Ken to return to the Premier League. I just hope I'm still there when he does. And as I said, I'm grateful to him for making me feel welcome at my first ever chairmen's meeting that summer of 2002, even though the dinner was not a good start.

After coffee the next day, Richard Scudamore and David Richards invited me, along with the chairmen of the other two promoted clubs, Manchester City (David Bernstein) and West Bromwich Albion (Jeremy Peace), to a short welcoming ceremony during which we were each handed our framed copy of a single Premiership share. Later on that afternoon one of the items on the agenda was a proposal to increase the parachute payments of relegated clubs in the future. At that time, relegated clubs received 50 per cent of the television revenue, amounting to approximately £4.5 million per year for two years. The reason behind this proposal to increase the payments was that relegated clubs were finding it difficult, if not impossible, to meet contractual commitments, particularly to players, a fact borne out by the majority of ex-Premiership football clubs going into administration. But there was some confusion as to whether this proposal to increase the parachute payments could be voted on without changing the founders' agreement, which is rather like a constitution.

David Richards asked for a show of hands to vote for a change to the founders' agreement. Fourteen votes were required to change it. Now of course I was very much in favour of increasing the parachute payments, as I was potentially a future relegated club. You can imagine how I felt when, at my first vote at my first chairmen's meeting, I found myself the only chairman in the room with my hand up. The tables are laid out in a circle, with the chairmen seated in alphabetical order of club, each accompanied by their chief executive or managing director – a total of 40 people, plus Dave Richards, Richard Scudamore and Mike Foster, making 43 people. Imagine the embarrassment of being the only person in such a room with his hand held aloft. Dave Richards then asked for 'those against' – zero; and 'abstentions' – zero. Looking towards me, David then announced that the proposal to change the founders' agreement had failed. Not a good start! I later discovered that the chairmen of long-established Premiership clubs fiercely protect the founders' agreement, based upon the fact that it had served the clubs well and had stood the test of time. Well, that was their opinion, and had it stood the test of time of half a century instead of eleven years I would probably have agreed with them.

After further discussion, it was decided that a vote could be taken on whether we agreed in principle to an increase in the parachute payments, without changing the founders' agreement (too late to save me the embarrassment of being the only chairman ever to vote for a change to the founders' agreement!). 'All those in favour of increasing the parachute payments in principle,' said David Richards. I raised my hand again. Shock, horror, my hand is once more the only one held aloft. I am completely on my own for the second time. 'It can't be,' I thought. 'This is madness!' I looked across the room, and to my relief the chairman of West Bromwich Albion slowly raised his hand, and from the corner of my eye I saw Bolton chairman Phil Gartside's hand go up as well. At least I was no longer isolated, but we needed fourteen votes to carry the proposal.

I could understand why the mighty clubs like Arsenal, Manchester United, Liverpool, Chelsea, Leeds and Newcastle didn't vote for the proposal; after all, they could never be relegated, could they? But what about Blackburn Rovers, without Jack Walker's money? And Middlesbrough – what would they do without the financial support of Steve Gibson? What would happen to Fulham without Mohammed Al Fayed's cash? Then there were Everton and Manchester City with their huge debts. Did Sunderland and West Ham believe, like Leeds, that they could never be relegated? At least I tried.

It would cost every club less than £700,000 of their TV income to make a full parachute payment to the relegated clubs in the first year at a total cost of £13.5 million, which would give the relegated clubs £9 million in the first year instead of £4.5 million. However, this vote was based only on the *principle* of increasing the parachute payments, so basically seventeen Premiership clubs were saying, 'Not an extra penny to the relegated clubs!' I can still see the disinterested face of Peter Ridsdale of Leeds, who was clearly finding the entire proceedings a bore. What an irony that two of the three clubs relegated at the end of that 2002/03 season, West Ham and Sunderland, were so sure of not being relegated that they did not vote for increasing the parachute payments. And of course the following year, 2004, the mighty Leeds went down with debts exceeding £80 million. How the fans at Leeds must wish that Peter Ridsdale and the new chairman Ken Bates had lobbied that day for an increase in the parachute payments. They will never know what might have been had they received an extra few million pounds in their first year in the then First Division.

Those Premier League meetings were nerve-racking affairs for me early on. From time to time David Richards or Richard Scudamore would ask the chairmen their opinion on some topic, in alphabetical order, starting with David Dein of Arsenal and Doug Ellis of Aston Villa, both eloquent, knowledgeable speakers and both vastly experienced in the machinations of football at this level. And then came me with my experience of the Premiership totalling a few days. How I wish the questioning had started at the other end of the alphabet, giving me an opportunity to assess the question and the answers. Sadly that was not the case, and my first address to the gentlemen of the Premiership was pathetic. 'I think David Dein and Doug Ellis have covered the issue,' I said, 'and it only remains for me to say that Birmingham City endorse their opinions.' To this day I still cannot remember the question. I was still smarting from the vote earlier on, after all.

Two months later, another chairmen's meeting was called following UEFA's recommendation for a January transfer window. The chairmen debated the pros and cons for some time before a vote was called. Again, fourteen votes were needed for the motion to be carried. I had been considering the issue for some weeks and felt this new rule would not be in the best interests of Birmingham City, or indeed any smaller club working within a budget with a small squad, in particular those recently promoted, and especially those promoted through the play-offs, as we had been. It was not until the Sunday evening of 12 May that we had been sure of our Premiership place, leaving only three months to prepare for the challenge ahead in the toughest league in the world. I thought to myself, 'What if we had a serious run of injuries in the first half of the season? We would have to wait until January to bring in replacements.' Even worse would have been a run of injuries in February, which would mean having to wait until the end of the season. Too late for some clubs.

Listening to the various opinions, and the fact that UEFA were going to impose the ruling on us, eventually left me unsure as to which way to vote. A show of hands was called for, and this time I waited for a few seconds before raising my hand to be sure I wasn't the only one going against the motion. The count was taken: thirteen for the proposal and eight against, including me. 'That can't be right,' remarked David Richards. 'We have miscounted. Can we start again?' There is no doubt that had they got the count correct (it was 13–7) the vote for the January transfer window would not have been carried. But between the original vote and the recount, I was doing some thinking, especially about the benefit to the club's board of directors, who would have four months without the pressure to buy players once the summer session had closed, and after the window at the end of January had closed the pressure would be off again. I was still unsure what was best for us, but I decided in the confusion to change my vote. When Dave Richards called for a second show of hands, my vote in favour increased the tally to the required fourteen and the proposal, recommended by the Board of the Premier League, was carried. I comforted myself with the fact that UEFA were going to pursue it anyway. All I would have achieved with a vote against was a delay.

On the Thursday before our match at Upton Park early in October, which I was looking forward to for all the usual reasons, I was in Steve Bruce's office. We were sitting one point above the relegation zone with eight points from eight games. One point per game throughout the season means a total of 38 points and a very fair chance of being relegated. Steve turned to me and said, 'We aren't good enough! Grainger is injured and out for the remainder of the season. I have Fagan, a nineteen-year-old, and Carter, an eighteen-year-old, on the bench. To be honest, chairman, we have too many First Division players in the squad and not enough quality, and there is nothing I can do until the January window opens. Chairman, this January window is a bloody nightmare!'

I couldn't bring myself to tell him that I, single-handedly, had brought it about.

'Yes, most unfortunate, Steve,' I said sheepishly.

CHAPTER THIRTY-TWO

NEW VISION, NEW STADIUM

We have a vision at Birmingham City Football Club, and it centres on a derelict 60-acre area just a mile away from St Andrews that is known as the Birmingham Wheels, which is surrounded by the highest unemployment rates (over 20%) in the country. The golden opportunity lies in the fact that the land is council-owned. It brings them no financial income and is surrounded by deprivation – which, of course, worsens with every passing day. It would cost the council £55 million to clear this contaminated site which is currently a health and safety hazard.

Birmingham City Football Club are desperate to move ahead and have a stadium to compete with the large clubs in the country. Look at Newcastle United, a 55,000 sell-out against Birmingham City, a club nearing the foot of the table; Manchester United with their ever-increasing number of seats; Arsenal with their new stadium – the list goes on. When you have a capacity of less than 30,000 you have to maximise the income in terms of ticket prices and everything else we do so that we can stay in the mix. With double the attendance we could reduce prices for certain matches and still come out on top with a greater income. People are talking about the cost of seating at the ground, but we want to be competing with those big clubs like Chelsea, Arsenal and Manchester United. We want to take that next step. I believe it is also an opportunity for the council to take a step forward.

When I was taking my eleven-plus at school, one of the few questions I could answer was this: what is the second city in England? I knew it was Birmingham because my uncle had told me, with pride, when he took me and Ralph to watch the Blues play in the FA Cup. I have become an adopted Brummie. I love the vibrant city and its people, but it does keep coming second. It was second when it came to a national stadium; it was second when it came to the European Championships; it was second to Glasgow for City of Culture. We are in danger of becoming the second city for all the wrong reasons. But here, I think, is an opportunity to lead the way. Let's build the City of Birmingham Stadium, where we would be the tenant, and it would be used for other sporting and cultural events as well. It would also allow Birmingham to host the Commonwealth Games in the future. It would be the first stadium in Europe with a fully retractable roof and a retractable pitch, so that grass can be taken outdoors for it to grow naturally, and to allow the arena to be used for concerts, events and shows with seating. We could even stage indoor cricket. It is a totally unique concept.

The city of Birmingham would benefit. Some 2,500 new homes will be developed on the site alongside other sporting facilities, entertainment centres, a casino and a 250-bedroom hotel. It would guarantee 6,000 jobs to start with, 3,500 of them ongoing after completion of the development, and it would regenerate an area of massive unemployment and rid the council of a piece of land that is a menace. It is a once-in-a-lifetime opportunity. The casino people are very excited and they are ready with the funding for the stadium. Blues are a willing tenant. All it needs now is for the council to grasp the nettle. It's not even a particularly nasty nettle as it would not cost the taxpayer a penny. All they need to say is, 'It's fantastic,' and give it the green light. I am convinced it's a compelling argument and I'm optimistic they will reach the right conclusion. The more people I speak to, the more they see the potential of the project and the keener they become.

It will be fantastic for the city, the football club and the wider community: it's only just down the road, a little closer to our pals from West Bromwich Albion and Aston Villa.

The partnership would be between Las Vegas Sands, who have built fantastic entertainment centres and hotels around the world, and Birmingham City Council. It would touch everybody, and the benefits are enormous. It would be easy to access too, as the train runs alongside the site. It would be just one stop from Snow Hill station, one of the main railway stations in the centre of Birmingham.

I'm a great believer that a club has to have a heart and soul. Look at towns like Swindon, Wigan and Reading, where my friend John Madejski and Steve Coppell have done such a fantastic job. Most people there would acknowledge the football club as being the living, beating heart of the community. Even in big cities like Newcastle and Manchester, the football clubs are their heart and soul. Aston Villa will be upset when I say this, but we carry the name of a great city; Aston Villa are the heart of Aston, a district between Erdington and the city centre, while West Bromwich Albion straddles the borders of Birmingham and West Bromwich.

If Birmingham City is the heart of Birmingham, then my predecessor Jack Wiseman was the heart of the football club. Jack is a wonderful man who did so much for the club over many, many years, following in the footsteps of his father. I hold Jack in the highest regard, and I feel extremely disappointed that he was never rewarded with an honour from the Queen. If Mick Jagger can get a knighthood for his music, surely someone who saved a football club, a very important public commodity, deserves recognition? I like the sound of 'Sir Jack', and I know what he would say in response: 'Swingin'!' Which, of course, is his famous catchphrase. The Blues were genuinely teetering on the brink and could have disappeared for ever but for Jack. He was chairman back in January 1993, when he took the helm after the crash of the Kumar brothers. He served the Football Association as faithfully as he served Birmingham City. He travelled around the world with the England team and was known to everyone by his 'Swingin'' greeting. Look what happened to Brighton and Hove Albion, left homeless and struggling, a club that had reached the FA Cup final, where they drew with mighty Manchester United before bad fortune overtook them. Thank goodness the government has at last seen sense and approved the site for their new stadium.

Jack kept Birmingham City alive when no-one else would, and thanks to him we can look to the future.

St Andrews is perfectly placed for development, but the only way they will cover the sacred turf is if Birmingham City Council support us in our vision to build a super stadium for the city at the Birmingham Wheels site. Now we need the support of the media, the fans and the people of Birmingham if the Blues are to grow and develop into a super-club. It is, I repeat, a once-in-a-lifetime opportunity.

CHAPTER THIRTY-THREE

FRIENDS AND ENEMIES

Football is a wonderful gateway to meeting all manner of people, from the hundreds of fans I have met, some of whom I know by name, to famous managers and chairmen, pop stars, tycoons, showbiz personalities, politicians and all kinds of celebrities. One of the nicest, warmest people football introduced me to was the former pop star, actor and businessman Adam Faith, who I met at Birmingham City when he came up for a game as someone's guest. We chatted for a while, and discovered that we had much in common.

One of the first things we discovered was that we were neighbours in Surrey. He told me he often had lunch in the Rendezvous in Westerham, a restaurant I used myself. Lesley and I arranged to have Sunday lunch there with Adam the next day, and we met at two p.m., after the lunchtime crowd had dispersed. It was a lovely day and we sat outside, enjoying the sunshine and finishing our meal some four hours later after a long and fascinating discussion. People came up to us as they passed by, asking for Adam's autograph, or just having a little chat. He had time for everybody who stopped. I have been with some so-called rich and famous people who are affronted by such a show of friendship and admiration and openly show their distaste. Adam was quite the opposite. Someone else very similar to Adam is my friend Jasper Carrott, Birmingham's favourite son, also a man who will find time for anyone. I quickly grew to be very fond of Adam; he was a charming person to be with at any time. Gradually we became firm friends, and he would come to my house for dinner or we would meet up at the Rendezvous.

Despite his fame, Adam was quite insecure in his way. He would sometimes call me at two in the morning. I would remind him of the time, and he would answer, 'Sorry, cock, I know, but I needed to have a chat because I'm a bit down.' I would talk to him for up to an hour, and afterwards he would say, 'Thanks, cock, I feel better now. You're pure Gold! Speak to you soon.' And he was gone. I remember one lunch at the Rendezvous when he told me a story about having made a fortune on the stock market and then a year later losing it all. He wasn't bitter, just philosophical. A couple of hours later he called for the bill, which I snatched from his hand, saying to him, 'Sorry, Adam, I can't let a man who has just lost £23 million on the stock market pay for lunch.' We both laughed.

I felt cheated when Adam was taken from us at the age of 62. Real friends come along rarely, and a new friend later in life is unusual indeed. When he came into my life, I struggled to name six or seven genuine friends, as opposed to acquaintances. I enjoyed his stories about the pop and business world; he was just a joy to be with. But sadly, just when I realised there was someone very special in my life, he died. I knew him for only a couple of years, and we enjoyed a close relationship for only a couple of months. It hit me hard because I had lost another great friend, David Tearle, only a year earlier. It was as though Adam had been sent along to take his place.

He was a remarkable man with a series of different careers spread over five decades, starting in the fifties when he rose from messenger to film editor. He was a huge pop star in the sixties, then he went into TV acting, management of other artists and record producing in the seventies, and he was a financial guru and journalist in the eighties. He re-emerged as a TV star in the nineties and throughout was involved in film and stage ventures, including serious dramas. Not bad for a lad named Terry Nelhams, born in Shepherd's Bush. His first number one hit was 'What Do You Want' in December 1959. He had a string of them after that and was as famous as Cliff Richard and Billy Fury until the Beatles and the Liverpool sound came along. He died of a heart attack while on the road with a play in the early hours of Saturday, 8 March 2003. I had spoken to Adam only the day before to arrange Sunday lunch at the Rendezvous. The following morning I was sitting with Lesley having breakfast and reminding her that we were having lunch with Adam the next day when it was announced on the radio that the actor and singer Adam Faith had died. We were devastated.

He died in the arms of his 22-year-old lover Tanya Arpino. Adam had just finished a stage show and had returned to his hotel room, where Tanya was waiting for him. Tanya, a waitress, said, 'It was like being in a horror movie. Adam was rushed through the hotel lobby and put into an ambulance. The paramedic said to me, "Don't worry, your dad will be all right." It was a nightmare: one minute he was fine, the next minute he was fighting for his life.' She continued, 'I was in this hospital room watching as they tried to save Adam, giving him a heart massage. I can't explain what it was like seeing the person you love die in front of you.' Tanya says Adam's wife, Jacky, was furious about the affair and banned her from attending Adam's funeral. Adam loved the ladies; he never missed an opportunity to flirt with them. He acted more like an eighteen-year-old than a man in his sixties. I lost count of the number of times he joked with me, 'Cock, when my time comes, I want it to be in bed making love.' Well, Adam got his wish.

Another friend is our old manager Barry Fry, and I don't want to see the same thing happen to him! He also suffers from heart problems, and even now is undergoing various tests, but if he does the right things and takes the right pills maybe he can go on until he's 90. I hope so.

Then, as I mentioned, there are the other 'superstar' personalities who find they cannot handle it because of their own self-importance. The film director Michael Winner falls firmly into this category. He is so full of himself, he would probably agree. His name came up during conversation over dinner one evening with Lesley, world-renowned chef Delia Smith and her charming husband Mike, and two of their American friends, Pamela and Colt, at the River Café in London. It was a kind of reunion, as Lesley and I had met Pamela while holidaying in an exclusive game park in South Africa. Remarkably, we discovered we were both friends of Delia and Mike. After pre-dinner drinks we were escorted to the best table in the restaurant where we ordered dinner. Then, who should arrive but Michael Winner, accompanied by two attractive ladies. 'It's Michael Winner,' I proclaimed.

Three years earlier, Lesley and I were planning a holiday in Morocco when Lesley told me she had read an article by Michael Winner that praised highly a Moroccan restaurant called Le Tobsil in Marrakesh. On arriving at our hotel, La Mamounia, I immediately booked the restaurant for 8.30 p.m. and arranged for a car to take us there. That evening, walking through reception, I was struck by how lovely Lesley looked, absolutely stunning in a beautiful evening dress, and wearing her new diamond watch which I had bought for her birthday. I must confess I looked quite dapper myself. We climbed into the chauffeur-driven car and set off for the restaurant through the old town of Marrakesh, drinking up the exotic atmosphere as we went. Before long we turned off into an even older part of the town. The narrow backstreets were swarming with Moroccans. The driver got out of the car, opened the door for Lesley, we stood on the side of the road, and the driver drove off. We felt extremely uncomfortable and fretful, but then a man with a lantern in one hand and a staff in the other, dressed in what looked like pyjamas, came up to me and said, 'Mr Gold?'

'Yes,' I replied.

'Follow me,' he said, and he proceeded to walk down a very dark and dingy alleyway with a number of beggars sitting against the wall. It was extremely intimidating. The alleyway twisted and turned, becoming gloomier and gloomier. It was littered with stray cats and barking dogs, and as the cobbled alleyway became narrower we could see a number of frightening-looking characters standing in dark doorways. Lesley, fearing for her safety, removed her new diamond watch and slipped it into my pocket. She subsequently confessed she was terrified. I was thinking, 'Michael Winner, I'll never forgive you.'

But then the man we were following stopped in front of two huge doors and banged on them very loudly with his wooden staff. A grille on the door opened, a face appeared, a few words of Arabic were exchanged, and the grille was slammed shut. I was still wondering what to expect when the double doors swung open to reveal the most stunning entrance to a courtyard complete with fountains, palm trees, beautiful lighting and soft music playing in the background. The food was magnificent and the service exquisite. It was a truly memorable evening. 'Michael Winner,' I thought, 'all is forgiven!'

Some months later Lesley and I went to Venice for a long weekend and arrived at the island hotel Cipriani. We were walking together in the gardens with our dear friends David and Karin Tearle when I spotted Michael Winner coming the other way with his then girlfriend Georgina Hristova. Making eye contact with him, I extended my hand, which he reluctantly grasped. 'Michael, do you have a moment?' I asked. 'My name is David Gold, and this is my lovely Lesley.' I wanted to share with Michael our adventure in Marrakesh, but within seconds I realised I had made a mistake. He was dismissive and rude. I removed my hand from his quickly as he made it abundantly clear he didn't wish to be engaged in conversation. Bizarrely, I thanked him and bade him goodnight. I disliked him all the more for ignoring my Lesley. I felt sorry for her, as indeed I did for Michael's girlfriend, who looked positively uncomfortable. We met Michael Winner and his girlfriend a number of times over the weekend while travelling on the small eight-seater boat that transported us to and from the island hotel. At no time did he sit with the rest of us in the cabin; he just stood outside in his arrogance. Despite this, I still read his column in the *News of the World*, and I love his 'calm down, dear' car insurance commercials.

To my surprise, that evening in the River Café, Delia Smith said she had a similar story about this pompous man, which she proceeded to tell, followed by her husband with yet another Michael Winner story. Finally, unbelievably, Pamela surprised us all with her own Winner story. Surely this makes Michael Winner universally the rudest man ever.

'Calm down dear, Michael, it's only the truth!'

We went on to have a most wonderful evening with warm and charming friends. Thankfully, Michael was not on our table but two tables away.

CHAPTER THIRTY-FOUR

MY BEAUTIFUL LADIES

I have always had the good fortune of being able to share the successes as well as the tragedies in my life with people like my lovely Lesley, my mother and my two daughters.

When I was in Malaysia a few years ago I accepted an invitation from Birmingham City fans to attend, as guest of honour, a farewell dinner party at their hotel in Kuala Lumpur. The club had just enjoyed a successful end-of-season tournament: they played well against Newcastle, but lost 2–1, and beat the national side 4–0. When I arrived at the hotel I was asked to pose for pictures and sign autographs even before I had crossed the foyer. Lesley said she could see I was busy; it might be best if she went back to our hotel. She knew from experience what happens when the fans monopolise you, talking football, a supporter with other supporters. But I told her, 'Lesley, you can't go because it's no fun for me without you.' It was exactly what I had told my brother when we went into business, and then into football. It is so much better to have someone with whom you can share your joys. I'll never forget what my friend David Tearle told me, how lucky I was because I was able to share everything with Ralph. It was the one thing he regretted, because he had no one to share his triumphs and setbacks with.

I am a lucky man to have four such fantastic women in my life. Jacqueline is well documented here and elsewhere, but I love her and Vanessa absolutely equally, and I cherish them both, although in different ways. Vanessa has been a great joy to me, full of fun and mischief. She recently married Nick, her soulmate; you can see the two of them are so content together. It gives me a huge amount of pleasure to see her so happily married, with a nice house and roses around the front

240

door. It is terrific for her and for me, and we remain great pals. She is also involved in the business, and just as Ralph and I were best friends, Vanessa and Jacqueline are very close. That bodes well for the family business. Ralph also has his son Bradley in the business; they work together and he guides and promotes him, while I do the same with my girls. We are, of course, involved in the Ann Summers and Knickerbox businesses, while Ralph and Bradley are in the development and property side of the business where we have a large portfolio. Bradley is also a director of Birmingham City Football Club, Broglia Press, Gold Air International and Gold Group Properties, and he is well respected within the company.

Vanessa was a tomboy as a child, and to this day is a fun-loving lady who doesn't take herself too seriously and is blessed with a great personality. Both my girls have lovable dispositions, but both remain very different, very much their own person. Vanessa is a little more reticent where publicity is concerned compared with Jacqueline. I guess Vanessa is very much like the Gold brothers were all those years ago, happy in her life, happy in her job and avoids the limelight. When it becomes a job and you have to do it, then you can grow to like it, as both Jacky and I have done. When you are comfortable with the media, there are parts of it you can enjoy. That is certainly true of Jacqueline, who wants to sell her products and promote the business. I can sit with Birmingham journalists like Colin Tatum, Graham Hill and Tom Ross, our local broadcaster, and enjoy just having a chat about football, regardless of the interview. I am genuinely interested in their opinions, and interviews often turn out to be two-way discussions. We talk about players, fans and the rest, and it is all immensely enjoyable, even though it means I am still working at nine o'clock at night. Vanessa, however, will always have time, despite having a passion for the business and contributing fully as a Director of Ann Summers and Knickerbox. She has time for Nick and the many other things that dominate her life. Different people, different styles.

Vanessa, Jacqueline and I make time for dinner every week, just the three of us. We have always found the time to be together. I am happy to say that it is orchestrated as much by them as it is by me. If we miss a week because, say, the two girls are on holiday, it is in my diary for the very next week, sometimes in a restaurant, sometimes at home, maybe at Vanessa's, or with Jacky at her place. Occasionally, though, we will break our golden rule and invite partners to be present, maybe when we order a takeaway and watch the football together on television.

Lesley is the lady I wish I had met when I was sixteen. She is my soulmate, my lover. Every Wednesday after work, Ralph and I, along with two friends, used to play tennis at my house. After the match we would go to the Las Fuentes Tapas bar in Purley. We were often joined by Janet, the wife of one of my friends. It was noisy but a great place to have a drink and a plate of tapas as an appetiser before going into the restaurant. Everyone knew I was single, and one evening Janet said she was in town with a friend the following week and would it be all right if she brought her along afterwards. There was no doubt in my mind it was a set-up, especially when Janet added, 'You would love to meet her!' Ever the gentleman, I said I would be delighted, even though over the years my experience had been that these things were more often than not a complete disaster.

When Lesley walked in, I was sitting at the bar on a stool. I was introduced to her, and although it wasn't love at first sight, what I can say is there was instant chemistry between us. I found her very attractive, scintillating, and as we stood at the bar we were captivated with each other. Because it was so noisy we were forced to stand very near to each other to talk, literally into each other's ears. Forced by circumstances into an encounter of the closest kind. My immediate impression was that here was a very elegant lady. I was comfortable with her straight away; it was as though I had known her for years. There was no difficulty, no clumsiness on either part.

Lesley will say I didn't call her for a couple of weeks after that first meeting, even though we exchanged telephone numbers (I'd discovered that she was single, having been divorced for about five years). But I was out of practice: this was something I hadn't done for twenty-odd years. I eventually called her and asked if she would have dinner with me. She had given up on me by then, even though it had only been a couple of weeks. I have to confess I was quite nervous. After all, this was very different from meeting in a noisy bar with lots of friends around. Telephoning for a date is decidedly unnerving.

I recall arriving at her bungalow at the prescribed time of 7.30 to discover that I had arranged to meet her at seven and to leave at 7.30 for the restaurant. She was calling her friend Janet when I arrived and was in the process of saying, 'Janet, David has stood me up!' Janet responded, 'He must be mad! Something's wrong with the man!' With that I knocked on the door and walked in with a bottle of nicely chilled champagne. Despite opening many bottles over the years, I sprayed it everywhere, all over the kitchen, as I released the cork. I made a complete mess of it, and left myself thinking, 'I'm like a teenager on his first serious date!' We went out for dinner, and enjoyed it so much we were soon doing it again.

Lesley lived with her little dog Monty, who had been her companion for many years. He was a very important part of her life, but he and I had a kind of love-hate relationship. I was the only person not to spoil him, so he dismissed me and made for Lesley all the time when we were together. He had this trick of squeaking and making a fuss at the bottom of the stairs when he wanted to go to bed, in order that she carried him up at around 9.30 or ten, regardless of whether we were ready for bed or not. In the bungalow it was all right – he could go off to bed whenever he wanted to – but now that Lesley is in her new house, or when she was at my place, he always wanted carrying upstairs to bed. We might have been listening to music, watching television or just talking, but when Monty wanted to go upstairs he would interrupt until someone took notice. That is how spoilt he was, though he knew he couldn't get away with it with me. I remember one evening at Lesley's bungalow. We had just enjoyed a wonderful evening and were sitting on the sofa when I put my arms around Lesley to kiss her goodnight. Monty jumped up in the middle of us and refused to budge. There I was, trying to embrace Lesley, but Monty was having none of it, leaving Lesley with the problem of whether to push the dog away or leave him where he was and ignore me. She left him where he was, and we said our goodnights around him. It was quite clear to both of us by that stage that this was a special relationship developing – despite Monty and his scant regard for my earnest courtship. I guess we were rivals for the lovely Lesley's affections, though I was somewhat dismayed at the fact that he won more often than me. I can whinge as much as I like and never get carried up to bed! Sadly, Monty is no longer with us.

About a year after meeting Lesley, we were both getting ready to go to a charity function in London when Lesley suddenly asked, 'How do I look?'

I replied, 'Lesley, you look stunningly beautiful. You could be taken for a teenager.'

Lesley blushed and said, 'I think you're fibbing!'

'Lesley, I would never lie to you.'

She put her arms around me, kissed me and said, 'I don't think you would. But there was a time just after we first met when I thought you did.'

I was intrigued, and pressed her to tell me more. Somewhat reluctantly,

Lesley explained.

'A month after we first met,' she began, 'I asked you what you did for a living and you told me, among a number of other things, that you were the chairman and co-owner of Birmingham City Football Club. Well, as you know, my interest in football was close to zero, so I told Paul because I knew he'd be interested that you were the chairman and co-owner of Birmingham City.' Paul, an avid Arsenal fan, is Lesley's brother. She has another, Philip, an equally keen Spurs fan. 'My Paul's response was that you might be a very nice man but you were not the chairman and co-owner of Birmingham City. He thought you were having me on.

'I asked myself whether you were lying to me, and a couple of weeks later, troubled by Paul's response, I asked you again, were you the chairman and co-owner of Birmingham City, and you confirmed you were. The week after that I was talking to Paul and, still confused, I told him I was sure you were what you said you were. But he told me he had been reading an article in the *Sun* that very morning which clearly stated that David Sullivan was the chairman and owner, and he also recalled some time earlier watching a programme, *Back to the Floor*, which was all about David Sullivan, the owner of the *Sunday Sport* and *Daily Sport* and the owner and chairman of Birmingham City. He told me he was sorry, but you were still teasing me.'

Stunned, I asked, 'So how long did this doubt go on for, Lesley?'

She told me right up until the day when we had Sunday lunch in the Pilgrim's Goose and in walked a client of mine and her son Marc, a thirteen-year-old who loved his football and supported both QPR and Southampton. On being introduced, he said, 'Yes, I know you, you're David Gold, the chairman of Birmingham City. I've seen you on television.'

So, thankfully, a smart teenager rescued me. Marc is now in his early twenties and has an amazing recall of players' and, fortunately for me, football club chairmen's names. He is still my friend to this day, and a guest from time to time at St Andrews.

When we first met, Lesley was working hard to survive, and financially things were difficult. I am proud of her for the way she kept her independence. She used to work six days a week, and I couldn't persuade her to quit, but at least she reduced her clients and her hours by not working from Friday lunchtime until Monday lunchtime so that we could spend more time together. She used to live 40 minutes away in her bungalow in Hurstpierpoint, but we bought a house this side of the village so she is now only 30 minutes away. It is a pretty house with amazing views, and we call it our country retreat. It is a picturesque village, and we happily split our time between our two properties as I tried to persuade her to spend more and more time with me. She has her loyalty to her clients and to her independence, but gradually my nagging saw her reduce her workload to give us as much time together as possible. Her skill as a beauty therapist can be judged by the way she has made me so incredibly young-looking and handsome!

I remember her telling me a story a while back. She ran her beauty therapy business from home, where she saw her clients. Most were mature ladies who took tea in the afternoon, but one young girl was bold enough to ask who was in the picture on the wall in her house. Lesley told her it was the new man in her life, and the young girl turned round and said, 'It must be really nice to have a companion at your time of life.' Which made Lesley feel about 100 years old! Little did the young girl know how passionate Lesley's new companion was! … don't you just hate the young!

Lesley had a small but exclusive clientele. She handpicked her clients, people she liked and got on with. She is so meticulous. She would spend half an hour preparing for her clients – hardly the 'next please' you normally get. She prided herself in her cleanliness and preparedness, so that her clients could walk straight in and find her ready to begin. I have no doubt she will still keep her special clients, even though she has unofficially retired.

Lesley is adorable. The impact she has had on my life is remarkable. Take my home, for example. Before Lesley came into my life it was very masculine, with paintings of warring battleships with exploding cannons; in their place now are pictures of flowers and gardens, which lend the place a softer, warmer, more feminine look. The house now feels lived in. Here's another example: I am not the sort of person to take a holiday because it interferes with my work and football, but Lesley took me away to South Africa, where she wanted to see the animals on safari. No one else could have got me to do something like that. She opened doors for me, and my eyes. She is persuasive and charming, and she knows what is good for me. Getting me out to South Africa for a ten-day break, the longest for some time, only she could have engineered. Though when we went I insisted I was not going to get up at five o'clock in the morning to see the animals.

We picked up a private plane in Johannesburg, flew to Victoria Falls and spent four wonderful days at the Royal Livingstone Hotel in Zambia. On our last evening, Lesley and I ordered drinks in the Colonial Bar, a magnificent room overlooking the Zambezi River; you could just hear in the background the water cascading over the mighty Victoria Falls. We were the only people in the bar as it was still quite early. The pianist was playing Lesley's request, 'Wind Beneath My Wings', when a man noisily burst into the room followed by a much older man. The younger man called out to Michael, the bar steward, in an extremely loud voice, 'No, no, Michael, not there. You know Sir Denis does not like sitting there close to the music. Over there, Michael, by the window.' Who could be so rude as to burst into a room barking instructions like that with no respect or care for the other guests and with no concern for the pianist, who was playing especially for Lesley. What a boor. I couldn't resist turning round to see for myself who this arrogant loudmouth was . . . it was none other than Mark Thatcher, with his elderly, frail father Sir Denis. Mark continued his loud and offensive diatribe at the waiters. Lesley and I found the whole thing quite embarrassing, so we finished our drinks and left.

We took a leisurely stroll alongside the Zambezi to the hotel restaurant, and about half an hour later Sir Denis arrived with his arrogant son. Lesley had purchased a copy of Margaret Thatcher's book and ventured over to Sir Denis to ask him if he would mind autographing it for her. He was extremely charming and signed it. However, Mark couldn't resist making an insulting remark about his mother's book. I wonder if he is a friend of Michael Winner, or did they just attend the same charm school?

The following morning we flew off in our King Air 200 to the Boulders Lodge, Singita Private Game Reserve. I was intending to spend the next six days flying around South Africa while Lesley was going to get up at five o'clock every morning to see the animals, but I never actually flew. The plane sat on the airfield by the hotel in the middle of Africa because we had a fantastic time on safari. It was a wonderful experience going out in the early hours of the morning, despite my original reluctance. I was captivated by the savagery and romance of it all. At six o'clock in the evening we would stop the open-top Land Rover at a high vantage point. Our two guides – Winston, the lead guide, and Lumumba – would prepare hot food, and Lesley and I would sit with some chilled champagne and watch the most amazing sunset. It was an awesome experience.

On the last day of our safari adventure we decided to take an adventure trail with our two guides – about a three-mile walk. We had seen Africa's Big Five: buffalo, elephant, leopard, lion and rhino. Now we were hopefully going to see the Small Five: the amazing dung beetle, the elephant shrew, the buffalo weaver, the ant lion and the leopard tortoise. Early on our two-hour walk we encountered three male buffalo who had been separated from the herd, and had to beat a hasty retreat back to our support Land Rover. Winston was concerned that if they attacked – and they certainly looked like they might – even a bullet from his high-velocity rifle might not penetrate the massive horn across the buffalo's forehead. Soon we continued our walk, but as we came round a bend, standing in front of us was a huge rogue male elephant. We were over half a mile from the safety of our Land Rover, and this huge elephant had only one tusk and looked ferocious. Winston instructed us to stand rigidly still. 'Don't move a muscle' was his instruction to Lesley and me. It reminded me of being with Norman Collins, my helicopter flying instructor: on one occasion when I'd lost control of the helicopter, just before we crashed he said calmly, 'I have control!' The elephant bellowed, and scraped his massive foot along the ground, raising clouds of dust. I saw beads of sweat appear on Lumumba's brow. 'Stay calm, everything is fine,' Winston repeated. I actually didn't feel that everything was fine. His voice wasn't as reassuring as Norman's. But then, to everyone's great relief, the huge old elephant raised his head and his trunk, bellowed defiantly, turned, and disappeared.

By this time I'd had enough excitement for one day and was looking forward to returning to the safety of the lodge. Winston was continuing to describe the various wonders surrounding us when suddenly Lumumba screamed out something in African and sprinted down the track, followed by Winston, who had grabbed Lesley's arm, leaving me standing on my own wondering what the hell was going on. 'Mamba, mamba!' screamed Winston. I looked to my right, and saw a dark olive-green snake about ten feet long rearing up at me no more than a few feet from where I was standing. 'Run mister, run mister!' called out Winston. I was already on my way! Winston explained that it was the deadly Black Mamba whose bite can kill a man within twenty minutes. There is no known antidote. He went on to say that he hadn't seen one in over two years, which was cold comfort to me. To think that we had made a decision to take a leisurely walk to see Africa's harmless Little Five and ended up with three life-threatening experiences!

Every couple of years Lesley and I have a charity open day in the grounds of my home, The Chalet. Lesley had done this once in the past at her bungalow in Hurstpierpoint, where she had a beautiful garden. For our first open day we delivered invitations in the form of flyers and organised everything, but when we woke at seven a.m. on the day it was overcast and pouring with rain. We were due to open the gates at eleven a.m., and with much to do our army of helpers soon began to arrive, with the rain still cascading down. Lesley, whose bungalow and garden would have fitted snugly into my hall, had twelve people waiting at her gate when she opened her garden to the public; at eleven a.m. at The Chalet, we had none. I had even advertised in the local paper as well as through the leaflets, but there was not a soul in sight as the rain continued to tumble down. What a disaster! Ralph and Jacqueline were due to arrive to do some book signings, but there was not a soul to greet them.

Thankfully, the skies lightened and the rain began to ease, and by midday we had people arriving. Because of the bad weather we'd set up seats and tables in the indoor swimming pool area. I'd put a cover over the pool, but as I was sitting talking to Kevin Black, the photographer from the local newspaper, a woman walked straight on to it and immediately sank up to her ankles. I couldn't understand it as I thought the cover was so obvious, but even so I decided to remove the cover so that everyone could see that it was a swimming pool, avoiding any confusion. I looked at this beautiful blue pool, all lit up with the Ann Summers apple logo at the bottom, and thought it was a good decision. Kevin then told me he was going outside to take pictures of people strolling in the grounds and putting on the golf green. Soon after he left I watched in absolute disbelief as a woman walked straight into the pool. I waited for her to swim to the side and climb out using the steps, but to my horror she sank straight to the bottom and began sliding down the slope towards the deep end with her handbag floating on the surface. As I watched open-mouthed in horror, Ralph, complete with Armani suit, gold watch, handmade leather shoes and crisp, new shirt, dived in the pool and pulled her out. The hapless lady, Mrs Daphne Winters from neighbouring Caterham, a non-swimmer, was full of apologies and explained that she was wearing new bi-focals and wasn't getting on with them. She could say that again!

It was, of course, the moment of the day, the event everyone talked about for weeks afterwards. But where was Kevin? He'd missed it all because he was outside – not taking pictures of the putting, but puffing away quietly on his Hamlet cigar. The sun eventually came out in the afternoon and everyone enjoyed the day. Meanwhile, we gave Mrs Winters a change of clothes and ran her and her soaked handbag home. Kevin wanted to make up for his absence with an interview with the woman and Ralph, but she declined, saying she didn't want people to know how stupid she was. Poor Kevin missed his scoop completely.

Lesley and I have since had several open days and golf days and raised a good deal of money for local charities.

As for my mother, I still have to pinch myself when I see her. I hug her and tell myself how lucky I am to still have her around, and to be able to give back some of what she gave to me when I was a child. Her suffering was at least twice as bad as Ralph and I put together, right from the days of the Blitz, when she refused to be evacuated despite the house being bombed twice, and the terrible business with the pyorrhoea, when all her teeth were removed. She is a remarkable woman who was treated badly by my father all his life. She endured him because she loved him in the traditional way, for ever, until death do us part. She adored him, and forgave him time and time again.

It is amazing the number of times my mother could have died when a lesser woman would have given up. Mum was a heavy smoker, as were a lot of people during that period between the thirties and the sixties when part of the publicity campaign by the cigarette companies was that smoking is good for you. She smoked 50 a day and suffered lung cancer because of it. I appreciate her all the more because I said goodbye to her once when I did not think she would last until the morning. Then she was in her fifties and looked as if she was in her nineties; now that she is in her nineties, she looks as though she's in her fifties. Her survival and recuperation shouldn't really have come as a shock or a surprise. She has always astounded me with her resilience and her ability to survive, despite having only one lung.

I speak to her two or three times a week, and a fortnight won't go by without me seeing her – providing I can get hold of her, such is her busy social calendar. I rang her a while ago to tell her that a mutual friend was coming to dinner and would she join us. She went through her social calendar for the day, saying, 'Shopping, hairdressers, the gym (!). I also have bingo, and although I could skip that, I definitely couldn't let down my darts team.' I simply held up my hands and wished her a pleasant evening.

When she comes to stay, we always have a few drinks. The next morning I will be up at eight a.m.; she will be up at six. By the time I appear in my dressing gown she has had breakfast, has dressed, and is raring to go. I have no doubt at all that she is making up for the lost years, and she treasures every second, saying, 'Why should I take it easy? I'll have plenty of time for that when I'm dead!' Hard to argue with a philosophy like that.

I can sense when she is down, and it's usually because she has had an evening in on her own. Normally she goes to her local West Ham supporters' club if she has nothing else to do, like darts, bingo, or a singsong with her pals. Mum is a Birmingham City Blue Nose, but all her local friends are Hammers, and have been all their lives. She still wants West Ham to win, but when we play each other she does not decide until the day. It usually depends on who needs the points most. For harmony, she prefers a draw. When we played West Ham in our first season in the Premiership, on the last day of the campaign, she wanted Birmingham to win but West Ham not to go down. She worked it out: if Bolton lost 8–0, Birmingham could still win and West Ham would stay up. She just wants everyone to be happy.

She has been an inspiration throughout, not only to the family but also to others close to her. She could be sitting in a nursing home being looked after instead of going away for weekends, watching football matches, going to Birmingham to the Senior Citizens Club to play bingo, playing darts and going to the gym. She went to a dance weekend and decided afterwards that she wouldn't go again because the other participants were all too old. If there was one person there older than her it would have been a major surprise. They were probably older than her in their attitude to life. At one stage, when she was in her early eighties, she was very friendly with a man named Charlie. When I discovered she wasn't seeing him any more, I asked her what had happened, and she told me he wasn't sexy enough! There isn't a minute spare in her life, and she has everything mapped out. When I call, her answerphone is stacked with messages; I have to wait while it goes through half a dozen of them before I can add mine. A truly amazing woman.

CHAPTER THIRTY-FIVE

LIFE JUST KEEPS ON
GETTING BETTER

It is quite remarkable that when you are a teenager you dread becoming 21 because, in your fertile mind, it's all going to come to an end in a few years. Fortunately, those few years seem to last for ever once you emerge from your teens. But it doesn't end there, because when you are in your twenties you worry about not being a success by the time you are 30, as you are convinced that by the time you are 40 life will be over and you'll be in your dotage. Of course, all those things are entirely wrong, but when you talk to young people they cannot believe life can become even more exciting, that it continues to ripen like a good red wine. The young believe that two 60-year-old people kissing passionately is about as disgusting as it gets. They think it is their sole preserve. But I can assure all those youngsters who think sex is great when you are a teenager but gross when you are older that they are absolutely wrong. Life does get better.

All right, I'm not playing football any more, and that was an horrific thought when I was young. I am sensible enough to know I cannot play at my age, but I can derive as much pleasure from watching and supporting football, and I have a wonderful time talking about the sport. If you are very lucky you could become a manager; with a bit more luck, a shareholder or a director; if you are really lucky after giving up football, you might become a chairman. The progression for me has been amazing. Here I am in the autumn of my life as excited about the game as I was when I was playing at Upton Park and was known as The Rabbit. With what we have achieved at Birmingham City and what the future holds, the excitement and the experience are just as satisfying as scoring those two goals against Bermondsey Boys at the Spotted Dog in front of 300 people when I was thirteen years old, or the winning goal against Glasgow for London in front of 12,000 at Selhurst Park when I was eighteen.

When I was trying to snog Millie as a newly arrived teenager, I could never have believed that kissing my lovely Lesley would be even more pleasurable half a century on. While I was probably close to being a millionaire when I was 30, I know of people who have broken down and cried because they hadn't made it at the same age. It was important to me to be a millionaire by the time I was 30 because I thought I wouldn't be able to enjoy it as a 40-year-old. I still hear the same thing being said by others all these years later. I remember Jacky's ex-husband Tony being upset because he felt he had not achieved his life's ambitions at 30. Thirty is fantastic, but rather than worry about being 40 I can tell everyone of that fragile age that it gets better. Honest. It is just as exciting to make it at 40 or 50. One of the best times of my life was in my fifties, and now I'm in my sixties I wake up in the morning and think how wonderful life is. My mother is in her nineties and is still optimistic about the future; on the other hand I know people of 50 who are positively old.

My life changed when I met Lesley, and I know I am happier now than I was when I was 40, and certainly happier than I was at ten! Life is rich, and it is what you make of it. I have been rich and I have been poor; I have been very happy and very unhappy; and being rich didn't mean being happy, and being poor didn't mean being unhappy. There were great moments of happiness when I was poor – although I was rarely happy when in poverty, which is different from being poor – and I have suffered while being rich. Riding my motorbike with the wind in my hair was happiness, even though I had no money. But I have to say rich is better. That is a plain fact.

Where am I today? I am as excited about the future as at any time in my life, and I'm always trying to convince other people that age isn't a barrier. You can only be your own barrier if you declare yourself to be too old. Age is only a real obstacle if you want to run a four-minute mile or play football for Real Madrid. But then unrealistic ambitions at any age and in any walk of life are destructive. I have discovered as I've moved through life that new challenges are surprisingly enjoyable. I do different things that are equally fulfilling. Ambitions change with age, but they can be hugely rewarding. I would say to someone who is 50 and wanted to become an airline pilot that it was too late, but that doesn't mean to say he can't learn to fly. I have been a fixed-wing pilot since 1972, a bizarre year for me: not only did I qualify as a pilot, I separated from my wife Beryl, Ralph and I purchased Ann Summers, and we went through three traumatic court cases. In 2004, when I was in my sixties, I passed my helicopter pilot test, which was far more difficult than anything I had achieved before, and without the patience and skill of my instructor, Norman Collins, I doubt whether I would have succeeded. I was also fortunate to have Arwyn Jones as my fixed-wing flight tester, and to do my annual checks with him. He is a 747 and an Airbus 300 pilot, a serious flyer with more than 20,000 hours under his belt. He has also learnt to fly a helicopter. He is my mentor. He flies a 747 on Monday and checks me out in my Cessna 182 four-seater on Tuesday. A wonderful experience, dare I say, for both of us. He was about three months behind me in his helicopter lessons, and we would talk about exactly the same struggles I went through, like learning to hover. I would keep reassuring him that he would be all right in due course. It was a great feeling, telling this icon he would be OK.

So here I am, at my age, achieving a lifelong ambition to fly a helicopter. I did not have the time in the past, and sometimes not the inclination, but then I had a window of opportunity and I took it. I now own my own helicopter, which I park in my garden and use to fly to games, training sessions, business meetings, hotels, golf courses, even to Karren Brady and her husband Paul Peschisolido's house for tea (they have a landing area for me). It is a great experience, so if you think at 30 these things are past you, you should think again. When you reach 40, don't say it's too late. As the sportswear manufacturer Nike cleverly says, 'Just do it.'

It would be very romantic to be able to say that flying stems from my poverty-stricken youth, that to be as free as a bird was a dream of mine, but the truth is I drove past Biggin Hill airport every day on my way to work and watched planes take off and land twenty feet above the car. On many occasions I would pull over into a lay-by to watch them land. I was simply captivated by the whole magic of flying. My first experience in the air, in a Cherokee 140 at Biggin Hill in my early thirties, was fantastic. It took me a year to achieve my pilot's licence, though it would have been a lot quicker had I devoted more time to it. Years later I did my instrument rating, which also took me a year to achieve. It is the equivalent to a commercial pilot's licence. There are only about 70 private pilots in the country who have instrument ratings.

Why had I taken so long to fulfil my dream? Well, Beryl, my wife, was terrified of flying, and I suppose it was because I wanted to be fair to her. My father had rarely shown the same feelings for my mother. If he wanted to do something he did it, regardless of anyone and anything. I started to take flying lessons in 1970, and it quickly became my hobby and my release. I would leave home an hour early twice a week for flying instruction. It didn't impinge on my business, and Beryl thought I was just going to work an hour earlier. I couldn't tell her what I was doing because she would have been traumatised. She did fly in the end because her second husband, who was considerably firmer than I was, insisted on her flying with him when they went abroad on holiday. Indeed, most people's experience of flying for the first time is as a commercial passenger, but I, of course, never took my children on holiday in an aeroplane. I took them by boat, train or car. When I fly I sense a freedom, more so in the helicopter than in the Cessna, and especially when I am on my own. When I'm flying with passengers, the pleasure for me then is in sharing the experience. Flying has undoubtedly been one of the great joys of my life, a fantastic reward for all those years of hard work.

So I am happier now than I have probably ever been, but two or three times a year I have a nightmare. I arrive back at Green Street in my Bentley – bizarrely, because in the nightmare I have lost everything. As I climb out of my car my mum is waiting for me, and I take out my tool bag and my spirit level. Later I drive to the building site at Baylam Street, where I once worked, and see the faces of people like Terry Green and old Ben the hod carrier. They cannot understand why I am on the scaffold, especially with my Bentley parked in the street outside. I'm wet and I'm cold. It is the same dream every time.

Unlike inherited wealth, with first-generation wealth there is a fear factor. During the climb, you always fear slipping back. That fear makes you aware not only of what you have, but what you could lose. As a result, I have always been a great protector of my business and wealth. That is the way it is when wealth is hard-earned as you claw your way up and face adversity from the very beginning, starting from abject poverty, reaching the first rung of the ladder then climbing to the second only for someone to knock you down to the first step again. It has never been a steady climb for me. There have been many downs, whether in the form of court cases or adverse business deals, but fortunately there have been more welcome ups. There are always failures along the way, but they act as a spur to bounce back and do better. The fear of losing everything is a driving force.

I can now speak in front of a couple of hundred people without preparation. In contrast, when I was thirteen and it was my turn to speak at assembly in front of the entire school I got up on to the stage with my notes to report on the school football match. After the game on Saturday I would be up all night and all day Sunday writing something that took me a minute and a half to speak. It was the most frightening experience. It was no better as a young adult. When Ralph married, I had to speak at the reception, attended by a dozen people I knew well. As best man I stood up for no longer than a minute and a half, but even in front of friends it was still a terrible experience because I was inarticulate, uneducated, and had no confidence. Ask me to rack out the shop or fix the van or work all hours and I was your man, but to speak in public was an ordeal. It was like fencing without swords. These were the experiences that brought about practising words in the car and developing my vocabulary, and I knew I had to get rid of my cockney accent. It would have been nice to be born into comfort, to have had a university education, but if that had been the case I doubt very much whether I could have succeeded in the same way as I have done because it would have taken away my essence, my driving force.

The ability to succeed requires a special desire – that driving force. It is in most of us, but some of us need a little bit of encouragement. Nowadays, one of my great pleasures on a Sunday morning is to rise at around 7.30 a.m. and have breakfast while I read the Sunday papers, particularly the sports pages. But when I first moved into my new house, which sits at the end of a mile-long road, my schedule was thrown awry as my papers did not arrive until 9.30 a.m. Keen to put my routine back on track, one Sunday morning I waited for the paperboy, whose name was Tom.

'Can you get my papers to me before eight o'clock on a Sunday?' I asked.

'No, mate,' replied Tom. 'I start at the bottom of your road and finish at your house. You are my last call, and that's the way I've always done it.' With this dismissal he rode off on his bike back up my driveway.

The following Sunday I put two pounds in an envelope marked 'To Tom the paperboy' with a note inside saying, 'Please find enclosed a two-pound tip for delivering my papers. Just for your information, at eight o'clock this morning there was a five-pound note in this envelope.'

The following Saturday night I left Tom a five-pound note in an envelope on my doorstep. At nine o'clock the following morning my papers had still not arrived so I removed the five-pound note, did not replace it with two pounds, and left the following message: 'Dear Tom, at eight o'clock this morning there was another five-pound note for you in this envelope.' At 9.30 a.m., Tom arrived with my papers, and from my vantage point I saw him open the envelope, maybe expecting another two-pound tip, only to find my note. Tom rode off up my driveway with an empty bag – I was his last call, remember – and an empty pocket.

The Saturday evening after that I placed a five-pound note in an envelope with a note saying, 'Dear Tom, thank you for delivering my papers early, please find enclosed a five-pound tip.' I am delighted to report that my papers arrived at 7.30 a.m. the next day. Tom was about fourteen at the time and he carried on delivering my papers at 7.30 for the next couple of years. From time to time I would leave him a five-pound tip, and always when Birmingham City won! Maybe Tom took his first step to becoming the next Sir Alan Sugar or Sir Richard Branson – who knows?

Ralph and I have evaluated our progress almost as if it were a sporting contest, going by the league table in the *Sunday Times* Rich List. We were first included in 1992, at number 458 and valued at £25 million, and we watched with interest as we climbed the table until we were in the top 100, which demonstrated how well we were doing by someone else's standards. My mum once said to me, 'I have just bought the *Sunday Times* and I see in the Rich List you have gone down nine places. I am very disappointed! What will my friends think?' I told her I was doing my best, and she mischievously answered, 'Well, it's not good enough!' Even to my mum the league table is a barometer of how well her sons are doing.

Are the figures accurate? They are written with great authority, but they do make judgements based on accumulatives. If you are a company on the stock market, worth is easy to calculate according to share values and how many you own. But the list is a barometer; it was never meant to be a totally accurate assessment. They may look at your business and discover your turnover is £100 million, and those kinds of businesses are selling for one year's turnover, but is it in decline or growth? The calculations can be out either way. With a company like Ann Summers, because it is a growth business, by the time the figures are published the turnover has gone up, along with profitability. In some companies there are huge changes over the years, with hundreds of millions of pounds' difference, but if you look at ours it is built carefully and studiously with no violent ups and downs in our growth pattern. We have a strategy of opening stores at a controllable pace. Some say, 'Why don't you double your shop openings when they are going so well?' Our answer is we always want to have it under control, as many businesses are at their most vulnerable when they are expanding. We ensure that our manufacturing and warehousing and the entire infrastructure can cope with the growth. There was a time when Ann Summers Party Plan was growing at such a rate the infrastructures couldn't keep pace, and ironically we were beginning to fail because we were so successful. It was only by slowing down the growth that we brought the business back under control. There is nothing in this world that pumps the adrenalin more than when a business is going along at an electric pace, with growth in every area. You are reluctant to slow it down, but we realised the dangers, and our business acumen overcame the adrenalin surge. Our suppliers couldn't keep up with the demand, so if we hadn't slowed down we would not have been able to maintain supplies to our customers. You have to supply your customer, or you die.

But there is more wealth in confidence than there is in money, a fact first brought home to me during my first business trip abroad, to America in 1966. As Beryl hated flying we crossed the Atlantic on the *Queen Elizabeth*, travelling second class, but we returned to Southampton first class on the *Queen Mary* because I couldn't bear being told I couldn't go here and couldn't go there. The leap up from second to first class was huge, rather like the difference between the Championship and the Premiership. On board the *Queen Mary* there were first, second and third classes plus steerage – the Premiership right down to the equivalent of League Two, or the Conference. Steerage was down in the bowels of the ship; there were no portholes, and it was very noisy and hot. It was mainly occupied by American teenagers coming to explore Great Britain and Europe – early-day backpackers. The film *Titanic* brought back memories of the *Queen Mary* with its wealth and splendour in first class and the poor in steerage. The ship was quite amazing, her grandeur a great experience for a young man of 29. I had never even been in a glamorous hotel before, so I found the trappings stunning. I was in my early twenties before I went into a decent restaurant, but this was a quantum leap. The ceiling in the dining room was 40 feet high; I gaped in awe at its splendour.

On that passage home we met a very wealthy American couple – not a difficult thing to do given the circumstances – the man around 40 and his wife about half his age. They were charming, and invited us to dinner along with Count Vladimir, another of the guests. He was a splendid fellow, and he and I went down in the lift together and then walked two more flights of stairs down to steerage to meet a girl he had met and fancied (just like *Titanic* again!). We danced the evening away, and the Count looked after his beautiful companion who wasn't in the least bit overawed by her surroundings. This was an experience for me – seeing a man with wealth, power, a title, and supreme confidence, just waltzing around and doing whatever he wanted to do. He didn't worry about whether it was allowed or not, he simply did it.

There is nothing in this world as satisfying as confidence, and I have to confess it came very slowly to me in my life. I would say that in my case it all revolves around my current house. Confidence, wealth, expression, success, recognition – this house was the beginning of the new feeling and a new life. It was the catalyst that changed many things. My former house was just a house; as long as it was close to my office and comfortable, it was all I needed. Those were the days before laptops anyway; the computer I had in my house then was so slow I was better off driving the four minutes to my office. Today I still print off a report identical to the one I was printing out twenty years ago. Now I press the buttons and it's complete in about five seconds; that same report two decades ago would have to be run overnight. I had to set it up at close of business, go back the following morning and hope it had finished running – and this was a single-page report! Sometimes I would return sixteen hours later and it was still not finished. It printed out a line, then spent the next couple of hours calculating things, going through all the company records, before moving on to the next line. Nowadays, anything that takes longer than a few seconds leaves you wondering what is wrong with the machine.

Also with the house came the beginning of my slowing down from the incredible work ethic I had pursued. I wouldn't change anything in my life, but if I were advising someone in the same position I would ask whether they are sure about working all the hours God sends, the obsession, the dedication, the risk, the fear, and ask themselves, 'Do I have the courage?' Give it some thought, and live a life. But if I'd asked myself the same questions at any stage of my life I wouldn't have changed a thing.

I have still never been away on a fortnight's holiday in my life, not only because Beryl wouldn't fly, but because I personally wanted to work, and the challenges were all there waiting for me. I felt it was a week wasted when I was away, and the only reason I went was to keep Beryl happy. I would suggest she take the children and her sister and then offer to pay for them all, as I would be too busy to go. My passion for my business was partly to blame for the collapse of our marriage. But I do remember my desire not to replicate what had happened between my parents. I was very conciliatory towards Beryl and I ended up spoiling her. We were just wrong for each other, two virgins at 21 who were simply not suited. Our marriage was almost procedural. We were asked, wasn't it time we were engaged, then wasn't it time we were married, and suddenly we found ourselves walking down the aisle. She wasn't in love with me and I wasn't in love with her, and we both knew it from the day we went on honeymoon. Now that I'm with Lesley I still don't take serious holidays, apart from that ten-day South African safari. I might go down to Marbella for five days with David Sullivan, but then we sit in the sun and catch up on business. We will usually end up meeting football people like Dave Bassett, Jim Smith and others, and talk about players and football. It is a bit of a busman's holiday, but it is a nice environment, sitting in the sun and going out for nice meals in the evening.

Regrets, as Frank Sinatra sang, I've had a few, but too few to mention. Obviously I wish I had met Lesley much earlier in my life. I wish I were writing here that I had been happily married for 40 years. But I am now enjoying the very best of things. As I progressed through life and started to make money, I began going to nice restaurants. I remember going to the Savoy, Mirabelle, the Ritz, and places like the Café Royal for dinner at a time when each venue was a new adventure. At the same time my taste in wines began to mature: I moved on from Blue Nun, the ubiquitous Liebfraumilch and the deep red Bull's Blood from Hungary to more sophisticated wines such as Premier Cru Chablis from France, or a Gavi from Italy. Lesley drinks champagne. When I go away I unashamedly look for the best suite in the best hotel, and the best table in the best restaurant. Some people like to spend their money on yachts and exotic holidays, but I have my lovely house with its indoor swimming pool, tennis court and nineteen-hole golf course, my plane and my helicopter, my Bentley and my Jaguar.

The aircraft are not just toys; they are used for business, as are my cars. My helicopter, in fact, is extremely cost effective. When launching a new catalogue, for instance, the helicopter means my daughter Jacky can get to two conferences in a day rather than one. It is a working tool, and super efficient. I can be in the helicopter and airborne in five minutes with no issues with air traffic control as I fly low level to Birmingham. I have the choice of all three methods of transport. I will be driven in the Bentley, say, to Chelsea, Charlton or West Ham; if I am going to Birmingham I will go in the helicopter; and if I am going to Manchester I will use one of the Lear Jets. The choice is all about efficiency and speed. They are not indulgences. I don't stay over and I don't drive for ten hours in a day. To me they are tools of the trade, and in business time is very important.

I've come a long way, and it shows how times have changed by the very fact that I have been invited on two separate occasions to meet and enjoy the company of the royal family. As a fierce patriot and royalist, both were very special visits for me, something I will long cherish. It is not, however, something I have broadcast. Once, when I was on local station BBC Southern Counties Radio reviewing the newspapers and answering listeners' calls, the presenter, Ed Douglas, asked me what I had been doing lately, and I told him quite innocently, 'I met Noel Edmonds at the Palace.'

'What was he doing at Crystal Palace?' he queried.

'Not Crystal Palace,' I retorted, 'Buckingham Palace!'

I enjoy my visit to the local station every couple of months or so. I was on soon after the tsunami on Boxing Day 2004, helping the station to raise money for the victims. I offered a trip in my helicopter as one prize and a day on my golf course at my house, things I could offer which were not easily obtainable elsewhere. It was very successful, and the chap who won the bidding for the helicopter ride more than had his money worth. I coupled the trip with an extra ride for him to Stapleford Tawney airport to have my rotor blades greased. The winner was really enjoying his day, getting much longer than he expected, and it was to become even more dramatic as we returned from Stapleford when I received a fire alarm warning on my instrument panel. It was the first time that had ever happened to me. Fortunately we had only just taken off, so I broadcast a Mayday and returned to the airport to be greeted by a full-scale emergency, with fire engines and attendant vehicles waiting for us to touch down. Mike, the prize winner, never turned a hair. He just looked on with interest, as calm as you could be. It actually looked a far bigger deal than it really was. The switches are ultra sensitive, and it was nothing to write home about, but Mike loved every minute of it.

I recall as recently as 1996 Birmingham City Council Trading Standards taking Birmingham City Football Club to court over an issue that could have been resolved with sensible dialogue. What was worse, Karren Brady faced a criminal conviction, and I knew exactly how she felt. It was all to do with away ticket charges, which hadn't been made clear in our paperwork. Eventually we had Karren removed from the charge and Birmingham were fined a derisory £200.

A disillusioned supporter who I had met on many occasions before brought the charge against us. Amazingly, he is a dyed-in-the-wool Blue Nose, but he issued forth a non-stop litany of complaints: the seats aren't comfortable enough, the bars aren't accessible, the toilets aren't correct, the gates aren't wide enough for his car to pass through. I quickly came to the opinion that this man, Chris Measey, was a professional whinger and complainer. The strange thing is, when I met him face to face he was always charming. I would tell him, 'Chris, you are mad. Your heart is in the right place but your decision-making is appalling. You should be helping us with these issues, not taking us to court. You should be making friends, not going to war. We are not enemies, we are on the same side.' I had the same conversation with him in Malaysia when we were attending that pre-season tournament. We bumped into each other at a supporters' dinner. Wherever the Blues were, Chris would be there too, and we spent our usual quarter of an hour together before parting, agreeing to disagree.

Both David Sullivan and I were furious over the case and felt that the local councils, local businessmen and local institutions, rather than being supportive of their local football club, were actually working against us. They were anti even before we arrived. When we did, the local media claimed, 'These spivs from the East End of London have taken over Birmingham City FC.' The fact that we had put an attractive young woman in charge endorsed it as far as they were concerned. They were asking, 'Whatever next – dancing girls on the pitch?' They were against us from the outset. Because of our background and the perception of us as businessmen, if anything their attitude hardened over the following few years, until they discovered that Karren was a talented managing director and the Gold brothers and David Sullivan were serious people with the future of the football club at heart. They saw that we wanted to rebuild Birmingham's reputation as a family football club, that we were rebuilding the stadium, and that we were relentless in the pursuit of success.

Happily, as I said, it seems we have finally been accepted as proper people, and now not a day goes by without my life and my business exciting me in some way, whether it's a new Ann Summers shop opening or Birmingham City chasing a new signing and wondering whether he will be successful. The excitement is never-ending. So, as I said at the start of this chapter, don't think too early on that you are set for the remainder of your days, because things happen. In my case it was Lesley, and the impact was enormous. She has changed my perspective, my aims and my ambitions. I am content, and I hope everything carries on as it is. My group of companies are flourishing, my lovely daughters are in the business, I have the nicest brother a man could ask for, and I have my football. In a sense, my life is complete. Lesley was the last piece in the jigsaw as far as I am concerned. If things don't change for the rest of my life, I will consider myself a fortunate man, having climbed a mountain that appeared at times insurmountable. Being at the top is an amazing feeling. That is not to say, of course, that I no longer have ambitions for my businesses, and in particular for Birmingham City Football Club. I am not going to dig trenches any more, but I will be encouraging others to pick up the shovel because I have been there before and done it. But if I don't move any further forward, I will be content, even though my mother may call me and tell me I have slipped down the *Sunday Times* Rich List by a few places and 'must try harder'. I can survive that.

EPILOGUE

BIRMINGHAM LAND
THE FA CUP AT LAST

I am not a collector of trophies, but occasionally something crops up in your life when you feel you have to stand up to be counted. In May 2005 I heard and read about the oldest FA Cup in existence coming up for sale at Sotheby's. I sent for the brochure, but with no real interest in buying it. There was a reserve of about £300,000 on the silver trophy, and I thought to myself at the time it was fairly cheap for a large slice of English sporting history. Just thinking of the names on that cup (with the exception of Aston Villa!) and the hands that had held it aloft sent shivers down my spine. But, sadly, never Birmingham City.

The first FA Cup, 1872–1895, was lost by Aston Villa when they allowed outfitters William Shillcock to display the trophy in their window in Newton Row, Birmingham, from where it was stolen on the night of 11 September 1895 and never recovered. The cup that was fascinating me was the one presented to the winning team between 1896 (Sheffield Wednesday) and 1910 (Newcastle United). It was a similar cup to the first because the silversmiths who made it, Messrs Vaughton's of Birmingham, had an exact replica to work from, commissioned by Wolves when they won it in 1893. One of their directors, Howard Vaughton, played for Aston Villa when they won the trophy in 1887. But the cup was withdrawn in 1910 after it was discovered that the design had been pirated. A new one was commissioned and the second, retiring FA Cup was awarded to Lord Kinnaird to mark his 21 years as president of the FA. The cup had been out of circulation for almost a century having lain untouched and unseen in the long-dead Lord Kinnaird's bank vaults. It dripped with history. Aston Villa,

Bury, Sheffield United and Sheffield Wednesday each won it twice, and seven other teams won it once each. The first cup had supposedly been melted down, so this was a really important cup in the history of the world game, never mind just our own Football Association.

In the build-up to the sale I heard rumours that the main bidders were going to be from the United States of America and Germany. I bridled at this, but did not believe it until a friend telephoned to tell me a newly refurbished hotel in Berlin was indeed planning to buy the cup and use it as their main display in a glass case in the foyer. Surely, I thought, we cannot lose a piece of history overseas; there must be a bidder from England. To my relief I heard that the National Football Museum in Preston was also planning to bid, which put my mind at rest. At this stage it had not entered my head to make a bid, not until I discovered that the museum had only limited funds and could only go as far as the reserve price of £300,000. I knew they could not possibly win the auction with that sort of money.

Slowly, I found myself becoming embroiled, and in a strange way annoyed, wondering where everyone was. What about the FA, or indeed the PFA, whose Chief Executive, Gordon Taylor, paid £2 million for a Lowry painting in 2002? Then he threatened to take his players out on strike when he was negotiating for more money from the Premier League. I had one of my agents check with Sotheby's, and we found out that the most likely winners were the Germans. Now, I am hugely patriotic. I have not gone off and become a tax exile, or set up offshore. I love this country and almost everything it stands for; I love its history, in particular its football history, and I couldn't believe this prize might slip through our fingers and finish up abroad. Apart from the museum, nobody seemed to care. I decided I had to bid for it if the museum couldn't go all the way, and sure enough, on the day they dropped out at £300,000. I was determined the cup would stay in the country. Henry Chappell from Pitch, my PR company, was on the telephone to me, instructing the agent as to what to bid. My valuation was half a million, and I told Henry to go that far, satisfied that it was a good investment – something to give me pleasure and something to leave to the country. I planned to enjoy it for the rest of my life and share it with as many people as possible.

I was at home in Surrey, not a million miles away from Crystal Palace where all the cup finals were played in those days. I had planned to remain anonymous so that people wouldn't bid me up. There were a number of other bidders on the telephone. There was a strong rumour that Roman

Abramovic was one of them, but he clearly wasn't because he would have bought it whatever the price. It finished with just three of us competing. The belief was that the hotel in Berlin was one and the other was from America, but nothing was official, although we ascertained later that the last bidder was indeed from Berlin. I carried on with my work while the bidding went on, and when Henry called I knew it was mine.

In the end I paid £488,620 for this piece of history. The following day Henry called me to say that Sotheby's had received the payment and would now release the cup to him. Unfortunately there was some delay and Henry didn't collect the cup until five o'clock that evening. I was on my way out to a charity function, so I told Henry to take it home and bring it to me the following morning. The cup was handed over to Henry in a tatty old carrier bag, and as he was leaving he was asked, 'Oh, by the way, you have insured it, haven't you?' Henry realised that he hadn't even thought about it. Concerned, he rang me back and explained. 'Well, Henry,' I said, 'take good care of it then. I'll see you tomorrow.' Apparently Sotheby's were worried about allowing Henry to walk out of the door with the cup and kindly offered to drive him home to Fulham, where he lived. Henry subsequently told me that he was watching the ITN news that evening, which led on the story of the whereabouts of the FA Cup and who the mystery buyer was. It was only then that he realised the enormity of what he had in his possession. He spent a sleepless night with the cup under his bed, though, as he has only recently admitted, on arriving home he couldn't resist taking a picture of his six-month-old daughter Agnes in the cup! Which is what the likes of Dennis Wise normally do when they win the FA Cup.

I was glad I'd secured the cup for the nation, and having pondered things since the sale I will almost certainly give it to the National Football Museum when I die – although I do not plan for that to happen for some while! In the months since purchasing the cup I have worked closely with the museum on a programme to display the cup, and at various other venues too. I'm planning to take it to the inaugural final at the new Wembley, and in October 2005 I was invited by the museum to go up to Manchester with the cup for the latest Hall of Fame inductions. Seeing the greats like the Charlton brothers and so many other top stars was wonderful. I was proud when they put my picture on the screen with the cup, and I was then invited up to the podium to say a few words about why I had bought the treasure. Another legend present that day was the German Bert Trautmann, the former prisoner-of-war and Manchester City goalkeeper who denied Birmingham the cup in 1956 despite breaking his neck in a challenge with Peter Murphy. When I was asked why I had bought it, I had to apologise to Bert before saying I was horrified at the thought of it going to Germany. All of the greats came up and told me how thrilled they were I had purchased the cup; even Sir Bobby Charlton came up and thanked me. Sir Bobby and other guests hadn't realised before the event that it was me who had rescued it.

When the cup is not being displayed I keep it at my Surrey home in a strongroom I had built when the house was originally refurbished. I have to confess I never used the room until I purchased the cup. I would not, in any case, put a picture or anything else in there for such things are hardly worth having if you cannot display them and look at them whenever you wish. I have to confess I bring the cup out for dinner parties and put it on the centre of the dining table. It beats a bunch of flowers. The cup, of course, now has blue and white ribbons to replace the red and white ribbons that came with it.

It is rapidly developing a personality of its own, as I discovered when I took it to a friend's golf day as a surprise. They normally raise about £500 for charity with raffles and a few bits and pieces after the golf, but we doubled the amount by having people pose with the cup for photographs for a small payment. The enthusiasm the guests showed that day endorsed my feelings about the trophy. Everyone wanted to touch it and have their picture taken with it. I also went to a workingmen's club in Birmingham where I do a question-and-answer session every couple of years with Tom Ross, the local radio presenter, as the host. As he finished with the players, two exes and one current, he called me on to the stage as the next guest. Out came the cup, rather like another guest, and everyone rushed forward to have a closer look. Such was the interest that afterwards Tom announced the first ten out of the raffle could have their picture taken for £10. Then he had twenty people at £20 a head, and eventually we raised over £500, and this at a workingmen's club! And it didn't finish there. When Tom called a halt to the event, one man rushed forward and was so desperate to have his picture taken with the cup that he offered another £250! This, for me, showed the absolute passion roused by this inanimate object.

I have, of course, been ribbed unmercifully by everyone in football, telling me Birmingham couldn't win it so we had to buy it. But I do believe we have the ability to win a trophy, and it would be unbelievable if it was the FA Cup.

INDEX